Life After Birth

Every Woman's Guide to
The First Year of Motherhood

WENDY BLUMFIELD

ELEMENT
Shaftesbury, Dorset ● Rockport, Massachusetts
Brisbane, Queensland

© Wendy Blumfield 1992

Published in Great Britain in 1992 by
Element Books Limited
Longmead, Shaftesbury, Dorset

Published in the USA in 1992 by
Element, Inc
42 Broadway, Rockport, MA 01966

Published in Australia in 1992 by
Element Books Limited for
Jacaranda Wiley Limited
33 Park Road, Milton, Brisbane, 4064

Cover photographs © Sandra Lousada
courtesy Susan Griggs Picture Agency
Cover design by Max Fairbrother
Designed by Roger Lightfoot
Diagrams by Taurus Graphics
Drawings by David Gifford
Typeset by Footnote Graphics, Warminster, Wiltshire
Printed and bound in Great Britain by
Dotesios Ltd, Trowbridge, Wiltshire

British Library Cataloguing in Publication
data available

Library of Congress Cataloging in Publication
data available

ISBN 1–85230–351–4

Contents

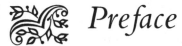 *Preface*

DURING pregnancy, women enjoy the extra attention paid to their physical and emotional needs. The focus of this and of their own expectations is centred on the birth itself and the welfare of the baby.

After the birth, and the initial euphoria and relief that the baby is born safely, most women feel totally spent. The focus of attention then moves to the baby, and the caregivers, concerned relatives and friends provide advice and counselling on every aspect of what the baby should eat and wear, in what he should sleep and with what he should play. The shops are full of books on pregnancy, birth, breastfeeding and childcare, and most parents have a sizeable library by the time they bring their first child into the family.

Meanwhile, the mother is exhausted and may be in pain from perineal stitches or engorged breasts. The ecstasy of those first few hours is replaced by the desperate need to sleep and let her body revitalize itself.

This book is intended for all who are concerned with the physical and emotional health of the woman after birth. It is not a manual on breastfeeding or child development, although no book on the postpartum period would be complete without some references to these important subjects.

My concern is to communicate with you as a new mother, or partner, parent, in-law or health caregiver.

Reading other parents' experiences of coping during this exciting phase in the lifecycle will, I hope, help readers to understand that they are not alone.

Examination of the research material that can be found in books and journals will provide some reasoning and logic behind all the changes and emotional upheaval that are being experienced just now. It is also important to understand the difference between normal adjustment difficulties and signs that the woman may be suffering from postnatal depression.

Both the personal experiences and review of research will also, I hope, be of value to professionals working in the field of maternity health. For it is indeed distressing to watch a young healthy mother experiencing insurmountable problems, unable to use her coping skills, and to see what negative influences this can have on the relationships within the family.

This book includes discussion on high-risk factors for post-partum disturbance. Without doubt, the woman whose family is not stable because of bereavement, divorce, job redundancy or being constantly on the move will find it harder to put down roots and develop support systems. Single mothers or abused wives, immigrants without extended family, all have their extra burdens to bear and the more society is aware of this, the more effectively can they receive support and practical help.

One of the most difficult situations to cope with is that of life after the birth without a baby to make it all worthwhile. I hope that the chapter on grieving after a foetal or neonatal death or coping with a baby in special care will provide some comfort and guidance for the parents and those concerned with their welfare.

However normal the pregnancy and birth, however stable and permanent the family relationships, this period does not stand alone in a hiatus of time. Each woman brings to her own birth experience and attitudes to parenting a heritage of beliefs, impressions from her own childhood, skills and talents which she has developed through her education and career. These values also influence her decisions after the birth of her child, issues such as whether or not to breastfeed, when to return to work, when to plan the next pregnancy.

If the mother may feel that the focus of attention has shifted to the baby after the birth, we can understand that the father can be feeling even more left out. My section on fatherhood began as one chapter. However, I express my grateful thanks to Martin Richards of the Child Care and Development Group of the Faculty of Social and Political Sciences at Cambridge University, who sent me his comments and suggestions for further reading. The subject became much wider and I decided to separate the emotional adjustment to fatherhood from the actual practical issues of parenting which are shared with mothers.

Since the new mother is also a daughter and perhaps a granddaughter, sister and niece, it is important to understand the complete family dynamic. The adjustment and emotional welfare of grandparents, for example, will inevitably influence how much they can support and assist the younger generation.

Many of the difficulties of adjusting to life after birth come as a surprise to the first-time mother. But those having babies in an established family have additional problems of coping with siblings as each child moves up the ladder.

So, together we shall explore the various aspects of what is sometimes called the 'fourth trimester' or the fourth phase in the childbearing year.

Books, like babies, are not born instantly, and the gestation period of this book was indeed much longer than a normal pregnancy. Through the years of working with couples during their childbearing year, I realized how little prepared they are for what happens after the birth and how useful a book on this subject would be.

I am therefore grateful to all the people who helped and encouraged me to meet this challenge. From the time I approached Element Books with the proposal of this book, I have been in constant postal and telephone contact with the Commissioning Editor and Editorial Manager, Julia McCutchen, and am grateful for the professional and efficient way in which she and the Element staff have worked on this book.

I also thank the National Childbirth Trust who started me on my career as a childbirth educator, and all my clients and colleagues who have shared with me their joys and problems.

Meeting a deadline is not always easy when one has a family and a work schedule to maintain, but every one of my family has contributed his or her very special talents to help me keep going.

Taking into account the content of the book, it is obvious that it could not have been written without the enrichment of being the mother of four very energetic and stimulating children.

And indeed, now that they are grown up, their involvement in this book has been tremendously heartwarming.

My specific thanks are due to my two computer managers, my husband David and son Anthony, who have initiated me into the mysteries of using a word processor, and handled my desperate phone calls during the day whenever my text got garbled. And to my daughter Sara who helped me obtain books from libraries all over the country. And to Jonathan and Daniel who were the inspiration for many innovative ideas on retaining my equilibrium.

My new daughters-in-law, Einat, Lilach and Galit, have changed the balance in this family of men and my involvement in their lives and work has reinforced my belief that motherhood is an active, unpensionable lifelong job.

David is, of course, not just my computer manager and his support and enthusiasm for my work over the years has enabled me to develop, to continue studying, with no complaints about a house which is always occupied by classes and meetings and a dining table which has to be cleared of books and papers before every meal.

Without all the distractions of family and work, this book could probably have been written years ago, but I hope that readers will agree that it is richer for the field experience which is contained in its pages.

1 ⚜ The Fantasy and The Reality

THE woman who is awaiting the birth of her first child is facing an unparalleled transition in her life. This transition will affect the structure of the entire family.

During the childbearing period from conception to the end of the postpartum period, which can vary in time, a total hormonal and physical change takes place. This in turn can exaggerate basic personality traits. A stable quiet woman may become lethargic and depressed; an energetic and creative person may suffer manic anxiety and agitation.

While postnatal depression (PND) has been widely documented and researched, few women or their caregivers are aware that these very same physical and psychological changes are also the reasons for the mood swings during pregnancy, the irrational fears and depression, bouts of crying and a general feeling that all is not right with the world.

When this does occur, the woman herself may feel guilty. 'What is wrong with me? I wanted this baby so much, I have a supportive husband, good job, comfortable home. Why don't I feel happy all the time?'

Of coure, if the pregnancy was not wanted, or where there is no supportive husband, good job and comfortable home, the mood changes may be more rational but no less distressing.

Many pregnant women do not recognize this period as a transition but rationalize their apprehension and ambivalence as fear of pain during the birth or concern for a healthy normal baby. These anxieties manifest themselves in extreme sensitivity and even in bizarre dreams. Fantasies about the outcome of birth, the taking over of the woman's body, loss of control, may be too threatening

1

to confront, and the subconscious dream world is invaded by unreal and fantastic situations. 'I dreamed I gave birth to a litter of kittens,' or 'We were all sitting on the bed eating the placenta,' are commonly heard.

Before the popularization of childbirth preparation classes, most women had little opportunity to express their fears; or if women attended the classes of even twenty-five years ago, the focus was on physical exercise. I cannot believe today that when I attended a hospital prenatal course before my first birth, I did not hear one word about emotional and psychological changes. The material of the course began and ended in the labour ward, with absolutely no information about breastfeeding or what happens after the birth.

During the past thirty years, childbirth organizations have attempted to present a method of education which gives the expectant father as well as the pregnant woman an opportunity to learn together about the processes of childbirth while at the same time providing an opportunity for the couple to express their feelings with a peer group. Both partners may have quite different expectations of the birth and postpartum period. Mood changes, diminished sex drive, anxiety about body changes are discussed or worked through in role play. Of course in every group there is at least one glowing pregnant woman who says, 'What's all the fuss about? I feel absolutely wonderful – this is the best time of my life'.

Interestingly, and perhaps understandably, the focus of all these couples is on the birth itself. When I welcome a new group to a course at about thirty weeks of pregnancy, I ask them to voice their expectations and what they want from the course. Very few express concern about not being prepared for what happens after the birth. At this point during the third trimester, their concentration is on the labour – and anything beyond that is on the other side of the hill.

Towards the end of the course, when we spend time discussing this issue, they find it hard to relate to the fact that there can be any problems. They cannot believe that they will experience anything other than relief and release.

Sometimes we try role play and act out a situation. One of my favourites is to reverse the role of husband and wife and present a scenario where the devoted husband, aware that his wife has been confined to the house with a new baby for two months, comes home with theatre tickets, having arranged for a friend to babysit. But he forgets that this is the day that the baby has had his first immunization and was rather cross and feverish; the washing machine has broken down and it has been raining for three days. His wife looks at him in disbelief when he presents her with his surprise and he is very hurt when she tells him in no uncertain way that all she wants is to get into a deep hot bubble bath and go to bed!

The group of expectant couples find this very amusing but do not believe that it can happen to them. Only when we meet after the birth at our reunion party do most of them admit that it wasn't so funny after all.

However, most women do give some thought to their role as mother. Some have fantasies of being Mother Earth, and view motherhood as a culmination of a dream; others are convinced that they will be supermums and will not let the baby make any difference to their lives. Again, there is often a conflict which causes guilt and anxiety during pregnancy.

Patricia was enjoying her pregnancy. She was particularly happy and relieved because she had reached thirty weeks and everything was progressing well. She had had several miscarriages previously, each one due to insufficient development of the foetus, and had been warned that it could happen again. Consequently she welcomed every foetal movement and eagerly awaited her visits to the clinic where she could see on the ultrasound screen a viable healthy baby.

Patricia had a very good and fulfilling job in a university department, and her husband George was a librarian in the same university. They also shared their leisure time, enjoying nature hikes and climbing expeditions.

As the birth approached, Patricia realized that all these activities were going to be limited for a time and she even felt some resentment. She was ashamed to admit it. 'How can I think of such things when all we wanted was a healthy full-term baby?' Patricia's self-awareness enabled her to cope and today she has three beautiful children, still enjoys her job, and all the family go hiking together with the latest baby in a carrier on George's back.

Women like Patricia who have a history of miscarriages or who have had a premature birth, a stillbirth or a history of infertility will be additionally sensitive and anxious during this pregnancy, however well it is progressing. This anxiety is often carried over into the bonding and caring for the new baby.

These concerns can result in exaggerated concentration on pregnancy symptoms and continuous calls for reassurance to the caregivers. Carol already anticipated this when recovering from a totally unexpected stillbirth. 'I shall never enjoy another pregnancy with such peace of mind as I had with this one.' As late as her thirty-seventh week she had noticed a lessening of the foetal movements and by the time she checked at the hospital, there was no foetal heart beat. 'I'll be counting the movements every hour in my next pregnancy', she declared.

CHILDBIRTH EDUCATION

While childbirth classes can prepare a couple for the changes in their life, most couples attend these courses in order to enable them to cope with the birth itself. 'We came to learn the breathing' is the most often voiced expectation.

And here we open a Pandora's box, for there is a direct link between the preparation and expectations of the pregnant woman and how her birth experience will affect her parenting and post-partum experiences. The impact of the birth experience will be discussed in Chapter 2, but here it is worth summarizing the methods of childbirth preparation and how they can mitigate or reinforce the fantasies and fears.

Exponents of childbirth education have developed methods over the past fifty years which vary from country to country. However, they all aim to provide updated information to the pregnant woman and her partner and to teach coping skills so that the couple have some control over the event.

One of the earliest pioneers of childbirth preparation as we know it today was Dr Fernand Lamaze[1] who taught controlled breathing on the basis of Pavlov's methods of conditioning. He then wrote a revolutionary book, *Childbirth Without Pain*, which depicted birth as a natural process which should not cause pain if the woman knows how to behave.

Up to then many women had been anaesthetized during labour, causing physical hazards and psychological dissatisfaction. However, Lamaze's challenge did create guilt and frustration in many women. 'It was painful because I didn't do my exercises properly,' is as inaccurate as it is psychologically harmful.

There are many reasons for pain in labour. Among them are the baby's position, the mother's hormonal activity, and other variables. It is true that the pain threshold is increased by aware-ness, relaxation and correct breathing techniques, but nobody can realistically suggest that pain is solely a figment of the imagination and that asking for drugs for pain relief is an admission of failure.

Dr Grantley Dick-Read,[2] a British obstetrician, was far more flexible in his philosophy. His book *Childbirth Without Fear* (note the difference in tone of the title) was written in the 1940s. His approach was that, by breaking the cycle of fear and tension, pain was reduced.

According to Dick-Read and his disciples, no woman should emerge from her birth experience feeling guilty because she requested drugs. Birth is a very individual experience and while some women will describe it as ecstatic and enjoyable, others will remember it as an ordeal. It is these memories which then influence her feelings towards her baby and of course towards her husband. And it is this experience which will influence her adjustment to her life after the baby is born.

In later years we have seen the approach of Dr Frederick Leboyer,[3] the French obstetrician who wrote *Birth Without Violence*. He concentrates more on the trauma of birth as experienced by the baby. It is also true that the remedies he suggests to reduce this trauma, such as quiet, dark, and placing the baby immediately on the mother's abdomen and reducing separation, are also key points in enhancing the beauty of birth for the mother.

Another French obstetrician, Dr Michel Odent,[4] suggested other innovative birth practices by encouraging women to spend their labour in a bath or to give birth in a squatting or standing position. But he did not offer any form of medicated pain relief in his hospital, however much it was desired. So while these birth positions are very close to nature and are recognized as easing the process, women did not have any choice if in the event there was more pain than they could handle. However, women who choose to give birth with Dr Odent, who now works in London, claim that his charisma and soothing voice are more relaxing than several doses of pethidine!

The effect of some methods of preparation and some of the literature on the subject is to present challenges and expectations which are not realistic. Instead of empowering the woman in labour and maximizing her participation in the birth process, she is left with reduced self-esteem. Once she feels that she has failed in this very important life event, she doubts her capacity to be a good mother.

Studies in one Toronto hospital[5] showed an increase in post-

partum neuroses and even psychoses in women who had participated in over-aggressive, consumer-oriented childbirth classes
which had influenced them against hospital procedures, and which
had undermined their confidence in the hospital staff. As we shall
see in some of our case studies of the birth experience in Chapter
2, this can lead to anger and frustration because the woman doubts
the integrity of her birth attendants. Should she have a caesarean
or forceps birth, her disappointment is further exacerbated by the
feeling that it was not really necessary, and that the judgement of
the duty doctor was at fault.

Today's childbirth educators, such as those trained by the
National Childbirth Trust, have had to find some compromise on
this issue, for it is true that if a couple go into labour prepared,
they can participate in decision-making in a more positive and
satisfying way.

It is perfectly acceptable to question medical opinion, but first
one needs solid and accurate information. Knowledge and control
will also provide more harmonious relationships with the staff
who know that they can discuss the options of treatment in a
rational way. In turn, the woman will know that her wishes are
being respected and that she has some control over how her baby
is born.

It is only this consumer pressure, after all, which has resulted in
today's trend to allow fathers or other support persons to attend
the birth, and it was only with the heightened awareness of the
benefits of early contact between mother and baby that rooming-
in or flexible access to baby nurseries was introduced into
maternity hospitals.

ATTITUDES TO BIRTH

Expectations and attitudes vary with class. At one time, it was the
working-class woman who was more likely to give birth naturally,
perhaps less hampered by academic inhibitions, and it was these
women who breastfed. While working-class women often could
not afford *not* to breastfeed, middle-class mothers were taught that
their social and working lives would be less disrupted if they
bottlefed.

From the middle 1960s, with the emerging movement towards
returning to nature, it is the less educated woman who is
influenced to be 'modern', who accepts more positively the man-

made benefits of epidurals and formula milk, while the middle-class woman will make a more conscious effort to go to prenatal classes and learn her options.

A study in the *Journal of Health and Social Behaviour* in 1982[6] reports expectations as follows:

> Two hundred and fifty women, at all levels of education, were interviewed in the last months of pregnancy.
>
> *Attitudes to medication during labour*   16% of working-class women preferred not to use medication compared to 62% of middle-class women.
> *Intention to breastfeed*   64% of working-class women compared to 86% of middle-class.
> *Preference for rooming-in during the hospital stay*   20% of working-class women compared to 30% of middle-class.

The problem here lies in the fact that antenatal classes, even though they are available in clinics and hospitals as well as in the private sector, are usually attended by middle-class women.

The other factor is that educated women traditionally investigate sources of information, whereas the less educated woman is more influenced by her peers and female relatives. When I speak to parents several months after the birth, I see two very varied trends.

The hospital cleaner told me about his wife's experiences. 'The clinic nurse said the baby wasn't gaining weight and my mother-in-law convinced her that it wasn't worth struggling with breast-feeding *and* bottles, so she went straight on to the bottle.'

The medical student, who was exhausted trying to study for her final examinations soon after the birth, but who was not content to listen to one opinion. 'The clinic nurse advised supplementary feeds, but I consulted my family doctor and we agreed to keep the bottles to the minimum. The breastfeeding counsellor gave me some good ideas for boosting my milk supply, and after a week the baby was gaining weight.'

Travelling through pregnancy, women do not always start the journey from the same place.

Some women have babies at a more mature age when they already have self-awareness of their limitations; others are younger and naive and either expect too much of themselves or of those around them. The mature mother has her own problems of adjustment, rather as related in the story of Patricia, but the younger mother may need to go through a process of learning about herself and her limitations before adjusting fully to mother-hood.

One of my programmes is organized as a seminar for ultra-orthodox Jewish women. The men do not attend these courses because they would consider it immodest for the women to discuss these issues and do exercises in the presence of other husbands. The women are on average very young, they marry straight out of school and begin as soon as possible to obey the commandment: 'be fruitful and multiply'.

Although being aware of physical changes during the pregnancy, many of them have not read or learned about basic care of the body, in spite of the fact that their extended families are large and their own mothers might still be giving birth at regular intervals. So, much of my work is focused on giving information about nutrition, foetal development and the birth process.

However, their psychological attitude is very positive and while they fear pain and, like all women, worry about the health of the baby, they accept that this is a normal part of the life cycle and that God will take care of them. 'My friends say that birth is like a very hard expedition – when you get to the top of the mountain, it's worth all the effort,' summed up Rebecca when we discussed their expectations. For many of them it is the initiation into an essential phase of the life cycle and they enjoy an elevated status in the circle of family and acquaintances.

Since the men spend a great deal of time in their *yeshiva* (academy) studying the Torah, the women look to each other for support. It is not unusual to see the streets of their neighbourhood thronged with young mothers walking together to the play-ground, wheeling a pram, with several toddlers in tow and a baby on the way.

In some strata of society, women have a less positive body image and face birth with some trepidation. 'I think being a woman is so messy,' says Rita, 'First of all we have to put up with menstruating every month, then there is all this effort in having a baby. I feel so heavy and hot and perspire so much, I can't wait to finish my pregnancy and get back to normal, but I dread the pain and mess in giving birth.'

Rita needed a lot of support and guidance in order to accept that there is some pain and bleeding after the birth too, and that small babies, adorable as they are, do not always smell so sweet. Added to Rita's own problems with her negative attitude was the fact that her husband 'cannot wait for me to get my figure back and doesn't want me to breastfeed so that I can go on a strict diet immediately after the birth'.

But even a woman with a positive approach to pregnancy may be thwarted by the physical discomforts. In the early months, the hormones, particularly human chorionic gonadotrophin which relaxes the uterus and helps to build the placenta, can cause vomiting and nausea as well as muscle weakness and an overwhelming tiredness. In bygone days when women of leisure took to their couches during pregnancy, these discomforts were inconvenient. Today, when women expect to keep up their fulltime activity in their work and family life, these symptoms can be devastating.

In the same way, as pregnancy progresses, the foetal movements may be interpreted as being like a 'butterfly' or, as time goes on, 'there's a Cup Final champion growing inside me'.

Some women really look and feel better in pregnancy; the hormone changes suit their skin and hair and they enjoy choosing pregnancy clothes. Others feel fat and ungainly, 'I feel like a non-person,' said one woman whose frustration with her body was intensified by the fact that she was preparing to leave her job and already resented the arrangements made to replace her, 'as if I was already gone'.

Women have expressed their feelings as being like an 'incubator' or that the baby is a 'parasite' drawing on all their resources in order to grow and develop. Frank Huyton[7], in his paper 'Metabolic adaptation of pregnancy in prevention of handicap through antenatal care', writes:

> The foetus is by no means a helpless little dependent . . . as soon as he plugs into the uterine wall, he makes sure that his needs are served by altering his mother's physiology and fiddling with her control mechanisms.

Sexual problems can occur in pregnancy because the woman may feel tired and heavy and emotionally drained. And yet she still wants the warmth and closeness of her partner. The usual signals which stimulate her partner, such as touching or hugging, may for her be enough by themselves and just a way of seeking comfort and reassurance. So her partner may feel that he has his wires crossed and suffer rejection.

Although modern childbirth education only developed in the 1950s, women in China attended preparation classes as much as 1000 years ago, in order to promote tranquillity which would in turn influence the baby.

Dr Aidan MacFarlane, in his book *Psychology of Childbirth*,[8] quotes the poet Samuel Taylor Coleridge who wrote in 1802, 'The history of man for the nine months preceding his birth would probably be far more interesting and contain events of greater moment than all the years that follow it'.

The subject of maternal influence on the foetus, while fascinating and interesting, can be another source of guilt for the pregnant woman. There is a lot of literature on the subject, including the famous book *The Secret Life of the Unborn Child* by Drs Thomas Verny and John Kelly.[9] It is indeed significant that the uterine environment provides warmth and food and the uterus is the most effective incubator in which the infant can develop.

It is also nice to know that we can sing to our babies, play music and think nice thoughts, and that the baby will be stimulated and benefit from this. But when conditions are less than perfect, it can be a source of frustration for the mother if she feels that her baby is not enjoying psychological and spiritual benefit because of inevitable outside influences.

My second son was born after a very difficult and traumatic nine months of pregnancy. I was already exhausted, coping with one very small baby, and my mother was terminally ill and died during that period. I spent more time grieving and crying during that time than in concentrating on the pregnancy or projecting positive thinking either to my first son or the one on the way. Fortunately for all of us, he was born with a smile on his face and he grew into a strong cheerful personality whose role in the family from childhood onwards has been that of peacemaker and sorter-out of all problems.

So I was particularly sensitive to the needs of my pregnant clients when, at the time I began writing this book, my Haifa home was in the midst of Scud missile attacks during the Gulf crisis.

On more than one occasion, my class was interrupted by the sirens and we ran into a sealed sheltered room and put on our gas masks. The women's anxieties were very rational. They worried that they would give birth during an alert and have to wear a gas mask, but most women expressed more the fear that the foetus would be affected by the crisis and periods of panic which inevitably occurred whenever they heard the sirens. We worked through this by concentrating on deep relaxation so that whatever the outcome of the anxiety peaks, there would be an opportunity immediately afterwards to release the tension and focus on positive thoughts.

However normal the situation during pregnancy and however well the pregnancy is progressing, most women express fears and anxieties. In Ann Oakley's book *From Here to Maternity*,[10] she writes about pregnancy being a 'state of health' but how, nevertheless, there were superstitions and traditions which instilled fear into the pregnant woman. She lists the fears in order of the number of times they are mentioned in her interviews.

Fear of deformed baby	39%
Change in lifestyle, giving up work	35%
Birth	32%
Miscarriage or stillbirth	29%
Money or housing	20%
Looking after baby	14%
Getting fat	12%
Other	20%

Presumably the 32% who feared the birth could be subdivided into fear of hospitals and being taken over, fear of pain, loss of control or even of dying in childbirth.

We have to remember that much as we regret the total take-over by technology in the labour ward and the phasing out of home birth, the woman of the 1990s and her baby are far safer than even fifty years ago. It is still not clear how much can be attributed to foetal monitors or methods of speeding up labour because when these techniques are used inappropriately they cause more trouble than they prevent. However, women do have safer options of pain relief, blood banks are available in cases of haemorrhage, antibiotics can prevent and treat infections, and regular antenatal examinations with the availability of more sophisticated procedures where needed can detect and prevent complications.

In *Maternity – Letters from Working Women*,[11] a collection of letters published by the Womens Cooperative Guild in 1915, there were horrific stories of ignorance and neglect where women worked in factories and farmyards during pregnancy doing heavy manual work, without any maternity health care, only to return to the workplace immediately after the birth. It was through the efforts of the Guild and Herbert Samuel that a State maternity care system was set up, available to every woman in Britain, providing antenatal clinics, nutritional supplements and maternity leave.

Women's fears focus perhaps less on physical danger than on the medicalization of birth, of taking birth out of the home and putting what is a natural healthy life process into an atmosphere of intensive care. In the same way as the family dog or cat will find a warm, dark, sheltered place like the linen cupboard to give birth and will stop labour if disturbed, so women fear the light, bright, noisy, alien conditions of hospital and many do indeed stop contractions on admission to the labour ward, only to restart when they have settled down and feel more at home.

The history of childbirth superstitions and traditions combined with the do's and dont's and old wives tales relayed by the neighbours and extended family have conditioned women to face this experience with fear and trepidation. So the childbirth educator or the nurse at the antenatal clinic has a responsibility to recognize these situations and reduce this fear, and, at the same time, to ensure that their clients do not go away with unrealistic expectations.

Whatever form of childbirth preparation the woman receives, the message should be clear that a prepared birth will be a good experience, whether it is straightforward without medical intervention or whether there is a need for inductions, epidurals or even surgery. But it will only be a positive experience if the woman is aware of what is happening and is able to use her coping skills. And it is this satisfaction with the birth experience which will carry her through with self-confidence into the days and weeks of bonding and caring for her baby.

As one of my favourite childbirth educators, Shulamit, based in Jerusalem, once commented at a teachers' meeting: 'We must make sure that our women come out of the labour room with their self-esteem intact, if not their perineum'.

2   *The Impact of Birth*

WOMEN who experience changes or difficulties in adjustment after the birth will not necessarily find the causes rooted in those hours, days, weeks or even months. One of the most powerful influences on the mental health of a woman during the period following the birth of a baby is the experience itself.

We have discussed in Chapter 1 how fantasies and expectations during pregnancy can affect the woman throughout and after the birth. But the birth is the culmination of all the hopes and fears, and the woman who emerges from the delivery room with her self-esteem intact will be able to handle the next phase of life with more confidence.

In the Book of *Genesis*[1] women are instructed to be fruitful and multiply, but already, part way through that great Book, there is mention of Eve's curse, *b'etzev teldi*, which is popularly translated from the Hebrew as 'in pain you shall labour'.[2]

In fact, the literal translation of *etzev* is not pain but sadness or toil. Any woman who has given birth knows that it is the hardest day's work she has ever done, but it is far from sad. It may be intense, ecstatic, devastating, orgasmic – but not sad.

Last year I was invited to facilitate a session for the local mothers support group, most of whom had attended one of my prenatal education programmes. All of the women had given birth six months previously and were in the midst of decision-making about where to go from here. I suggested that before they discuss these decisions, we should first go backwards and examine feelings and reactions about the birth itself, in order to feel that that period of life was completed, thus enabling them to go forward.

It was a stormy winter afternoon and we sat warm and cosy, the mothers and babies in my living room, deeply engrossed and oblivious to the rain lashing against the windows and the waves crashing on the shore far below. And the session which had been scheduled to last a couple of hours went on into the evening.

At first the women shrugged their shoulders: 'It's such a long time ago – we've forgotten all about it'. I smiled, for my children were born far more than six months ago and I have not forgotten one moment of those births. Maybe for some of the women, it was easier to forget the immediate past.

And then the floodgates opened. Each woman expressed her feelings of wonder, awe, ecstasy, thanksgiving mixed with anger, frustration, helplessness and loss of control.

Surprisingly, the woman with the least anger was Miranda who had endured the most complicated birth. A rare situation of a last-minute diagnosis of placenta praevia had resulted in an emergency caesarean during which there had been a severe haemorrhage. She had been in intensive care for two days, wired up to intravenous infusions and monitors, much to the consternation of her family and friends. And yet when I visited her the same evening, she was actually smiling through it all.

When we discussed this long after the event, Miranda said that although the situation was frightening, she felt that she had had some sort of control. In fact, during pregnancy she had attended the course, read a lot of materials and was aware of her body. Therefore it was not bleeding, which is the usual warning of placenta praevia, but other symptoms which took her to the hospital for a check-up and she felt that she had helped the situation by being aware of what was happening to her.

Interestingly, during her pregnancy she had been adamant about natural birth and was very apprehensive about high-tech maternity wards. In the event, she was thankful for modern technology and her recovery was quick and uneventful.

The other women in the group had experienced less dramatic births but each had a story of adjustment.

Ellen and her husband had endured seven years of fertility problems, with three miscarriages during that time. This pregnancy had progressed normally and she entered her last trimester hopefully. But at thirty weeks she was hospitalized with toxaemia (pre-eclampsia) and spent the next few weeks alternating between resting at home and receiving treatment in hospital. Eventually, the birth was induced at thirty-seven weeks and although technically this is not a premature birth, the toxaemia had caused low birth weight. The labour was long and Ellen agreed to an epidural anaesthetic because the pain was beyond endurance.

Although she had worked through all the aspects of medication during the pregnancy course and discussed the benefits as well as disadvantages of epidurals, Ellen had been very keen to give birth naturally after the long years of infertility and continuous medication.

On the day Ellen came home, her husband was out of town and she had no immediate family in the area. 'I had coped with those weeks so calmly,' said Ellen, 'but that homecoming just broke me up. We thought that I had one more day in hospital so my husband took the opportunity to do a day's work which took him away overnight. I had just arrived home and was trying to decide what to do first when the van arrived with all the baby equipment. The driver just dumped it on the pavement and I was sitting there in tears, not knowing what to do, until some neighbours came to help.'

By late evening, Ellen was exhausted, and she and the baby were crying it out, until in desperation she called for help. It was not only the difficult homecoming which had triggered off this reaction, but the fear and feeling of being out of control which she had experienced during the decision-making about inducing the birth. 'I knew that it was logical to induce, my blood pressure was high, the baby was not growing and it was obvious that at thirty-seven weeks, the baby was not in any danger if born at this point,' she said. 'I know that after all those years of desperately wanting a baby I should be grateful that everything was all right, but suddenly I was overwhelmed with disappointment that I again had been dependent on technology and medication.' The loneliness on arriving home and the stupidity of the delivery man had been the last straw.

For many women there are 'missing links', inconsistencies in procedures or routines in the labour ward, lack of sufficient explanation as to why it was advisable to induce the birth or use forceps or, in more rare cases, drugs given without permission.

Karen Stolte's 1986 work[3] discusses the missing pieces in women's obstetric history, factors such as not understanding what happened during the labour or receiving treatment without consent. In these cases, there is often difficult adjustment after the birth until the jigsaw puzzle is complete.

Debbie had been eagerly anticipating the birth of her first baby.

She was young, healthy and the pregnancy proceeded normally. She would have preferred a home birth but understood the logic of having a first baby in hospital. Debbie is a committed vegan and claims that she always managed to cure aches and pains with the right herbs and teas. If she did occasionally take a prescription for antibiotics or other drugs, the reaction was very strong. She therefore was apprehensive about being given drugs during labour and was assured by her caregivers that the use of analgesics or anaesthetics was an option which would only be given with her permission.

Debbie gave birth in a hospital which is known for its liberal ideas and positive communication between staff and the woman in labour and her partner or support person. However, in the best of departments there are always one or two staff members who prefer to take control, and in this case, Debbie was given a dose of pethidine without realizing what was happening. Her husband asked the doctor what injection he was giving, and before he could prevent it happening the doctor replied that it 'is good for her pain'.

Up to this point, Debbie had happily relaxed and breathed her way through the first-stage contractions, had kept mobile and coped optimistically. After the pethidine, Debbie was so sleepy and disorientated that she could not move from the bed. The pain was worse and she could not concentrate on controlled breathing. She felt very depressed and the effects of the pethidine lasted into the second stage. She was unable to push effectively, was given a large episiotomy which required a lot of stitches, and the baby was born floppy and sleepy. The midwife put the baby onto Debbie's stomach for her to cuddle, but Debbie had no interest in anything. This lack of interest lasted for six months!

While she was still in hospital, Debbie felt that she was disintegrating. She started to tremble and shiver and cry, and the psychiatrist was called. He asked her a multitude of questions about her family history, indicating that somewhere there was some mental instability. But he did not ask the most important question. What happened during the birth?

Debbie had badly wanted to breastfeed and in spite of her lethargy and distancing from the baby, she did try to persevere. But the psychiatrist who followed up her depression advised her that the situation was aggravated by the hormones of lactation.

So at four weeks after the birth, Debbie had experienced a nightmare contrary to all her expectations. She had wanted a natural birth, had been able to cope with pain, had enjoyed the control. Her labour had progressed normally and there was no reason at all to give medication. Debbie had been very enthusiastic about immediate infant bonding and breastfeeding for the first year of life. All these hopes and dreams had been shattered with one injection of a drug given without her consent. And it took over six months for Debbie to recover sufficiently to function normally.

While the use of medication for pain relief is a blessing for many women in labour, it is known that there are sometimes less desirable side effects, not only because of how the drug works on the physical systems of mother and baby but also on their psychological well being.

Aidan MacFarlane's *Psychology of Childbirth* quotes Eugene Marais[4] who, in *The Soul of the Ape*, recognizes that higher animals do experience pain during labour but that in certain species where drugs were given, there was radically altered behaviour towards the young after the birth. Marais observed a herd of buck in which for fifteen years there had been no case of a mother refusing to care for her young. He took ten of these animals and during their births administered analgesics. In all cases, the mothers rejected their newborns.

He hastens to add that we should not immediately make comparisons with human mothers, but this does perhaps suggest caution when administering drugs in the labour ward. Had the doctor got to know Debbie and found out more about her, there were clear warnings here that she might be adversely affected by being given pethidine at a time when she neither requested it nor felt that she needed any form of pain relief.

EXPERIENCES OF MIDWIVES

'I had a wonderful midwife who was really caring and positive,' says Sheila. 'She helped me keep moving, encouraged my husband and brought him cups of tea. She was like a mother.' This midwife went off duty two hours before the baby was born. 'The next midwife acted totally contrary to what I wanted,' continued Sheila. 'She made me lie flat, and I went through a painful transition which could have been eased if I could have crouched on all fours or sat upright.'

Helen's husband had called me from the hospital to ask if I

would visit them in the neonatal intensive care unit. I was surprised because I knew that this was not a premature birth, and when we had last met, the foetus had been a good weight.

Helen was sitting next to the baby's cot crying. 'I haven't stopped crying since I gave birth. It's all my fault. I can't live with this guilt.' Her husband told me that during the birth, there had been some foetal distress but not sufficient to warrant a caesarean. The labour was progressing well and the staff told them that once the baby was born, he should recover spontaneously and quickly.

The transition stage was long and Helen felt more comfortable on all fours but the midwife was adamant that she must lie down, lie still and not push, several negative inactions which do not go easily together. The contractions were so overwhelming, and in that uncomfortable position, Helen felt her control slipping and started to push. 'You're harming your baby,' the midwife kept reminding her. The baby was born with a low Apgar score and respiratory problems. Helen was convinced that it was her fault and was distraught with anxiety and guilt.

After arranging a meeting between the doctor who had been on duty at that time, the head midwife and the parents, it was clear that the problems were temporary. There was a good chance that the baby would be out of intensive care within a day or two and that there was absolutely no link between this problem and Helen's behaviour during the birth.

Reading *The History of Midwifery*,[5] it is hard to believe that such an unkind and insensitive midwife managed to graduate from nursing school. This book was written as the final thesis at the end of the author's midwifery course and should perhaps become compulsory reading for all nursing students. It tells us that the tradition of midwifery goes back to the beginning of recorded history. In *Exodus*, we read of the midwives of Egypt who tried to conceal the male Jewish babies whom the Pharaoh had decreed should be slain at birth.

Papyri have been found dated to 1950BCE with recipes for fertility taught by midwives who worked with priests and physicians.

In *The Birth of the Royal Children*, Papyrus Westcar 1650–1550BCE, three midwives prevent intervention by saying 'We understand childbirth,' and close the door on the father who is impatiently suggesting ways of speeding up the birth.

In ancient Greece, midwives were called *omphalotoma* or 'navel cutters' and enjoyed a high social status.

Soranus (AD98–138) wrote the first textbook for midwives: 'She should have given birth herself and not be too young. She should be literate, industrious, have a good memory, be patient'.

More up-to-date guides for midwives include the British John Maubray who wrote in 1725: 'The midwife should be patient, pleasant, soft, meek and mild in order to encourage and comfort women in labour'.

The medicalization of birth began in France with the introduction of male midwives at the time of Louis XIV. It was this king who, wanting to 'observe' (not participate with) his concubine in childbirth, requested that she lie with her legs raised so that he could sit at the end of the bed and watch with as little effort as possible! Margaret Stephen, a mid-eighteenth century midwife to Queen Charlotte, wrote: 'By using men in the business of a midwife, ladies have been induced to dispense with delicacy'.

Of course, in English nineteenth-century literature, the midwife is sometimes depicted as gin-swilling and less than hygienic. In 1902, efforts were made to ensure a high standard by initiating a register and midwives in England could only work with a licence.

Midwives were much in demand during the First World War, when there was a dearth of physicians, but today Britain stands almost alone as a country where midwives, not obstetricians, deliver babies in uncomplicated births.

HOME OR HOSPITAL?

With this battle for equality, one would therefore expect the best of quality care from midwives in the labour ward. The problems which occasionally arise are caused by lack of communication and are perhaps a reflection of the inadequate system of care, not so much in terms of skill or equipment, but in insufficient concentration on the continuum of care.

The pregnant woman attends an antenatal clinic, either with her family doctor or at the hospital. Her family doctor knows her and understands her fears and anxieties, but the hospital clinic will be staffed by different doctors and nurses at every visit.

On admission to hospital at the onset of labour, the staff of the labour ward are entirely unknown to her. Just at a time when she is at her most vulnerable, the only familiar face is that of her partner or support person and some women do not even have that.

In many hospitals, the staff midwives do meet with clients before the birth, to answer questions, accompany them on a tour of the ward and introduce them to some of the staff. But invariably, if a woman is admitted at night or at times when these midwives are not on duty, they will again meet a set of strange faces.

It is no wonder that many women prefer home births where they establish a relationship with the midwife months before the birth. It is quite a different feeling, giving birth in one's own home with all its familiar comforts, not having to share a bathroom, and with the baby at one's side constantly. But there is also a shift in the relationship between the family and the caregivers because the doctor and midwife are guests in the home.

In countries like Britain and Holland where home births are available within the health service many women and childbirth organizations are fighting to retain this right.

Professor G. J. Kloosterman of the University of Amsterdam writes: 'Childbirth in itself is a natural phenomenon and in the majority of cases needs no interference . . . This job can be done in the best way if the woman is self-confident and stays in surroundings where she is the real centre . . . a healthy woman who gives birth spontaneously does a job which cannot be improved on'.[6]

Not all women are suited to home births. The advantage of home birth being an integral part of an established health system is that women are screened so that they can be advised if they are at all at risk and should therefore give birth in the hospital.

In many countries, the health system does not offer planned home births, and in Canada it is even illegal for a midwife to work on her own.

A recent television programme about birthing alternatives in Israel described the lack of infrastructure for home births because hospitals are considered a sign of progress not only by the caregivers but by the women themselves. Many Israelis are refugees from undeveloped countries and consider that giving birth in a modern high-tech maternity ward is the ultimate in birth conditions.

Since family doctors in Israel do not supervise pregnancy care, the obstetricians are very interested in keeping birth in the domain of their hospitals. During the programme, it was explained that while birth should be a natural phenomenon, the transition from a normal to a pathological emergency situation can be very fast and if there are no specialized facilities, such as in Britain and Holland, for transporting women urgently to hospital, then home birth is hazardous even for the supposedly low-risk woman.

Britain's Domino system is perhaps an ideal compromise in that the woman's own familiar midwife and GP accompany her to the hospital, attend the birth and return home with her the same day. It is perhaps a sign of regression that succeeding government health departments have tried to phase out home births and close down cottage hospitals and GP units.

Whether or not home births are available, it is clearly the task of hospital managements to make the maternity departments more homelike with adequate privacy, choice of support persons and unlimited access to the baby.

CULTURAL CONSIDERATIONS

To return to the stories of the women who sat in my home that rainy afternoon, we can see that many of these women suffered disappointment or frustration through things being done without their knowledge or consent, or with a lack of sensitivity.

There are deep-rooted reasons why some women themselves do not behave rationally during their birth experience.

Maggie is a university graduate with a very high level of intelligence. She studied the stages of pregnancy and birth with the same diligence as she had studied chemistry at university.

For Maggie, pregnancy was an awesome and wondrous period of her life. She was a dwarf and had never anticipated that she would have a normal married life and bear children. Her husband was of normal height and was very protective and tender to his wife.

She was anticipating a vaginal birth because although her arms and legs were very short, her pelvis was sufficiently wide for childbirth. She was determined that everything would be normal.

At the beginning of the ninth month of pregnancy, Maggie attended the local antenatal clinic, and the nurse, shocked by the rise in Maggie's blood pressure, advised her to go straight to the hospital and gave her a letter of referral. Maggie did not go to the hospital but went home without saying anything to her family.

The next day, the clinic nurse phoned the hospital to enquire about Maggie, and was very anxious when she heard that she had not checked in. She went to her home and urged her to go to the hospital without delay. By the time Maggie was examined, her blood pressure was dangerously high and there were signs of placental separation. An emergency caesarean was the only way of averting a disaster to both mother and baby.

Maggie recovered quickly from the operation and the baby was well. But her anger overwhelmed her and she could not stop weeping. Again her body had let her down and she felt a prisoner within its limitations. The staff patiently explained that the problems encountered in this pregnancy could happen to anyone and that there was every chance that her next pregnancy would be uneventful followed by a vaginal birth.

It took over a week for Maggie's anger to subside and by that time she was breastfeeding happily. The baby gained weight and was very content with mother's milk. The breastfeeding experience was so positive and enjoyable that Maggie's faith in her own body was renewed. Maggie's baby was still breastfed one year later and Maggie was at peace with herself and optimistically planning another pregnancy.

These stories come from women from all walks of life. For some of them there was a communication problem, either because they were giving birth in a country where they were not using their mother tongue, or because their expectations had been established during their childhood in a place and time where conditions were very different.

In every hospital, women from many varied ethnic groups and cultural norms give birth influenced by their origins and the expectations of the society in which they have been raised. Take simple issues like food taboos, modesty in dress, exposure of the body to male doctors, and already we can see the root of many conflicts. In both Islam and Judaism, certain foods or combinations of foods are forbidden. The very orthodox will make sure that their bodies are hidden, which is rather a problem when the standard gown handed out in the labour wards is skimpy and buttock-length.

In some religions, orthodox men are forbidden from accompanying their wives to the maternity ward and even where they participate in the first stage of labour, they may not touch or massage her.

The interpretation of religious laws is very varied. Many orthodox Jewish men, for example, are directed by their rabbis that helping their wife in labour by physical contact is '*pikuach nefesh*', life-saving, in the same way as one may break the Sabbath laws and drive a car if a woman is in labour or if a sick person has to be taken to the hospital.

Muslim women prefer only to be examined by female doctors or midwives, and will avoid as much as possible being seen naked or partly undressed.

Brigette Jordan has written extensively on the anthropology of childbirth. In her paper 'The hut and the hospital',[7] she writes: 'As the tools of birth change from familiar household objects such as hammocks and beds to delivery tables and foetal monitors, significant changes occur in the ability to give physical support to women during labour'.

There are basic superstitions which may not be comprehended in a modern maternity unit. Oriental Jewish communities, for example, keep vigil over the male child, and the 'evil eye' was averted by asking the neighbourhood children to visit the house with nuts and sweets and to recite prayers. Jeremiah and Micah constantly refer in the Bible[8] to the intensity of pain. In the Talmud there is emphasis on death in childbirth as a result of neglect of family purity.

Not only in Judaism are there so many superstitions. In Salonika, for example, all doors and cupboards are kept open during pregnancy to prevent miscarriage. A difficult birth was made easier by undoing all knots and ties in the woman's garments and again by opening all the doors.

In Kurdistan, the mother is not allowed to leave the house at night for forty days after the birth. There are Judaeo-Christian myths about the spirit of Lillith entering the body of the mother and this leads to the custom of not leaving the woman alone after the birth.

These myths and superstitions die hard and it is no wonder that modern women also face birth with some trepidation, which is not immediately assuaged even when the birth is safely over.

If a particular ethnic group is transferred from one environment to another, as happens with refugees in this turbulent world, this transition can cause severe anxiety and fear at a time when a woman is at her most vulnerable.

If one takes all these cultural factors and places them in a modern hospital, there may well be problems of communication. If individual sensitivities are threatened, then this poses a severe identity problem which in turn can also be a cause for difficulties in adjusting after the birth.

The Bloomsbury Health Authority[9] recently published a useful guide to caregivers about the cultural taboos and expectations of minority groups. The message was clear that not only foreigners and aliens are 'ethnic groups with cultural norms'. The native Briton too has been moulded by environment and will demand a situation according to expectations which have been imprinted throughout childhood.

STRESS AND CHILDBIRTH

Nature has a clever system of helping women cope with the memories of labour. During times of stress, including during childbirth, the body produces endorphins, hormones which help us to 'fight or flight'. It is these which cause us to react with unbelievable speed to an emergency and afterwards we wonder how we ran so fast. The endorphins produce the energy and ability to act fast, and afterwards the event is slightly foggy and cannot be remembered in detail.

One day, I went to the VAT office, which in my town is situated in the Customs and Excise building in the port. I came away with an enormous incorrect bill which had to be paid in fourteen days and I was trying to fathom out how to get this bill investigated as I left the building.

In order to get back to my car I had to cross the railway line which runs through the port. I was so preoccupied with this problem that I did not notice that a train was approaching. Suddenly I heard a frantic whistling and hooting, and looking up, I saw the engine almost on me. I do not know to this day how I ran so fast and reacted so quickly, but certainly my endorphins saved me and I was left only with a racing pulse and a rather foggy recollection of those seconds of reaction.

Endorphin release in stress is accompanied by increased adrenaline with the attendant dry mouth, rapid pulse, butterfly tummy and sweating. This is not desirable for extended periods and while an optimum level of arousal is necessary for achievement, too much impairs performance and leads to exhaustion.

During labour, natural endorphins are released, providing unexpected energy and optimism. This enables the woman to cope with the enormous effort of giving birth and to a certain extent blocks out pain.

Professor Arthur Eidelman, head of the neonatal unit at

Jerusalem's Shaare Zedek hospital, has researched how endorphins affect labour. In one of his papers given at a conference on perinatal education,[10] he produces the interesting fact that drugs given during labour affect the natural endorphins.

This means that instead of women using their own 'fight or flight' mechanisms, the drug dulls the senses, intending to block out the pain. However, it does not produce the energy, wellbeing or euphoric aftermath which result from the woman's own natural resources. In extreme cases it results in the sort of depression suffered by Debbie.

In Jane Madders' *Stress and Relaxation*,[11] she describes the 'human function' curve (Figure 1), the swing of healthy tension and exhaustion, and how the 'fatigue point' reduces actual performance drastically as compared with intended performance. For this reason, much of Jane Madders' work in this field concentrates on deep relaxation and how to control the 'fight or flight' instinct and use it constructively during the efforts of labour and other life crises.

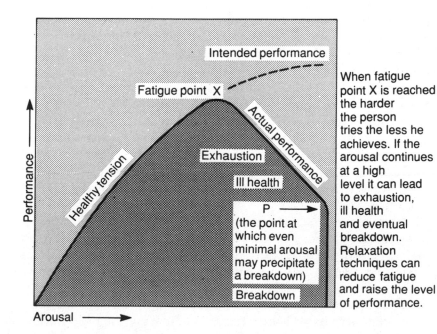

Figure 1. The human function curve (reproduced with permission from *Stress and Relaxation* by Jane Madders, published by Martin Dunitz, 1979)

BONDING AFTER BIRTH

While most methods of childbirth education and books dealing with childbirth concentrate on the pregnancy and labour, it was Dr Frederick Leboyer who brought the world's attention to the importance of those precious moments following the birth.

Until he wrote *Birth Without Violence* in 1976,[12] not much attention was paid to the reaction of the baby to all this activity. In many hospitals throughout the world, babies were turned upside down, smacked on their bottoms to stimulate breathing, wrapped up and whisked off to the nursery, leaving their exhausted mothers wondering what it was all about.

Mothering is not always a spontaneous reaction, and in maternity units where mothers and babies are separated for long periods of time, not only is breastfeeding difficult but the natural bonding between mother and infant is delayed.

Since Dr Leboyer published his work, many hospitals have changed their systems. Much of the credit is also due to conscientious caregivers, midwives, educators and, of course, to the parents who have demanded change.

If the baby is born without problems, he will normally breathe spontaneously with the rush of relatively cold air which greets him on emerging from the warm safe uterus, rather like the gasp you give when you get into a cold shower.

The baby's airways sometimes need to be cleared but after this the baby will give a good hearty cry, turn pink and all is well with the world. There is therefore no good reason not to put him straight on his mother's abdomen so that he can relax after his hard work, feel his mother's warmth and fragrance. He may well start rooting round for the nipple and start sucking. The milk that he receives at that point, the colostrum, is rich in nutrients and antibodies.

This experience is of the utmost satisfaction to the mother, however tired she may be after labouring for several hours. Again there is a rush of endorphins which enhance her euphoria and a release of prolactin which is the lactation hormone. The baby's sucking releases another hormone, oxytocin, which in turn helps the uterus to contract. If there have been any problems in expulsion of the placenta, this hormone will facilitate the procedure.

Mothers who are deprived of this immediate bonding may have to wait several hours before receiving their baby, by which time the relief of the birth has worn off, her stitches may begin to hurt and she is feeling the aftermath of exhaustion and lack of well-being.

While researchers such as Marshall Klaus and John Kennell[13] write about the effects of early bonding on infant–mother relationships, many studies show how this natural period of 'getting to know you' after the birth is a factor in preventing depression.

Many hospitals now offer rooming-in, where the mother and baby spend most of their time together. Some pregnant women feel that it will impose an unreasonable burden on them at a time when they need rest and recuperation. But indeed, if a baby is quietly tucked up in his crib next to the mother's bed, she will feel far less anxious than trying to identify his cry among all the screaming babies in the nursery along the hall.

The staff in these units need to be specifically trained to give guidance and to teach the new mother how to breastfeed and care for her baby.

By the time she leaves the hospital, she will have much more confidence, her milk supply will be established without the routine intervention of supplementary bottles, and she will feel that she is already acquainted with this baby instead of bringing home a strange little parcel.

THE SEX OF THE BABY

The bonding period also helps a mother to cope with any residual disappointment if the baby is not the desired sex.

Sophisticated ultrasound techniques which can detect the sex of the baby early in pregnancy are available to most women. Amniocentesis, a test of the amniotic fluid which measures alpha-foetoprotein as well as the chromosome count, is recommended to a selected category of pregnant women and also detects the baby's sex as early as sixteen weeks.

Some couples say that it is good to know this in advance and stop all the speculation and old wives' tales. But it is not unknown for a woman in a third or fourth pregnancy to be so disappointed and depressed that she is having yet another son or another daughter that she seriously considers abortion.

After the baby is born, most of this ambivalence disappears and it is hard to imagine that one was ever the slightest bit disappointed with this baby who has in the end turned out to be beautiful and healthy.

My first two sons were born a year apart, and two years later our third child was born. During the pregnancy I certainly hoped for a daughter. This birth was longer than the previous ones and during the pain and hours of patient waiting I remember thinking that it had better be a girl because I wasn't going through this again!

My son was born and in a daze of exhaustion I didn't show very much interest for the first half hour. Fortunately, this birth was at home and I was left with the baby after the midwife and doctor finished their work. He too had suffered a long labour and was restless and fretful. Half alseep myself, I leaned over his crib which was next to my bed and laid a hand on him. Somehow I made contact with his hand and he grasped my finger and held on for dear life.

The foundations for our beautiful lifelong mother–son relationship were set in that hour or two. As I watched him grow into a lively, healthy child with a very individual and interesting personality, I cannot imagine how I could have experienced a moment of disappointment.

Had I known in advance the sex of my baby, I am sure it would have affected my feelings and anticipation during the pregnancy. As it was, during this very special period of being at one with my baby immediately after the birth, the wonder and thankfulness took over from the initial tiredness and let-down feeling.

Of course it does not always work out that way. There are case histories of children who are abused and their personalities irreversibly twisted because they in their innocence committed the crime of being born the wrong sex.

In some cultures, as we discuss in the chapter on parenthood, the birth of another daughter may make the mother a social outcast, rejected by her husband. The mother's reaction at the time of birth is one of fear.

I was working in the Rambam Medical Centre in Haifa during the early days of the war in Lebanon. Pregnant women who lived in the south of Lebanon were unable to travel for medical care because of the cross-fire of the various fighting factions. When labour began, they were rescued by helicopters and taken to the Haifa hospital to give birth. Although their physical safety was assured, they nevertheless suffered separation trauma because their families and support network were still in the war zone.

One evening, I tried to help a young woman who was alone in the labour ward. She spoke no English or Hebrew and we communicated by sign language. Young as she was, this was her third birth, and she still did not seem to understand the stages or progress of labour. She began bearing down long before the cervix was dilated and the baby was becoming distressed.

We tried to demonstrate with body language how to breathe and relax and she did try to cooperate. However, the birth was long and difficult and the baby was born with a low Apgar score and breathing difficulties. The paediatrician rushed her away for resuscitation and after a tense ten minutes, brought the baby back looking pink and healthy. There was relief in the room, except from the mother who was horrified that the baby was a girl, her third daughter.

Fortunately, in that hospital, babies are kept in constant contact with the mothers and by the time I visited her again on the day she left hospital, she was smiling and happy with her baby who was indeed a beautiful healthy girl.

THE PLACENTA

In all the discussions on birth, very rarely is attention paid to the rituals and significance of the disposal of the placenta.

Theoretically, there is no more use for the placenta once the baby is born. It separates from the uterine wall within 10–30 minutes after the birth and is expelled. The umbilical cord is cut before this, by which time the baby is hopefully breathing freely. The placenta is checked to make sure it is complete, and then often thrown away with all the soiled pads in the incinerator.

Some hospitals sell the placenta to cosmetic companies who use it for rejuvenating face creams. It can in fact be donated to a burns unit because its antibiotic and antiseptic properties are very beneficial for patients who have had skin grafting. The placenta has also been used for research into genetic diseases and some life-saving drugs are being developed using placental matter.

There are many traditions and superstitions surrounding the placenta and in some agricultural cultures, it is planted under a tree in order to improve the fertility of the village. Others eat the placenta, and it is thought to be beneficial in preventing postnatal depression.

New Generation, the journal of the National Childbirth Trust, published an article by Mary Field[14] on placentophagy, the eating of the placenta. The article quotes a case history of a woman who suffered very severe postnatal depression after her first birth, following a normal event-free pregnancy. After her second birth, in an effort to prevent a recurrence of the depression, the woman ate the placenta which is rich in natural progesterone, zinc and vitamin E, all of which are known to promote wellbeing and efficient function of the central nervous system.

This may sound very gruesome to many of us, but in fact most female mammals cut the umbilical cords with their teeth, lick their babies to clean them and stimulate their breathing, and finally eat the placenta.

When my second baby was due and a home birth planned, we saved old sheets for the bed and newspapers to cover the carpet. Our female cat was pregnant also and we were not sure who would give birth first. As my own births were always late, I was quite jealous of Delilah when she curled up on our bed and started to purr with the first contractions.

We hastily covered the bed with the old sheets prepared for my labour, and watched as she quietly and with great dignity produced three beautiful little kittens. By the end of the birth, there was not one drop of blood or placental tissue left on the sheet, and she had cleaned herself and the kittens and settled down to the serious business of feeding them.

Needless to say, Delilah did not suffer from postnatal depression!

3   Three-Day Blues – or Postnatal Depression?

M OST of us have heard of women who suffer from depression after the birth of a baby. In very rare cases, a woman may be so ill that she needs hospitalization or a long course of anti-depressive drugs because her behaviour is unpredictable and bizarre or she is totally cut off from reality.

Since most pregnant women and their families fear that this will happen to them, it is perhaps a comfort to know that only 0.2% of women are so severely affected. While 80% of new mothers experience some degree of depression or weepiness during the days or weeks after the birth, 10% are somewhere in the middle, suffering a longer period of emotional disturbance but this is not sufficiently serious to need long-term treatment.

In later chapters we shall discuss the normal difficulties in adjusting to motherhood, but it is important to understand the aetiology and treatment of postnatal depression or disturbance (PND) in all its forms.

Monty Python fans might have been amused by the film *The Meaning of Life*, when the poor labouring woman was hooked up to 'the machine that goes ping' which got far more attention from the obstetricians than she did. When she asks what she should be doing, they chorus in astonishment: 'But you're not *qualified!*' This was followed by a sequence in which the doctor hands the woman a packet of pills, warning her: 'You may feel rather depressed after all this – we call it PND'.

This excerpt was intended to be funny, but it is really too near the truth. Obviously the Monty Python team had had some real-life hair-raising experiences in the labour ward. It does show, however, that PND is in fact a common term, albeit misunderstood and misinterpreted. Women should understand that they are not alone with this and should seek support and help.

The birth itself is followed by a feeling of euphoria, unparalleled by any other life experience. It is worth giving birth just for that glorious feeling of release and relief. The mother then settles down to a well-earned rest and wakes up feeling refreshed and that all is well with the world.

Temporary weepiness or a let-down feeling are very common in the days after the birth, very often while the mother is still in the hospital. For that reason, it is called the 'three-day blues'.

During this period, several physiological and hormonal changes are taking place. There may be stitches which are painful, the breasts will feel full and heavy, there will be bloody lochia discharge as the uterus contracts and sheds the lining which has built up over the past nine months. The stomach feels like an empty sack and the skin of the abdomen looks like crepe paper.

At the same time, the hormones, oestrogen, progesterone and human chorionic gonadotrophin, which have nurtured the pregnancy are being replaced by oxytocin and prolactin, the lactation hormones. In the same way as women have mood changes during the premenstrual period and in menopause, this hormone swing after birth often causes a sort of seesaw between anxiety and depression, surplus energy and fatigue.

A few days after the birth of our first baby, my husband walked into my hospital room and found me sitting on the floor, in floods of tears, with the contents of my bag scattered all around me. All that had happened was that I couldn't find my hairbrush!

If these changes only last a few days, they are accepted as a normal result of the tremendous physical and emotional effort expended during pregnancy and birth.

Dr Ulla Waldenstrom of Uppsala University, Sweden,[1] links fatigue and emotional overreaction with hospital discharge. Her study showed that it did not matter whether it was early or later discharge, the 'three-day blues' were often at their worst on the day or two after return from hospital.

Reports from fifty women who were discharged 24–48 hours after the birth, with domiciliary midwives visits, showed a tiredness peak 2–4 days after the birth. Fifty-four women who were discharged after six days reported a peak at 5–7 days. There was no significant difference in the severity of fatigue and tearfulness in these two groups during the two weeks after birth, but increased depression was reported in the first six weeks in the group who were discharged later.

There does seem to be some logic in this, for although it may seem advantageous for a woman to get the extra day of hospital care, in actuality, women do not get much rest in a busy ward.

In a typical situation, Amanda records: 'I gave birth at 2 am but having suffered from toxaemia, my blood pressure was checked every hour after the baby was born. For this reason, I was left, cold and uncomfortable on the hard labour bed until 5 am when I was taken to the ward. I thankfully settled into a comparatively comfortable bed hoping to catch up on some sleep.

'By 5.30 am the ward was full of crying babies latching onto their mothers; women who had not yet had their babies were woken up to have their temperatures taken.

'At 6.30 things quietened down and I thought I might get an hour's sleep before breakfast when the paper boy came round asking who wanted the Telegraph or Express. After breakfast, I got up and showered and went to look for my baby, spent some time breastfeeding her and returned to bed with a drink, ready for some sleep before lunch.

'Out in the corridor could be heard an ominous crashing of buckets and in came an army of cleaners, moving beds, and pushing bedside lockers to one side.

'And so that day progressed until my husband visited in the late afternoon and I begged him to get me out of there.'

Amanda's previous births had been at home with organized home help, the baby slept next to her and she could rest between feeds or cuddle the other children on the bed. Nobody woke her up to take her temperature and if her home help saw her sleeping, she stayed out of the room and kept the children quiet.

Toxaemia is a contraindication for home birth, but Amanda requested discharge from hospital at the first opportunity.

The correlation between day of discharge and weepiness or fatigue is also understandable because it is indeed overwhelming to come home with a new baby. The phone doesn't stop ringing, neighbours drop in, and if this is the first birth, the baby is sensitive to the fact that he has to depend on his learner parents.

It is therefore quite normal for a woman to experience an emotional and physical reaction during those hectic days. But for some women, this period is extended into months, and it affects her mothering experience and her relationships with her partner and her family. If PND lasts more than a couple of weeks, it is worth getting professional advice because the longer it continues the harder it is to cure.

At a seminar in Australia, Dr Derrick Dodshon, a London psychologist,[2] said: 'The diagnosis is often missed because the woman is seen as having a personality defect, she may be slovenly, untidy, incompetent, when in actual fact she is depressed. In most cases, this depression is self-limiting and lasts for a few weeks or months, but researchers in the United Kingdom would allege that it can last for as long as twenty years.'

Dr Dodshon warns that this depression may not start immediately after birth but may emerge at a later stage, for example when the mother stops breastfeeding or starts taking the Pill again.

Dr Bruce Pitt, in his studies at St Bartholomew's, London,[3] reinforces the need to control the time span of PND. Out of 305 women he examined after birth, thirty-three (the accepted 10%) suffered depression more severe than the three-day blues. Six to eight weeks later, 10.8% of the thirty-three were still depressed. One year later, 43% of the 10.8% had still not recovered.

Beverley and Bernard Chalmers of the University of Witwatersrand in South Africa[4] write:

> PND should be called 'maternal depression' rather than postnatal depression because it is not isolated within the few weeks or months of birth but is an integral part of the changes of pregnancy and childbirth.

Looking through the research literature on three-day blues and depression, there does seem to be an overlap of symptoms although their severity and duration vary considerably (Table 1).

Table 1. Comparisons between three-day blues and PND

Three-day Blues suffered by 80% of women, usually within first days or fortnight after the birth. *Symptoms:* weepiness, sensitivity, fatigue, let-down feeling.

PND suffered by 10% of women, starting at any time during year after childbirth. *Symptoms:* similar to those of three-day blues, plus anxiety, dependency, compulsiveness, apathy or lack of energy, irrational fears, over- or under-eating, insomnia, loss of interest in sex, difficulties in making decisions.

Postpartum psychosis suffered by 0.2% of women can emerge at any time in the first year, for example after weaning. *Symptoms:* cut off from reality, rejection of baby, violence, hallucinations.

According to the Chalmers studies, all three conditions can be caused by hormone changes, while psychosis is more tangibly linked to previous mental health and personality. The varied aetiology of PND and the three-day blues is very similar in that high-risk factors include environment, history and impact of birth, but the severity and duration of disturbance is far greater in cases of true PND.

Three-day blues is usually self-limiting and treatment is not needed. PND can continue for weeks, months or even years and, depending on its severity, can be treated with progesterone therapy or antidepressants together with psychotherapy and counselling. Both conditions benefit from family and peer support.

Unfortunately, many women will agree with the Chalmers study that first-aid treatment tends to go on the lines of, 'Pull yourself together, you have a baby to look after now,' or 'You have a lovely baby, what are you complaining about?'

Other sources quote additional symptoms of PND such as insomnia, lack of appetite, difficulty in concentrating or making decisions, inadequacy feelings, withdrawal from the family, difficulties relating to the baby, introspection and self-hatred.

One must also remember that depression can be a symptom of a physical illness so a thorough investigation should be made. For example, a woman who is severely anaemic after the birth will feel exhausted and drained. Correct nutrition and iron supplements will soon restore her energy together with her blood count.

Dr B. Harris of the Caerphilly Miners Hospital[5] found cases of PND caused by thyroid dysfunction.

A woman suffering from PND may not seem visibly depressed. She may not be crying or sad, but may in fact appear to be on top of the world. However, a close look shows that she is agitated, abnormally energetic, over-excited, finding it difficult to sleep.

Susie had her first baby when she was thirty. She was a social worker and very aware of the psychological needs of herself, her baby and her husband. She went to a childbirth course, read all the books and was looking forward to the birth.

About a week after the birth, she called me to tell me that life was so exciting that she couldn't sleep one moment – she didn't want to miss anything! She had set herself a deadline to finish an article and had decided to make a big dinner that weekend to celebrate the birth. She did mention that the house needed cleaning and maybe it was time to paint the living room!

I warned her and her husband that this surplus energy would exhaust her and advised her to visit her family doctor. Together we were able to catch her as her mood plummeted a day or two later and she sat in the middle of her living room, among the paint pots, sobbing that she just couldn't cope.

There is some controversy about the influence of hormone levels on PND. While Dr Katharina Dalton[6] has brought about a breakthrough in treatment by her approach to progesterone therapy, other researchers have linked PND to the high prolactin levels during lactation.

Elizabeth Alder and John Cox[7] report that prolactin affects the production of progesterone and oestrogen. That is of course why there is less chance of getting pregnant while breast-feeding, but they also claim that the disturbance in progesterone production caused by high prolactin can extend the period of PND.

Some women who have fertility problems because of high prolactin levels need medication to reduce this in order to stabilize the oestrogen and progesterone production for conception. These women will retain a high level of prolactin even after they stop breastfeeding and this has been linked with longer periods of PND.

This is treading on rather dangerous ground because for most women, breastfeeding is the peak of their birth experience from which they derive tremendous emotional satisfaction. Combined with the benefits to the baby, the mother is very reluctant to stop breastfeeding solely because of the disturbed hormone levels. In fact, on an emotional level, early weaning may aggravate the depression.

In our story of Debbie in Chapter 2, I related how she had reacted very strongly to pethidine given during labour and had suffered months of PND. Her disappointment with her body's behaviour was exacerbated further because she was also advised to stop breastfeeding. Far from benefiting from this advice, she felt herself totally cut off from her baby.

It is known that prolactin is the 'mothering' hormone which is the reason why some women feel very calm and tranquil during the breastfeeding period. Sometimes a very active woman will say during pregnancy: 'I can't imagine being cooped up in the house with a baby, I'll probably be scrubbing the floors three times a day'. It often happens that that same woman quite naturally winds down and is perfectly content sitting dreamily in a rocking chair nursing her baby and listening to music, while the dust and the dishes pile up around her. It is prolactin that is reponsible for this change.

Dr Dalton finds no link between breastfeeding and PND and points directly at progesterone deprivation as the source. Women who have a history of severe PND after previous births are usually more at risk of recurrence. Dr Dalton therefore prescribes 100 mg of progesterone a day, produced naturally from the root of yam or soya beans, from the time of delivery for seven days, and then 400 mg twice daily for two months or until the onset of menstruation.

One hesitates to point at one medication as solving all ills, but there have been many cases of amazing recovery after the use of progesterone. Of course at the same time one has to examine other root causes.

New Generation published the story of Linda,[8] who married at an early age and coped equally with three pregnancies and the redundancy of her husband who remained unemployed for an extended period of time.

Eventually their life stabilized, they bought a house, the husband was promoted to a better job and with optimism they embarked on their fourth pregnancy.

'I felt depressed and unwell right through that pregnancy, regularly catching colds and flu,' writes Linda. 'The crisis came after the birth. I marched around the kitchen pulling my hair out, hitting furniture, screaming and crying.' Linda took vitamin B$_6$ supplements but there was no improvement.

She received support from her husband, mother, GP, midwives, health visitor, hospital social worker and NCT counsellor, but she felt no better. 'I wanted to explode and I was afraid I would hit the baby. Finally I went to see Dr Dalton and she prescribed progesterone and high levels of carbohydrates in my diet.' Within a month, Linda was back to normal, functioning as a woman, wife and mother and enjoying her family.

Some women are considered more at risk of PND, and this can be divided into categories of environment and personality. Ann Oakley, in her book *Women Confined*,[9] relates a higher incidence of PND in women who have had little previous contact with babies. This in turn can reduce confidence in decision-making.

G. Brown and T. Harris in *The Social Origins of Depression*[10] discuss causes such as lack of intimate marital relations, housing and employment problems, three or more children under the age of fourteen which increases the load on the mother, and a historical factor of loss of mother before the age of eleven.

This link with maternal deprivation was confirmed by Drs Frommer and Pratt at St Thomas's Hospital, London.[11] They investigated the emotional health of first-time mothers who had been deprived as children, either because of separation from parents or because of the death of their own mothers before the age of eleven. Sixty women were matched for age and social class, with a control group of women who had not been deprived of a solid relationship with their mothers.

There were clearcut differences between the groups in their attitudes and behaviour towards their children. Not all these differences were negative because in fact the deprived mothers were more concerned about breastfeeding and anxious to care for the infant in the best possible way. But there were more coping problems after the baby reached seven months and a tendency to early weaning.

One third of the first-time mothers and two thirds of mothers of more than one child had depressive symptoms or marriage problems. This confirms research done in the field of maternal deprivation. F. T. Melges[12] found more psychiatric symptoms in new mothers who had poor or no relationships with their own parents.

R. Kumar and K. Robson[13] linked neurotic disturbances with ambivalent pregnancies, meaning those of very young mothers or newly-weds who perhaps would have preferred more time, or older last-chance mothers who are more vulnerable to fatigue and stress.

It is obvious that some women will be more at risk of emotional disturbance due to environmental factors. Drs Dyanne Affonso and Thomas Arizmendi of the University of California[14] analysed the questionnaires of eighty women three weeks and eight weeks after the birth (Table 2). They discuss the psychosocial risks that promote PND. Top of the list is changes in daily activity. Following this is self-judgement, interaction with the baby in terms of pleasure and comfort as against fear, anger and negative emotions.

These researchers found a very logical correlation between PND symptoms, particularly mood changes with reduced energy, lack of appetite and effects on relationships with the baby.

If we examine the following paradigm from the Affonso/ Arizmendi paper, we can see that there are certain basic factors

Table 2. Percentage of women reporting problems in certain areas of postpartum adaptation (reproduced with permission from D. Affonso and D. Arizmendi, 'Disturbances in postpartum adaptation; depressive symptomatology', *Journal of Psychosomatic Obstetrics and Gynaecology*, March 1986)

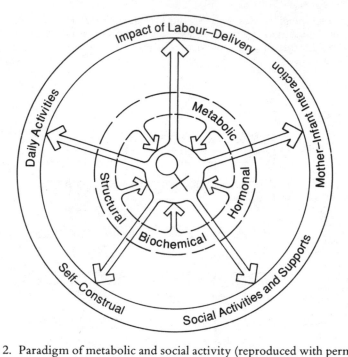

Figure 2. Paradigm of metabolic and social activity (reproduced with permission from D. Affonso and D. Arizmendi, 'Disturbances in postpartum adaptation: depressive symptomatology', *Journal of Psychosomatic Obstetrics and Gynaecology*, March 1986)

which do not change although they do vary from woman to woman. These are biochemical, hormonal, metabolic and structural. On the outer circle we see circumstances which are much more variable, such as impact of the birth experience, daily activities, self-construal, social activities and support and mother–infant interaction.

LIFE EVENTS INCREASING THE RISK OF PND

While we cannot consciously change our metabolic and chemical body functions, it might be worth being aware of the consequences of some of the inevitable life events which can indeed throw women out of tune. These include:

Moving house
Isolation from extended family

Bereavement
Divorce
Redundancy of partner
Previous stillbirth or infant death
Death of woman's own sibling at birth or in infancy
Death of woman's own mother during childbirth
Woman was herself adopted.

It is easy to understand why a woman in these situations may be more at risk for PND.

Moving House and Isolation From Extended Family

It is only during the past fifty years or so that young couples have been mobile, upwardly or otherwise. It was quite common for a couple to live in the same street as the bride's mother or at least in the same neighbourhood.

Therefore, when the first baby arrived, there was a network of female relatives to give support and practical help. Grandmothers, aunts, sisters would help with the cooking and cleaning after the birth and, later on, could keep an eye on the baby while the mother went to the shops or so that the parents could pop out to the pub in the evenings.

In addition, the new mother enjoyed the infrastructure of familiarity, the corner grocery, the neighbours, all of whom welcomed her into the Mother Club. Her former schoolfriends would also be having babies at roughly the same time and they could all push their prams together to the playground and chat while the children played in the sandbox.

It was only in 1966 that awareness was aroused by the publication of *The Captive Wife* by the late Hannah Gavron.[15] She wrote of the loneliness of women in new towns, claiming that a mother's involvement in society depends on familiarity with the area and people, women neighbours based at home during the day and a street-level front door.

In many ways, the slum clearance projects in Britain had disastrous results. True, families were moved out of dismal housing conditions, from damp, dark, cold and crowded houses into sparkling new flats with indoor bathrooms, but the spreading out of families to new towns separated the generations. However clean and bright the home is with modern labour-saving appliances, it can be very lonely for a new mother up there on the sixth floor with only a view of the clouds.

In these newly developed residential areas where most apartment blocks stand at least eight and sometimes twenty storeys high, the young mother is unable to open the back door and offer her small child the opportunity to go out and play. The child has to wait until she is free to take him down to the playground. Even if there are communal gardens, she cannot give him the freedom to play on his own because of the proximity of traffic and the danger of intruders.

As a mother who brought up small children in an old family house with a garden, I feel even more strongly that these high-rise families are missing out on peak fun experiences. One autumn day in England when Daniel, our second son, was two, he woke up from his nap feeling out of sorts and grumpy. It was cold outside but sunny and bright, so I wrapped him up well and opened the door for him to go out.

From the window I watched him as in sheer delight he tramped through the grass, feeling the leaves crunchy and crisp. He tried to catch a falling leaf and chuckled with joy. He came back into the house rosy-cheeked and happy, his after-nap mood quite forgotten.

The problems of the captive wife exist in all strata of society, but the mother who feels part of a village or suburb community can involve herself in local pressure groups and social organizations until she is ready to return to work. But the woman looking out of her tenth-floor window in a strange town may find it too much of an effort to get out and meet neighbours and make contact with local society.

In warmer climates, high-rise tower blocks are also a problem for family living but the weather brings people out into the streets well into the evening. In towns and villages, one can see families strolling along the streets and through the parks, enjoying the cooler air of the late afternoon or early evening.

One cannot, of course, always generalize about reactions to a given situation. Esther, the mother of two small boys, was delighted with her sparkling new flat in a ten-storey block in a new town. Her husband was a blue-collar worker and they both came from poor large families. During the first years of their marriage, they had lived in a small back-to-back in a very rough neighbourhood. 'No sunlight ever got into the house and even the weeds between the paving stones couldn't grow.'

At last, they managed to take out a mortgage and move to the new flat. The view from the window of the clouds gives Esther a feeling of space, and indeed sunlight did flood into the white-painted rooms. Esther is thrilled with her tiled kitchen and bathroom and the neatness of the flat. Every cupboard and unit is filled with neatly folded linen and clothing, and the window-sills are covered with healthy and thriving plants.

Apart from visits to the family, and participation in the local Townswomen's Guild, Esther is very happy to close the door of her flat on the outside world and spend time polishing and cleaning her new furniture. For Esther, it is the realization of a dream.

Bereavement

It is a sad fact that sometimes as a new soul arrives, another departs, and it may well be that the joy of childbirth is overshadowed by the death of a parent or grandparent.

Mourning and grieving are normal reactions, but in fact this may precipitate a very extensive period of PND even quite a long time after the event.

Soon after Anne's first baby was born, her mother became ill and it was clear that she would not recover. There followed several months of family anguish during which Anne's mother was hospitalized, had surgery and treatment and eventually died. Meanwhile Anne discovered that she was pregnant with her second child.

She and her husband had moved far away from the family after their marriage and each weekend, they travelled to London to visit her sick mother. Anne also made the journey by train with her first child mid-week. She did not connect her exhaustion and difficulties with the baby with this tremendous expenditure of time and emotion and was angry with herself for not coping.

When Anne's mother died, the family gathered together in their grief. Their main concern was their father and in concentrating their support and concern for him, Anne did not allow herself to grieve. During the rest of her pregnancy, she worried about her father and about the difficulties she was having with her first child. Fortunately she had planned a home birth because at that point she only associated hospital with her mother's illness.

From the moment the baby was born he was full of joy, a happy, smiling baby who ate enthusiastically and slept peacefully.

As he grew into toddlerhood, he was amazingly responsible and seemed to want to make life good for his mother.

Anne thought that her grieving was over, and her older child too seemed to be easier. But one morning, six months after the birth, she woke up with a feeling of dread and was unable to get out of bed. There followed three months of very deep depression and it was only when her family doctor, who was very understanding and supportive, helped her to understand that she was suffering from delayed mourning, that she could see that there would be a time limit to her distress.

Anne recovered and her father came to live with them for a couple of years. She loved him dearly but as so often happens when three generations live in a suburban semi, it was very difficult to balance the needs of an elderly man who had been uprooted from all that was familiar to him and those of her two very lively sons.

When her third pregnancy was visible, her father decided that it was too much for her and moved into a hotel. Her conflict of guilt and anxiety about him was mixed with a little relief to have the burden lifted from her. Her third and fourth children were born within a year of each other, and it was during her fourth pregnancy that her father died.

This time she was aware of how this could affect her after the birth and watched out for any signs of depression. It was only fifteen months later, more than a year after the birth of her fourth child, that she felt that familiar dread and anxiety.

She began to associate the cycles of life and death and was obsessed by morbid fears and anxieties. Combined with her grief that both her parents had died was an inescapable guilt that she had not looked after her father properly. It took Anne more than five years to recover from this second attack of PND.

In this situation, distressing as it is, Anne did at least have the support of her husband, her doctor and very good friends.

For Tessa, her grief was solitary. Her husband became ill towards the end of her pregnancy, and he died one week before the baby was born. She had married a man from a totally different religion and background and her in-laws rejected her. Their one concern after their son died was to reclaim the flat where the young couple had lived, and, without any justification, to have charge of the child.

In this case, Tessa had to cope not only with real intense grief for a husband whom she had loved deeply, but also with fighting off the demands of her in-laws. At a time when both families could have handled their grief by enjoying the new baby, relationships were further embittered.

Tessa was quite prepared to give up her flat but certainly not her child, and she managed to get a living-in job where the baby was welcomed, sufficiently far away from the in-laws. At last, when everything was settled, Tessa disintegrated, and it was only through the support of her employers that she was able to stay in her job and fight the panic and depression that followed.

Previous stillbirth or infant death

Every child is a precious child, but the baby who is born after a history of pregnancy or birth complications is especially cherished. It is therefore natural that this baby will be over-protected and that he will be watched for any sign of illness.

It may seem strange that a mother who has desperately wanted a baby now seems so tired and listless and even disinterested in the baby. She may, without anyone realizing it, be lying awake at night listening for the baby's cry, and getting up at intervals to make sure that he is still breathing. This leaves her so exhausted and irritable that she finds no pleasure in everyday fun experiences with the baby.

There is also the element of avoiding the 'evil eye'. A parent may say: 'Last time I shouted my joy from the rooftops and look what happened. If I keep a low profile this time maybe nothing will go wrong'.

The research studies show that to a certain extent, anxieties can cause PND even when the previous death was many years before; for example if the woman's own sibling died at birth.

Adoption history

Children who are adopted are usually brought up in loving dedicated families and come to terms with the fact that the people who have nurtured them are not their biological parents.

In her book *Postnatal Depression*, Vivienne Wellburn[16] describes the conflicts and questions that an adopted woman may face when she herself gives birth.

When a woman who was adopted gives birth to her own child,

it awakens a great deal of anger and pain. 'How did my mother give me away?' she asks as she looks at her own child. She may harbour fantasies that she was given away because she was unworthy and doubt her own mothering skills.

Mental Health Factors

The health history of the new mother will also influence her reactions to these body changes.

Women with a history of physical or mental illness will be particularly vulnerable during this period. Women who have suffered from emotional crises during adolescence or periods of depression should stay in contact with their mental health care workers throughout the pregnancy, so that they are ready to help her if the need arises.

A woman who has suffered from neurosis is particularly at risk after the birth because symptoms such as anxiety, phobias, compulsions and physical complaints develop very quickly when the woman in any case is coping with a heavy physical and emotional load.

Bathing the baby, setting a routine, feeding, can all become compulsive if they have to be done in a certain way with no room for flexibility. Fear of open spaces can keep a new mother confined to her house until eventually she is afraid to go out with the baby and it is easier just to sit around the house in a dressing gown. While most women do feel tired and suffer from some discomfort after the birth, the neurotic woman will worry more about these complaints and indeed be more prone to headaches and stomach upsets.

A neurotic person is not necessarily submissive because in an effort to escape, she may be antisocial, pick fights, stimulate neighbourhood gossip, or appear selfish and not be prepared to share. This is very different and much easier to treat than psychosis which affects functioning and links with reality. Psychosis includes childhood autism, severe withdrawal and schizophrenia resulting in delusions and hallucinations.

Depression usually happens to neurotic rather than psychotic people, but psychosis does cause manic depression with extreme shifts in mood.

The Marce Society, a research body, was formed in 1980 in the name of Louis Victor Marce[17] who in 1958 published the first substantial treatise on mental illness during pregnancy and the puerperium. In relation to this, more research was carried out at St Thomas's Hospital in London, in which 250 woman were interviewed twice during pregnancy and again after the birth. A link was found between PND and psychological disorder during pregnancy and also, again returning to the impact of birth, with poor obstetric or foetal outcome.

So again and again the opinion is reinforced that if high-risk women could be identified during pregnancy, and if PND were predicted, the possibility of prevention through progesterone therapy would be increased.

Both neurotic and psychotic symptoms can overlap and be linked with varied personality traits.

Rachel was a very creative, energetic woman who loved painting and music and generally enjoyed life. During adolescence she had experienced anxiety and depression but nobody spending time with her would believe that she sometimes watched the moon sailing through the clouds in the night sky and feared for the universe.

She grew up in a peaceful town in the north of England in an observant Jewish family, far removed in time and distance from the tumult of wartime Europe. In her teens she began to read about the Holocaust and was shocked by the depths of bestiality that mankind could reach. Nevertheless, it was for her at that point only a period of history; none of her family had lived in Europe at that time and in fact it was hardly mentioned in her immediate circle.

Rachel married young and was eager to have a large family. She loved children and put all her creative energy into running her home and enjoying her children. After each birth, she suffered a short period of PND, but it did not deter her until she was totally overwhelmed by fear and anxiety after the birth of her fifth child. She could not read newspapers or watch the news on TV because if she heard of a starving child in some far-off famine-ridden Third World country, she would start to shake and cry. If she saw pictures of terrorist attacks or border skirmishes anywhere in the world, she would fear for the safety of her children.

Sometimes she had nightmares that she was running with her family from burning buildings. She tried to conquer these fears until one day she had such a terrifying experience that she decided to seek help.

She and her husband had taken the children to a party to celebrate the Jewish festival of Chanukah. This is a children's holiday and the room was filled with noise. She watched with pleasure as her own children enjoyed the games and food, and almost forgot the dread and anxiety lying heavily on her chest.

There were a few moments of quiet as an elderly man thanked the organizers of the party. He had a gentle European accent and he spoke of the joy of the little children at this festive time. Rachel watched to her horror as the children and the old man sat, surrounded by barbed wire. The delusion only lasted one or two moments, but she ran from the room out into the car park where she stood in the cold, perspiration pouring from her.

'I was so angry with myself that my instability was spoiling my enjoyment of my family,' said Rachel. 'The anxiety would rear up every time something beautiful happened.

'For example, one day my daughter, then aged two, was rolling out pastry. She shaped and reshaped it until it was grey and sticky. I watched her concentrate, observed that exquisite curve of her cheek as she solemnly stretched the pastry, and her sudden smile as she scraped it off the board and offered me her precious gift to eat.

'I started to cry because I did not know how long I could keep those precious moments.'

A long period of psychotherapy followed, and although this frightening episode never repeated itself, it took many years for Rachel to overcome the nightmares and the anxiety. Eventually she could see war films and read the newspapers without immediately relating it to a threat to her own family.

'One of my most memorable sources of support was a neighbour, who was already in her early forties with grown-up children. She had also had a history of extended PND when she agonized about the world, and she was through it, out on the other side of the hill. She was having a cup of coffee with me one day and I asked how she had conquered this illness.

' "You know what I concluded, Rachel," the neighbour said, "I can't control the future for my children but I can have some influence on how they cope."

'From that day my fears became controllable. Instead of feeling impotent, I concentrated on preparing my children for life. And indeed, in the next few years they weathered many storms and came through as complete and integrated young people.'

Physical Health Factors

Becoming a mother brings tremendous responsibilities and if a woman has suffered serious physical illness in the past, she will fear its recurrence and its effects on her ability to be a parent.

Brenda was treated for cancer after the birth of her first child. She had endured a great deal of pain and anxiety but was confident about her prognosis. She had been told that this particular cancer would not be affected by pregnancy and she and her husband decided to have more children.

They were optimistic during the pregnancy and Brenda started breastfeeding as soon as the baby was born. Six weeks later, Brenda was physically strong but was enduring agonizing bouts of anxiety and fear. All her negative memories of her hospital experience had lain dormant during this time but now she was having recurrent nightmares in which she fantasized that the disease had returned.

'It was really a test going through that pregnancy,' said Brenda. 'Although the oncologists said that pregnancy would not accelerate tumour growth, I found very little in the research literature on the subject.'

Brenda's milk supply had dwindled during this period of anxiety, and she was already giving supplementary bottles. However, throughout this period of tension, she focused on re-establishing the milk supply and she was soon back on to full breastfeeding. She was still nursing her baby two years later when she again became pregnant.

'I felt a real accomplishment when I was able to re-lactate successfully,' she said. 'It symbolized the return of my self-confidence.'

Very often, illness makes one lose faith in one's body, and it is hard to come to terms with the limitations.

Life Events

With all the variables of family history and dynamics, it is hardly surprising that many women undergo a severe identity crisis during childbirth. So how much more difficult is this transition if she does not enjoy the support of her partner, if her husband is leaving her, or if he is unemployed and they have to cope with an unpaid mortgage and family expenses? Strangely enough, people usually cope with the crisis at the time. But if it coincides with such a drastic life change as becoming a parent, the symptoms may lie dormant until a later stage.

PERSONALITY ORIENTATIONS

Although environmental factors play an integral part in the risk factors of PND, personality orientation without doubt has an influence on mental health after the birth of a baby. While it may sometimes be possible to provide the optimum social and environmental conditions for a woman to become a mother, one thing that cannot be altered is the basic personality.

In J. Eysenck's work on the personality, *Fact and Fiction in Psychology*,[18] he presents a paradigm based on four personality groups: melancholic, choleric, phlegmatic, sanguine.

At the four poles, we see how these personality groups interact with introvert, extrovert, stable, unstable. There is probably something of all these groups in all of us, and sometimes they overlap, but one can look at one's friends and neighbours and roughly classify them within these groups.

Each of the four personality groups has its stable and unstable elements. For example, one might know somebody who is very quiet and reserved and sober, in themselves not negative qualities. But the darker side of that nature is rigidity, anxiety, moodiness, pessimism. There is quite a narrow gap between the phlegmatic stable with his passive, careful, peaceful control and the melancholic unstable at the other end of the spectrum. Likewise, the sanguine stable who is easygoing, a leader, outgoing, sociable and lively can cross over the border into the choleric unstable who is touchy, aggressive, excitable and impulsive.

Eysenck's model was used in a study in Edinburgh and Birmingham.[19] By conducting retrospective surveys on links between personality ratings and PND, the researchers found that the majority of disturbances were self-limiting. In general, the disturbances peaked at five days after the birth and declined by twenty-one days, and it was hoped that this information would open up a possibility of predicting vulnerability in women before the birth.

Reports were kept on day-to-day mood changes as described by an unselected group of eighty-one women in the first three weeks after birth. The researchers then interviewed women three years later and conducted personality ratings with the Eysenck Personality Questionnaire (EPQ), without the influence of the childbearing period.

The fifth day peak was more pronounced in women who scored high on introversion–extroversion and there was a striking relationship between the fifth day peak and neuroticism in the EPQ.

In addition, they found that the higher peaks of fifth day mood disturbances correlated with the development of a longer period of PND at a much later stage of the first five months. No significant difference was noted in women after caesareans even though they were exposed to the extra stress of healing. But they did note that there was a significant difference among those women who left hospital within twenty-four hours, which made them question the view that postpartum blues are caused by the hormone status.

In conclusion, there were so many false positives in the Edinburgh and Birmingham studies that it was not felt that the Eysenck Personality Questionnaire could effectively be used to predict PND.

However, B. R. Sakes of Yale University[20] did find that depressive symptoms during pregnancy could usually be correlated with depression during the six weeks after the birth. Therefore women who show symptoms of disturbance during pregnancy should receive supportive care then and be observed carefully during the puerperium.

Obstetric nurse Judith Petrick[21] discusses the identification of high-risk mothers for PND. Relating to atypical depression, with symptoms such as tearfulness, despondency, anorexia, sleep disturbance, impaired concentration, anxiety, guilt, lack of energy, loss of sex drive, obsession with death or suicide, she states that if four symptoms are observed each day for at least two weeks, this is an indication that the woman is suffering from PND. It might therefore be helpful if women were given questionnaires during their hospital stay which should be followed up by their GP for the next few months.

Nancy Donaldson, a maternity nurse at Hoag Memorial Hospital, California, describes what she calls the fourth trimester follow-up.[22]

'We telephone each mother during her first week at home. This contact confirms and supplements previous impressions and provides an opportunity for further assessment.' She continues: 'If there is no problem, we do not continue the contact but assure the mother that she can call us 24 hours a day.

'If we feel that there is a potential for disturbance, we call again and we can communicate the results of the follow-up assessments to the appropriate community resources or agency. Fifty-six per cent of families need more than one telephone call!' concludes Ms Donaldson, adding that there is specific follow-up after still-birth or neonatal death.

MOTHERING ORIENTATIONS

London-based psychoanalyst Joan Raphael-Leff, in her papers in the *Journal of Psychosomatic Obstetrics and Gynaecology* and in her recent book *Psychological Processes of Childbearing*,[23] discusses vulnerability to postpartum disturbances in terms of two basic orientations to mothering: the Facilitators and the Regulators.

The Facilitator embraces pregnancy and motherhood as self-realization, the high point of feminine identity. She adapts herself to the baby's demands and believes that she has a special capacity to interpret the needs her baby communicates and meet them spontaneously The Facilitator sees this intuitive understanding as exclusive to the mother. She enjoys the symbiotic relationship but in turn may experience problems in separating and weaning.

The Regulator views the infant as pre-social and sees her maternal task as regulating and training the baby to realistic routine. She regards mothering as a skill and she may feel threatened by the baby's dependency on her and fear becoming overwhelmed by the demands of the baby and domesticity.

Table 3 shows us the problems of adjustment and peaks of vulnerability in the context of these two orientations.

Raphael-Leff finds a higher incidence of symptoms of disturbance such as crying fits, less interest in sex, anxiety about baby, feelings of inadequacy, depression, both in interviews at six weeks and after that up to one year, among home-based Regulators. On the other hand, the Regulator reported more communication with the baby in the later months and was able to make life a little easier for herself by being prepared to share childcare. In the context of enjoyment of the baby, the Facilitator expressed more satisfaction at six weeks and the Regulator's rating was higher at nine months to one year.

This also may seem logical because a Facilitator may find her

Table 3. Percentages of groups reporting items present during different time periods postnatally (reproduced with permission from J. Raphael-Leff, *Journal of Psychosomatic Obstetrics and Gynaecology*, September 1985)

	Facilitators (n = 11)				Regulators (n = 16)			
	First 6 wks	Up to 1 yr	Over 1 yr	Prevalence	First 6 wks	Up to 1yr	Over 1 yr	Prevalence
1. Tearfulness (crying easily)	3 (27%)	2 (18%)	2 (18%)	5 (45%)	8 (50%)★	5 (31%)	1 (6%)★	10 (63%)
2. Less interested in sex than previously	7 (63%)	5 (45%)	4 (36%)	9 (81%)	8 (50%)	7 (44%)	7 (44%)	10 (63%)
3. Anxious about baby	3 (27%)	3 (27%)	0	4 (36%)	7 (44%)	8 (50%)	4 (25%)	10 (63%)
4. Feeling unlike your normal self	3 (27%)	2 (18%)	2 (18%)	5 (45%)	5 (31%)	7 (44%)	4 (25%)	12 (75%)
5. Feeling inadequate	1 (9%)	1 (9%)	0	2 (18%)	4 (25%)	5 (31%)	5 (31%)	8 (50%)
6. Self-critical and reproachful	1 (9%)	1 (9%)	1 (9%)	2 (18%)	3 (19%)	3 (19%)	7 (44%)	10 (63%)
7. Feeling unable to cope	2 (18%)	2 (18%)	2 (18%)	3 (27%)	4 (25%)	5 (31%)	7 (44%)	10 (63%)
8. Feeling depressed	2 (18%)	4 (36%)	1 (9%)	5 (45%)	5 (31%)	6 (38%)	4 (25%)	10 (63%)
9. Feeling able to communicate with baby	6 (54%)	8 (72%)	9 (81%)	10 (90%)	7 (44%)★★	13 (81%)★★	10 (63%)	13 (81%)
10. Enjoying mothering	7 (63%)	9 (81%)	10 (90%)	11 (100%)	6 (38%)	11 (69%)	10 (63%)	14 (88%)
11. Feeling confident in yourself	6 (54%)	7 (63%)	7 (63%)	9 (81%)	3 (19%)	6 (38%)	6 (38%)	9 (56%)
12. Feeling another person can look after baby in your absence	9 (81%)	4 (36%)	6 (54%)	6 (54%)	5 (31%)★★★	8 (50%)	12 (75%)★★★	12 (75%)
13. Feeling your presence is essential to baby	9 (81%)	8 (72%)	5 (45%)	10 (90%)†	8 (50%)	6 (38%)	8 (50%)	9 (56%)†
14. Finding the baby exciting	9 (81%)	8 (72%)	9 (81%)	11 (100%)	7 (44%)	12 (75%)	11 (69%)	14 (88%)

★ Fisher's exact P = 0.008.   ★★★ Fisher's exact P = 0.016.
★★ Fisher's exact P = 0.033.   † Fisher's exact P = 0.056.

energy and enthusiasm wearing thin if she is still demand-feeding, getting up at all hours of the night and completely out of routine when the baby is over six months. At that stage, the Regulator is more likely to have weaned or at least has attempted to educate the baby to conform to the family's needs.

The Regulator is more likely to return to work if she has a choice; if she has no help and has to stay at home, she shows more depressive symptoms and less self-esteem.

The Facilitator does not always find it easier because she needs constant support and boosting and has a need to be mothered and protected herself in order to concentrate totally on the baby.

When I met Diana during pregnancy, I was not sure about forecasting a long period of breastfeeding. She seemed to be a stickler for routine and knowing what each day would bring. However, after the birth, she spent the entire first year concentrating exclusively on the baby, fully breastfeeding and resisting all pressure to return to work. Her mother and mother-in-law came in daily to cook, clean and do the shopping. This is an ideal situation for the woman who has the extended family living in the neighbourhood. But it might have been much more difficult for Diana to be a Facilitator and concentrate solely on the baby's needs if she had not had so much help.

Fortunately, it suited her husband too, for while she believed that only she could perform tasks of baby care, he was very achievement-oriented and worked long hours in his office.

Sometimes, however, a willingness to share tasks is not because of a flexible approach and acknowledgement that these tasks can be efficiently delegated, but because the mother herself is lacking in self-confidence and is afraid to take responsibility.

When I worked and lived for a year in a kibbutz, the babies' house, as in most kibbutzim today, was a daycare centre and the babies were taken home by the parents in the afternoon and returned early in the morning before work.

Because most women in the kibbutz, and fathers too for that matter, work on site, it is usual for the parents to drop by during the day, feed and bath the babies and spend some period playing with them. Breastfeeding mothers are contacted by beeper so that they can come on call from wherever they are working. This is far from the original ideology of the kibbutz where the children were educated by the community and not by the parents, and in some cases parents were actually not permitted to visit during the day. Those children of the past are now parents and have demanded change so that with few exceptions today, children do live with their parents and their primary influence is the nuclear family. However, because both parents work a full day, the influence of the staff of the babies' house and kindergartens is also very important, not only in terms of caring for the children but also for educating and guiding the parents.

We were concerned about one of the mothers, a very young woman, who was reluctant to perform even the most simple tasks during the time the baby was in the daycare centre.

We noticed that her little boy, aged eight months, seemed sad and depressed and soon connected it with the fact that his mother did not once visit during the day. She was not breastfeeding and did not come in to give him his lunch or bath him or interact at all. She did not always arrive on time at the end of the workday to collect him. The father was working out of the kibbutz and came home an hour or two after the babies' house had closed for the day, so he too did not make these casual daytime visits which the other babies enjoyed so much.

The mother seemed to have no confidence in her own ability. She said that the staff of the babies' house were much more knowledgeable than her and that there was no reason why she should come and perform the tasks of feeding and bathing when we were the experts.

Of course, there were very deeprooted causes behind this attitude and it took a lot of support and counselling until she built up her self-confidence and understood that mother-love, even that of a 'novice', was preferable to all the expertise of the staff. In fact, the mother herself was facing a great deal of conflict because she had come to the kibbutz only when she married and still felt very lonely and outside the social mainstream. Her own family lived abroad and she missed their support, feeling that her husband who was kibbutz-born had advantages far above hers. It may seem strange that somebody living in such a community can be lonely but in fact in that situation the isolation is even more intense.

Women living in towns and villages can make new friends when they go shopping, go to the baby clinic or join a support group. But the kibbutz is a closed community and if one does not feel part of the group, the isolation is far greater.

Continuing the study of Raphael-Leff, she found that the Regulator has a peak of vulnerability at one year when the baby is less easy to control and toddlerhood is a challenge. The Facilitator experiences a peak at two years because she is more severely affected by weaning or separation, such as when the toddler goes to playgroup.

By examining these orientations, it is sometimes easier to understand women's reactions, which can be surprising.

Sheila is a grandmother and her two daughters gave birth to their first children within a few months of each other. During pregnancy, Sheila voiced concern that Elizabeth, the older one, would have a much harder time in adjusting than Margaret, the younger. 'Elizabeth is always in chaos – she was a messy child and her house now is always in a muddle. She has no routine and I don't know how she'll cope,' said Sheila.

On the other hand, Margaret was always very fastidious in the house, and by nine in the morning her floors were washed, the dishes finished, the laundry on the washing line. She worked half-day and each afternoon cooked varying and delicious dinners set on an immaculate table. 'She's very capable and will handle motherhood easily.'

In fact, the opposite was true. Elizabeth took each day as it came. If the sun shone, she put the baby in his pram and went off for long walks, visited friends for coffee, stopping each time the baby cried to feed him and change his nappies. When the baby slept, she unplugged the telephone, closed the curtains and got back into bed either to catch up on sleep or to read a good book. When her husband came home from work, together they bathed the baby, handled the basic household chores, put the baby in a kangaroo front carrier and again went out to enjoy any activity where they could take the baby.

For Margaret it was much harder. She very much wanted to breastfeed but she would sit upright in the chair, watching the dust gather while the baby fed. She visualized the unwashed dishes and was besieged by guilt when her husband came home to a convenience meal. When the baby slept, she cleaned and washed and by the time the baby was three months old she was totally exhausted.

It is not always possible to identify the personality orientations and it does not necessarily mean that the woman who is always happy-go-lucky does not get depressed or that low-key women suffer more.

Jennifer was a pillar of her community, secretary of the Towns-women's Guild, chairwoman of the PTA. She ran a car pool for old people, baked cakes for the church bazaar, and her house was a hive of activity, full of children, dogs and cats.

Nobody knew that Jennifer suffered acutely from phobic anxieties for at least a year after each birth and that in fact she was in a state of depression during the intervening periods. Her family doctor helped her both with psychotherapy and with juggling doses of suitable medication, and she believed strongly that if she kept busy, she would conquer her illness.

Occasionally, the anxieties were so overwhelming that she felt that she was literally climbing the wall, but onlookers were only aware that she was very energetic and always ready to take on more tasks. On one occasion, her family doctor was on holiday and she went to his partner to get a prescription. He looked at her in amazement. 'You – with PND! I don't believe it.'

Only her husband and closest friends knew that there were days when Jennifer was so low that she couldn't cope. One of them would take the children off her hands and she would spend the day in bed in tears of despair and anger at herself. It was like living in a grey fog and she felt that she was always on the edge of an abyss. She dared not feel too happy because the next day, her mood would drop and she would be exhausted.

In Jennifer's case, progesterone therapy may have been suitable, because four years after the birth of her last baby, the longest period in which she had not been pregnant, there was a sudden release.

'It was just before Christmas. I used to get very anxious before these festivities because I was afraid I would get an attack and spoil it for everybody. One afternoon, I left the children with a neighbour and went into town to go to the library and then get my hair cut. I walked through the town square, where the Christmas tree was already lighted up in the dusk. The sound of carols was clear even above the traffic. A gloomy twilight on a cold December day seemed hardly the setting for leaping out of depression, but suddenly the sky seemed to lift and I felt as if the sun was shining.'

Jennifer had turned the corner, and after that she found that she did not need to lose herself in such frantic activity in order to be at peace with herself.

CONCLUSION

Whether PND is caused by personality or environment, life events or history, there is not nearly enough attention paid to the prevention and treatment of this distressing illness.

Dr Bruce Pitt, whose work was listed earlier in this chapter and who has extensively examined this subject for many years, states: 'If a man presented himself with the symptoms displayed by women with moderate PND it would be viewed as a psychiatric emergency'. Instead, women are often treated with scepticism and patronizing attitudes, they feel guilty, inadequate and isolated.

'When a woman attends her gynaecologist or GP for a postnatal check-up six weeks after the birth, there is little time to assess her mental state,' says Dr Peter Holland, an Edinburgh GP.[24] For this reason, health visitor Jenny Trotter and psychiatrist Dr John Cox developed the Edinburgh PND Scale aimed at identifying depressed mothers and making treatment available immediately.

PND is not a modern-day illness but awareness has been aroused by these researchers and writers and it may be possible to prevent a deterioration of a depressive condition if the mother and the people around her understand the risk factors.

Today, there are many organizations working on prevention, research and treatment of PND. There are support groups such as the National Childbirth Trust, the Association of Postnatal Illness, and MIND, while some psychotherapists concentrate on working with women during the childbearing period.

But even recognized treatment methods such as psychotherapy can be humiliating and destructive if not done by practitioners who are expert in this particular field.

Nancy recounts her story of years of depression after and between the births of her children. 'I was just never well and was always tired and irritable. That was at its best. At its worst, I experienced a terrible dread for the safety of my children.' There was some logic to this because she had been brought up in India and had been exposed to scenes of violence.

Although she now lived with her husband and four children in a tiny, peaceful Welsh village, her anxieties caused her nightmares and panic attacks. Years later, after her recovery, she recounts with some humour her one and only encounter with a therapist.

'I was recommended to a psychiatrist and I arranged for baby-sitters and took the train up to London, leaving time spare to do some shopping. I went into a department store and bought yellow oilskin raincoats for the children, ideal for the wet Welsh holidays.

'I was called into the doctor's office and placed my carrier bag on the chair next to me. He asked me to describe my fears and his body language was so unsympathetic I just dried up after five minutes. He sat looking at me, his gaze switched to my carrier bag and back to me, and again at my carrier bag. I felt a hysterical bubble of laughter rising in my throat. Did he think I carried my anxieties in a carrier bag? After I stuttered a few more sentences he pronounced judgement. My anxieties were caused by my own inner aggression and that I enjoyed being ill because it provided me with attention. I picked up my carrier bag, walked out of his office, and went home. All I had to show for my journey and my hopes were four yellow oilskin raincoats.'

4 🎝 *Getting Acquainted*

FROM the moment of birth, the bonding between parents and baby establishes a relationship which, unlike among animals, lasts a lifetime.

Even though animals are separated from their mothers at an early age and do not even know who their fathers are, they nevertheless experience a critical period of imprinting – the establishment of perception. Animals who miss this bonding period are observed to display abnormal emotional development and their behaviour is often bizarre.

There is a famous study by the Harlows[1] who separated baby monkeys from their mothers after birth and found that those who were kept with their siblings or even a surrogate mother in the form of a soft doll with a bottle, were less disturbed than those who were totally isolated and could not afterwards even relate to members of their own species.

Dr John Bowlby's work on attachment in the 1950s and 1960s[2] was responsible for arousing awareness that human emotional development was as dependent as that of animals on that early sensitive period.

The human baby is keenly aware of his environment and of the presence of loving care. The American specialist on infant development, Dr T. Brazleton, wrote that even though the baby cannot focus his eyes, his first visual perception is of the round shapes of a human face or breast.[3] He soon makes eye contact and will even mimic facial expressions, and although he has little control over his body movements, when he is held, he snuggles up and soon learns to use his arms to hold or cuddle. For a parent, this precious moment of bonding may not be immediately after the birth but in fact when holding the baby and feeling him make this contact. The tactile sensation of the fuzzy down of his head snuggling up towards the parent's chin, the smell of that unique perfume of innocence and cleanliness which is that of a tiny baby, may be the start of the love affair between mother and child.

In 1946, Dr R. Spitz, who had over a period of time been visiting physician at two children's institutions, noted a very important and interesting phenomenon,[4] and this has since been the basis of much research on infant development.

One of the institutions was for orphans and foundlings without their mothers. Because of the primitive and crowded conditions, the babies were kept in their cots all day, with sheets draped over the sides so that they would not be stimulated, cry or want to be taken out. The ratio of nurses to children was one to twenty.

In another institution, unmarried mothers cared for their own babies, and even though conditions were poor, the baby enjoyed the ongoing relationship with the mother.

The general health and socioeconomic background of the two groups were similar, but Dr Spitz found that at one year of age, the babies in the first institution were far behind the second group in emotional, intellectual and physical development.

Aidan MacFarlane, in his book *The Psychology of Childbirth*,[5] discusses the effects of early bonding on easy breastfeeding. Not only does the immediate physical contact release lactation hormones but it also raises the mother's awareness of the baby's needs.

Dr MacFarlane was following up the studies done in the USA by Marshall Klaus and John Kennell, 'Human maternal behavior at first contact with her young'.[6] Drs Klaus and Kennell had filmed mothers' spontaneous behaviour if left with the baby immediately after the birth. There was an 'orderly and predictable' pattern of physical supporting and cradling, eye contact, facial and verbal expression.

This early contact and involvement correlated with a follow-up two years later when they found that those children were more stimulated by their mothers, there were fewer behavioural problems and their IQs were higher than children who had not experienced the early contact.

Most animals receive their young in a different way and in fact a puppy's survival depends on being licked and cleaned by the mother because the stimulation of the tongue facilitates the breathing mechanism. Rhesus monkeys do in fact also display instincts for cradling and grooming. In the case of animals, this contact establishes recognition so that for the next few weeks the mother is fiercely possessive.

Dr MacFarlane's observations were in agreement with those of Kennell and Klaus' work. He carried this further by noting other influencing factors such as whether or not the mother had received drugs during labour, if the baby was still floppy and did not provide the reciprocal attachment, whether the father was present, and the positive or negative element of relationships with the attending midwife or doctor.

Parturient women are more proficient in recognizing their newborns by smell and touch as compared to auditory or visual cues, was the conclusion of Professor Arthur Eidelman[7] of the neonatology department at the Shaare Zedek Hospital in Jerusalem. His data supports the hypothesis that women after childbirth utilize more basic instinctual processes in recognition than nonmothers. Professor Eidelman, who supports the policy of rooming-in or at least unlimited access to the nursery, points out that as infant recognition serves as the basis for the ultimate maternal–infant attachment, these results have particular relevance to practices and policies of perinatal care.

Another study of forty-six mothers at that hospital showed that 69% of the mothers who had spent more than an hour with their babies immediately after the birth were able to identify them by touch in the following hours. This was compared with recognition skills by touch, testing one group of non-parturient women and a second group of men. Neither of these two groups was able to identify by touch with the same success as the new mothers.

We have referred before to the work of Frederick Leboyer[8] and how the baby responds to quiet and touch. But the fact remains that in many hospitals throughout the world, the baby is born in harsh light, often to the sound of loud voices and a bedpan crashing to the floor! The umbilical cord is severed, his nose and throat are assailed by tubes to drain fluid, and stinging drops are put in his eyes. After a brief period with his parents, he is taken to the nursery where he is weighed, washed, injected and tested for some hours before being reunited with his mother. Women do not always have access to a hospital where there is rooming-in and even today some institutions maintain strict four-hourly schedules for feeding.

Testing the newborn is necessary. The eye drops are to protect the baby from dormant venereal diseases to which he could have been exposed as he came down the birth canal. The draining of fluids is essential to make sure the lungs are clear. Examining blood, urine, bone formation, heart function and reflexes can help to make early diagnoses of diseases which can then be investigated as soon as possible. Life-saving decisions can then be made early, or procedures started to control and improve the quality of life in conditions which can be detected at birth and successfully treated.

But there is no reason why the parents cannot hold and comfort the baby in the early hours, during which he is suffering the trauma of separation from the warm, dark, comfortable uterine environment.

In recent years, pressure has been put on hospital management to reduce this separation and it took a great deal of time to effect any change in the attitude that mothers and babies need rest after the birth – in separate rooms.

Dr Martin Richards writes in his chapter in *The Father Figure*[9] that these attitudes were reinforced by the earlier studies, in which the focus on attachment was based on the theory that the most harmful effects of separation were in *breaking established relations*, and that it took several months for a baby and parent to become attached.

I was visiting the maternity ward one day and stayed to help a woman who was giving birth unaccompanied by her partner. She had a difficult labour and finally gave birth to her third son.

She was so disappointed that it was not a girl and felt tired and irritable, taking no pleasure in the baby. She did not want to hold him and the baby was put in a cot in the corner of the room while the midwife dealt with the placenta.

There was an interval while waiting for the doctor to come and put in a few stitches and I wheeled the cot over to her. The baby's eyes were open and he seemed to be watching her through the transparent side of the cot. This aroused her interest and she stared back at him. Slowly she put her hand into the cot and took his tiny hand. His fingers closed around hers. Her tiredness and disappointment were forgotten. She was at one with her baby.

When the father is present at the birth, he can take this opportunity to get to know his baby. Even while the mother is concentrating on expelling the placenta or being stitched, the father can sit quietly holding his baby, making eye contact. For many men this is a very intense emotional experience.

During the next few days, the mother learns some of the practicalities of baby care, such as how to look after the umbilical stump until it dries up and falls off four or five days later. One of the advantages of rooming-in is that the mother gets used to handling her baby before coming home.

During the first couple of days, the baby's bowel movements will be black and sticky. This is called meconium and is composed of all the mucus and discharges he has swallowed prior to and during the birth. Early breastfeeding helps the passing of this meconium because the first milk, the colostrum, is a laxative. After a couple of days the bowel movements are then soft and mustard-coloured. It is thought that the early expulsion of the meconium also reduces neonatal jaundice.

The staff of the nursery will discuss the tests the baby has been given and when the mother leaves the hospital she will receive a report. Sometimes the parents will be invited for a return visit to check up on a question or if the baby has had jaundice.

LEARNING TO CARE

The next milestone is the first bath. The district midwife or health visitor is available to help with these first-times. It is also helpful if the father can take time off so that the parents can learn together and work out how to arrange the baby's room. This gives the father an opportunity to share in those first days without the pressure of getting to work in the morning.

Most family practice groups have a doctor who specializes in paediatrics or it may be that the family prefer to continue the relationship with the doctor who has treated the woman throughout the pregnancy.

It is interesting that the British system of family medicine has been used as a model in many parts of the world where specialization has caused an over-compartmentalization of health facilities.

But most important is that the parents can call on the doctor at all times and trust his or her judgement. Sometimes a small thing can cause a lot of worry to a new parent and it is a great help to have someone to give counsel. It is also an asset if that same doctor is familiar with the family structure and knows the health history of the child and his parents.

But the main responsibility for bringing up this child rests on the parents and this can be a formidable task. Parenting instincts do not always immediately emerge. You can spend a number of weeks caring for the baby until you feel that he is really yours.

Parents should not feel guilty if they don't melt every time they see their baby, especially in the small hours of the morning.

When a baby cries, it is difficult to know if it is hunger or thirst, wind or other discomfort, or simply a cry to be held and cuddled. But as parents become more attuned and sure of themselves, they start to enjoy their baby's development and his reaction to the new world that he has come into.

Dr Richards sees this more as a growth of communication between parent and infant.[10] At first the mother's relationship with the baby is one of total identification and withdrawal from other relationships. There is almost a recreation of her own infancy experiences which protects her child from the harsh reality of daily life. As primary maternal preoccupation begins to recede and the baby's dependence is less total, self-identification separates the relationship between the baby and the parent.

Much of the literature on infant development gives mixed messages. While some of the older books advise about routine and discipline and not spoiling the baby, the more modern approach is to make sure that the baby's demands are recognized.

Small babies can only communicate by crying and it takes time to understand whether it is a cry of hunger, pain, boredom or disgust at lying in a soiled nappy. But whatever the cause, the baby will be easier to handle, healthier and more contented if his needs are answered without delay.

As trends swing from one extreme to the other, parents can be very confused. We have all seen the impact on a family of a very demanding child who seems, as he grows up, to rule the house and does not even let the parents converse with friends without constant interruption, and displays temper tantrums if every request is not immediately answered.

However, it is usually the child who has had all his needs answered in that first year who grows up to be more independent, considerate and resourceful.

I always felt some degree of guilt about my children because they were born so close together that each one had a very short period of being the baby in the family. I tried to compensate for this by providing a stimulating and flexible lifestyle, made easier by the fact that at that time I was not working outside the home.

When the sun shone, we left the chores, packed a picnic and went out for the day. When the rain fell, the playroom was a refuge of chaos, with the paints and the modelling clay and sand trays spilling all over the place. I was often criticized by my in-laws and the tidier neighbours for allowing such disorder in the house, but that's how it worked with us.

Clearing up, true to the Montessori method, was part of the fun of making a mess and at the end of the day, each child had a bucket and cloth and brush to clean the tables and floors and tidy up the toy shelves. Washing dishes and making pastry were fun experiences and although at the time it created even more mess for me to clear up after the children were in bed, I reaped the benefits years later. When I started to work again and spent more time out of the house, the children, then of school age, took their turn clearing the table, washing dishes, emptying bins, making beds and cooking interesting and nutritious meals.

In the same way as we always welcomed the children's friends into the house and included them in our meals and holidays, so our children learned to welcome our friends in a way that sometimes bowled them over.

We had been living in Israel for two years and our children were then aged between eight and twelve, when we received an unexpected visit from friends who were on tour from England. They had intended dropping in for coffee one Friday evening but confessed when they came in that they had not found any restaurants open for dinner because the Sabbath had started.

In the time that it took to establish this fact and make them welcome, the children had gone into the kitchen, investigated the refrigerator and produced two plates piled high with delicious sandwiches and a pot of steaming coffee. This gave my husband and I time to talk with our friends and we all enjoyed the unexpected visit.

It does, however, take time and experience to set down these priorities and I must confess that most of my mistakes were made with our firstborn. We all try to be Supermum with our first babies and only a few of us succeed.

The Impact of Separation

The effects of early separation and the need for a constant warm relationship with the parents or a substitute is the leitmotif of Bowlby's book *Child Care and the Growth of Love*.[11] Written in the early 1960s, it was not coincidental that in the years following, parents and educators changed their ideas about the emotional needs and awareness of the very young child.

As an example of the impact of separation on children under five, he records studies done in postwar Britain by Anna Freud and D. Burlingham[12] showing that the young children who were evacuated out of the danger area without their parents were more traumatized than those who had stayed at home and been exposed to the sounds and sights of the Blitz.

As the baby grows and both mother and child begin to enjoy a harmonious relationship – or some may call it a truce – the mother may well ask: what is separation?

Long periods away from the baby while the mother is at work need not be significant for the baby if the childminder is permanent and loving; an evening at a concert or theatre leaving a reliable babysitter will not cause irreversible damage. But there can be separation even when the parents are physically in the house.

In modern families, babies usually sleep separately from the parents and sometimes it is the mistaken belief that a baby needs to be based in his quiet room and only taken out for feeding, bathing and outings.

A child needs to be with his parents even if he is not hungry. If the mother is baking a cake, using her computer or practising the piano, the baby will enjoy watching from his babychair, or he may enjoy cuddling up with his father during an intensive game of Scrabble.

The baby under a year has little perception of the future. His needs are egocentric; 'if my mother or father is not with me, he or she does not exist'. Therefore the cry of loneliness or fear or insecurity, interpreted by some as the spoilt cry for attention, if left unanswered can lead to intense grief because the child lying in his quiet isolation cannot understand that in fact his mother is in the next room finishing a job and that she will come in a very few minutes.

Stimulation

Small babies enjoy sound and movement because after all they have been jogging around in the uterus for nine months and have become accustomed to the actions and sounds of the mother's body. When one becomes attuned to the baby's needs, one can observe that while babies are often happy in a room full of people with a background of television, conversation and the dog barking, they sometimes reach a tiredness peak, or state of over-stimulation, perhaps caused by being handed from one to the other.

For the first six weeks, babies have an inbuilt screen or barrier to external overload, but parents may notice that the baby becomes extra fussy or cries more with a peak at six to eight weeks as that barrier disappears. They are still soothed by monotonous background noise such as the vacuum cleaner or the washing machine, and of course the motion of riding in the car or pram still works magic. But they will respond to sudden movements or noise with distress and it is often at that time that the baby does enjoy the quiet and peace of his own cot in his own room away from the source of bustle.

An infant needs to gratify his oral needs by sucking. Unlimited periods at the mother's breast with the use of a dummy when he is fretful will not result in protruding teeth or establish lifelong habits. The sucking instinct is developed in the uterus and he depends on this sucking for his survival. A baby needs to suck not only when he is hungry but also when irritated or tired.

At about nine months of age, this need overlaps with the newly awakened curiosity of the infant. He enjoys playing with sand and clay, mud and water, develops the tactile sense and differentiates between rough and smooth, hard and soft, the feeling and sensation of plastic, wood, velvet, silk and wool, water, sugar and mud. He will make a horrible mess with finger paints and clay, but the chaos soon turns to creativity.

Unstructured play, such as making an orchestra out of saucepan lids or rolling pins, playing at shopping with cans and packets and real money, using real tools and real cooking utensils under supervision, teaches a child to cope with the real world. Gardening, cooking and cleaning can be done together with a child. It may take longer at first, but the day will come when he will have his own vegetable garden or window box, will offer to cook the lunch if you don't feel well, or bake a surprise cake for your birthday.

The houseproud parent may despair as the child takes over the home, but it is very rewarding to encourage a child through this stage of development. A walk in the park is fun, but the mess he makes with sand and water in the playground gives him a great feeling of achievement. Learning to recognize and eat foods of different textures, tastes and colours will give him an appetite for life, even though you have to bath him after every meal – and wash the table, chair, walls and floor!

However, the bath should not be emphasized as a necessity for washing off that mess. Bathtime is for splashing and relaxing, with time spent afterwards for massage with bath oil or lotion. He will then equate all the adventures of life with love and touching and security and not consider bathing as a punishment for getting so dirty.

Toilet Training

One of the most controversial points of conflict between different generations is the issue of toilet training. Undue pressure on an infant under the age of two to use his potty is not only a complete waste of time but can be positively harmful.

One does not usually see a child going to primary school in nappies, so one should not be frantic about training a child to control his bowels and bladder. Some children show very visible signs that they are about to produce a bowel movement so they can be gently guided to the potty – and if you are both lucky, praise them. But following the child around the house constantly with potty in hand will only aggravate him and give him very negative impressions of his body functions. Likewise, a sour face and disgusted comments from the parent when changing the nappy will instil in him feelings that his parents are angered by his body.

It is sometimes a problem when one of the parents is absolutely overwhelmed by the sight or smell of a soiled nappy and just cannot handle it. It is important to recognize this so that the other parent can take on more of the nappy-changing, leaving another task to the parent who gags and retches if given this job. This is not a shortcoming of the parent, but some people are just more sensitive to smell. Others were brought up with such strict ideas about personal hygiene that they cannot cope with the bodily functions of even their small infant.

During the daytime a two year old can be encouraged to use his pot if he is dressed in pants instead of nappies. It is easier for him to undress himself and he will soon learn that it is more comfortable to use his potty than to walk around in dirty or wet pants.

Only when he relates the sensation of a full bowel or bladder with the relief of sitting on the potty will he be in full control. If he is made to feel dirty or nasty, the child will feel guilty and cannot graduate to the next stages of development.

So, as he grows out of the symbiotic needs of the first year, he builds his confidence and works through the learning phase of development. Slowly, he will be ready to experiment and separate.

The Outside World

At six to nine months he will have learned to relate to other people around him, testing their reactions. 'If I drop my toy, will they pick it up – again?' as he throws it out of his cot for the umpteenth time.

But by eighteen months he is prepared to take more risks. The peek-a-boo games are a sign of this. However, his perception is still immature. 'If I can't see her, she can't see me,' he thinks as he hides behind a curtain – with his feet sticking out!

On the one hand he is saying: 'Let me go and do it myself,' and on the other: 'stay with me, don't leave me'. The parents need to take the cue from the infant and plan the transitions to be as gradual and natural as possible. Since our life is governed by schedules and routines, this can be difficult.

Many children are ready for playgroup by the age of two and a half, and enjoy the play activity and companionship of other children. But there is ambiguity about this separation.

Daniel, my second son, was nearly three when he started play-group in a small school very near home. He was a very adventurous and outgoing little boy, but still very attached to me. The play-group was in a pleasant room with windows on all four sides. Each day we had the same ritual. As I waved goodbye, he ran from window to window to give me a kiss. If I was busy talking to another mother and forgot one window, we had to start all over again.

So while we are concerned about the development of the infant in these first years, it is important to note that the growth and maturing of a small child can only progress healthily if his parents, particulary his mother, are in tune with themselves.

MOTHER–BABY RELATIONSHIPS

There have been other references in this book to Joan Raphael-Leff's work on the Facilitator and Regulator,[13] and it is interesting that while there are basic orientations, one does see a changing

Table 4. Early maternal orientations (reproduced with permission from *Psychological Processes of Childbirth* by J. Raphael-Leff, published by Chapman and Hall, 1991)

	Facilitator	*Regulator*
Daily babycare experience		
	Adapts to baby	Baby adapts to mother
Feeding	Permissive, frequent	Schedule, limited duration
Crying	Communication/appeal	'Real' vs. 'fussing'
Sleep	Parental bed/room; night feeds	Own room; sleeps through night
Proximity	Close physical/spatial contact	Baby in own 'container'
Excretion	'Gift'	'Mess'
Maternal beliefs		
re Newborn	'Baby knows best'	'Mother knows best'
	Newborn is alert and knowing	Newborn is undiscriminating
	Newborn is sociable	Newborn is asocial
re Mothering	Mothering = intuitive 'instinct	Mothering = acquired skill
	Mothercare exclusive and monotrophic	Babycare shared and interchangeable
	Security = mother's continued presence	Security = continuous routine
	Babycare should be spontaneous	Babycare should be predictable
	Mother must gratify baby	Mother must socialize baby
Underlying unconscious fantasies		
	Baby = mother's ideal self	Baby = split off weakness, own mother denigrated/dismissed
	Wish to recapture idealized state of 'Fusion'	Mother threatened by lack of separateness
	Fear of hating	Fear of loving
Maternal defences		
	Idealization/vicarious compensation	Dissociation/detachment
	Altruistic surrender	Excess control/rigidity
	Manic reparation (guilt denied)	Defence against fantasy
Precipitants of postnatal distress		
	Enforced separation from baby	Enforced 'togetherness'
	Obstacles to being 'mother'	Obstacles to being 'person'
	Non-supportive partner	Non-egalitarian partner
	Deep disappointment re birth	Reduced adult competency

pattern of behaviour sometimes after a difficult beginning with the first baby.

Probably all the traits and attitudes in Table 4 are interchangeable, when analysing motherhood.

The two components of motherhood, emotional factors and physical caretaking tasks, are discussed in *Postpartum: Development of Maternicity* by Dr Susan Ludington-Hoe from the University School of Nursing, Dallas.[14]

The emotional component is termed 'maternicity', a synonym for the characteristic quality of a woman's personality that provides her with the emotional energy for feeling that her infant occupies an essential part of her life as determined by bonds of affection. These bonds include feelings of warmth, devotion, protectiveness and concern for the infant's wellbeing and pleasant anticipation of continuing contact.

> Maternicity is to be differentiated from mothering which is the physical caretaking component of the maternal role. Activities such as feeding, bathing, burping can be done without experiencing the emotion that makes the infant an essential part of her life. But a woman who has developed maternicity cannot avoid mothering at the same time.

Dr Ludington-Hoe continues that a healthy mother–child relationship does not automatically follow the birth of a child. It has to develop as the mother and child learn to respond to each other.

'There is small pleasure in caring for someone who responds by taking and consuming and who acts passively and indifferently.'

But this lack of recognition soon transforms into a rewarding relationship the more the mother interacts with her infant. The author writes about the identification process which begins prior to birth and is intense during the third trimester when the mother relates to the foetal movements and reactions.

In the first phase of identification after the birth, the mother relates fantasy to reality. If the new baby fulfils her fantasies the identification process is facilitated. But the physical contact is vital in order to realize that she really has a baby: active reaching, touching immediately after the birth, examining the baby, reassuring herself that he is complete and eventually snuggling up with the baby and smelling his newborn fragrance.

During the immediate period after the birth, according to Dr Ludington-Hoe, women undergo definitive stages of maternal role change. The first is taking in the fact that they are in need of care for themselves, by being helped to the bath or toilet, given food and at the same time being instructed on when and how to feed the infant.

If this dependency stage is handled by her caregivers with tenderness and efficiency, the woman will then graduate to the next stage of identifying with her baby, relating his appearance and characteristics to family likeness, and referring to the baby by name.

According to this study, the mood swings in the next ten days are caused by a juxtaposition of taking hold and letting go. The mother has to let go of her pregnancy and her fantasies and take on the tasks of mothering.

So again we come full cycle and can note that adjustment to motherhood is easier if there has been a close contact immediately after birth.

ADJUSTMENT TO PARENTHOOD

Jean Clark, addressing a seminar on postnatal expectations in Australia,[15] said, 'In our enlightened age, we are not educated to be parents. In fact very few parenting skills have been taught. We arrive home from hospital expecting to know and understand the new baby. Both parents are tired after the months of pregnancy and the hours of labour, they may not have support from the family and may feel isolated in a new community or a high-rise flat.

'They do not understand why the baby cries and may feel that the crying is labelling them as failures.'

Ruth relates how she and her husband moved to a bright new flat in a new town during the last month of pregnancy. Her husband's factory had been moved and although he had some previous connection with the people in his workplace, Ruth had left her job on moving and intended to stay at home until the baby was at least one year old.

'The birth went well and we were very happy with our son,' Ruth continues. 'The hospital was rather strict on routines but I didn't know of any other options. We had been so busy with the move, I missed out on childbirth classes. We came home in the middle of the morning after feeding Thomas and we looked forward to getting things settled and having a quiet lunch before the next feed.

'Thomas had other ideas. He cried all day and he cried all night. I fed him and no sooner did he settle than he cried again. I found out afterwards that they gave him lots of bottles in the hospital, but I didn't understand at the time why he was so fretful.

'During the move my next door neighbour, an older woman with two grown-up children, had been very kind and helpful. But after the birth, she kept giving me advice and was very critical.

'Our balconies were adjoining so she could see the baby in his pram when I put him out in the mornings. If he cried, she would poke her head out: "Oh dear, there he goes again," and if I ran to pick him up in order to avoid this confrontation she would call out, "It doesn't do to spoil them you know."

'Her own son used to play the trumpet at all hours of the day and night but the message was firm and clear: that a crying baby was a disturbance. I found myself apologizing or going for long walks just to get out of the flat.

'The worst feeling was that inadequacy of not understanding the baby's needs. He always seemed more difficult than other babies. He fed very quickly and often brought up his feeds, leaving him hungry again.

'I used to walk to the baby clinic with another mother I met in the hospital. It was nice because we would go back to each other's houses for a cup of tea. But her baby always looked crisp and shining in an immaculate pram while Thomas was always dribbling and bringing up his food over his clothes and bedding.

'Her house was always tidy with lines of sparkling white washing hanging on the line – even the garden was neat with trim lawns and weeded flowerbeds.

'She was like one of those TV ads for floor polish. And there were we, Ian and I, with this little monster who cried day and night and we were just too exhausted to even clean the flat or water the window-boxes.'

It took a long time for Ruth and Ian to understand Thomas's needs and this external pressure added to their feelings of inadequacy. This story is so typical of the experience of new parenthood in the Western world.

When a woman has a baby, her lifestyle changes dramatically. She leaves or interrupts the routine of her working framework and, at least for the first few months, her life revolves round the home and the care of the baby.

Some women accept this change gladly. They enjoy putting their energy into homemaking and, like Ruth's friend, derive pleasure from making the house look clean and pretty and take pride in the lines of clean washing flapping in the breeze.

It is not necessarily a difficult or demanding baby which causes frustration because for other women, even those with quiet babies, the constant repetitious chores deprive them of the intellectual stimulation they get at work.

There is nothing wrong with either of these attitudes. We cannot change the colour of our eyes and we cannot change our basic personality traits. So instead of feeling guilty that one does not live up to a self-image of Mother Earth, it might be more productive to learn to adjust one's lifestyle so that there is still time for an interesting course of lectures, a morning at the library or an evening out with friends.

The natural homemaker also has her frustrations. The baby takes up so much time and energy that the house is not as spotless as she would like it to be, and by the time her husband arrives home from work, she has not even thought about dinner.

We discuss in Chapter 7 how to cope with these situations but it is also relevant when we learn how to get acquainted with the baby and enhance the bonding experience.

Adjustment is far easier when the baby's father has flexible working hours. A short holiday after the birth will give him time to get to know his baby. The mother can then concentrate on establishing breastfeeding and helping her own recovery period, while the father can establish a relationship by bathing the baby, taking him for a walk in the park, lying in a warm bed with the baby on his chest. If the mother is exhausted by the constant disturbed nights, the father can occasionally give a bottle of expressed breast milk and also enjoy sharing in the experience of that blissful milky contentment of a young baby after a feed.

The juxtaposition of roles is a healthy development for the baby also as it teaches the child that parental tasks are interchangeable. Dr M. Ainsworth, writing on infancy in Uganda,[16] points out that infants can recognize a primary attachment figure and this could be the father. This model acts as a haven in times of stress and the focal points to which the child looks for answering his needs.

Often the question 'When does the baby begin to be a person?' can be answered when the parents can say, 'When I feel like a person again'. For with the return of self-confidence and self-esteem of the parent, so the child can grow and mature in freedom and in love.

5   *A New Life for Fathers*

M EN who read this chapter may justifiably complain that it is written by a woman, and for this reason I have consulted with Martin Richards of the Child Care and Development Group of the Faculty of Social and Political Sciences at the University of Cambridge. Martin Richards is a father himself, who has written and researched extensively on the subject of fatherhood.

Additionally, I have over my years of teaching shared the experiences of many fathers. It is true that some of them came reluctantly and unwillingly and ambivalently to the first session of the prenatal course. But once they realized that I was not going to pressure them into attending the birth or threaten them with fantasies of ideal fatherhood, most of them relaxed and enjoyed the course and the interaction with other couples.

'Somewhere at the dawn of history, males started nurturing females and their young . . . males appreciated that the female found it harder to climb trees when about to give birth or with an infant round her neck.'[1] Margaret Mead reminds us of our origins.

In 1927, Bronislav Malinowsky[2] discovered that fathers in the Trobriand Islands in New Guinea were oblivious of the part they played in procreation. Sex was for pleasure and Malinowsky calls their life a 'blissful egalitarian paradise'. And yet there was total equality between men and women in work and in childcare, completely uninspired by any biological drive or awareness as to whose child the man was nurturing.

While the Greeks worshipped full-breasted female goddesses, most religions focus on a male supreme being. Interestingly, the most family-oriented of the Mediterranean countries follow the

Catholic religion where the Madonna is revered along with the male Trinity.

In her field work in Jamaica, Edith Clarke[3] found that while the father recognized paternity, he did not accept the obligations which are usually associated with this role. Mothers and grand-mothers often set up home together with children fathered by more than one man. As a consequence, male children grew up with a primary duty to their mothers, even into old age.

'Most cultures excluded fathers from birth and active fathering, but they did nevertheless have some sort of role, whether it be dietary restrictions or sexual taboos during pregnancy,' observes H. Heggenhougen in the *Journal of Nurse-Midwife*.[4]

'Unlike these cultures, the Western world views paternity as a kind of symbolic object,' writes Dr Richards in *The Father Figure*.[5] 'The emphasis on biological paternity may provide the means for the father to assert this link with his children while remaining physically and psychologically distant from them.'

In Britain, too, fathers were distant figures and the Victorian attitude to sexuality prohibited any involvement of men in what was after all a direct result of sexual relations.

The psychoanalytic approach pre-World War Two suggested that pregnancy would kindle old emotional conflicts among men, especially inhibitions connected to sexual relationships and behaviour. It was not so long ago that obstetricians resisted fathers' admission to labour wards with the threat: 'But he will be impotent afterwards if he sees what he has done to his wife'.

Data can always be manipulated to suit the hypothesis as we see by the following example of research.

The British and American psychiatrists, T. Freeman,[6] J. Carter,[7] A. Hartman and R. Nicolay,[8] and W. Wainright[9] reported case histories of expectant fathers who displayed depressive and psychotic reactions, severe anxieties, abnormal psychosomatic symptoms, impulsive behaviour disorders, anti-social reactions and fears of homosexuality.

But a commentary on these researches by Katharyn Antle May and Steven Paul Perrin[10] criticizes that most of these studies were done with a population already under psychiatric treatment and did not correlate the mental health of a control group of non-expectant fathers.

They conclude: 'Pregnancy may represent a time of significant emotional disturbance for many men who otherwise appear to be functioning adequately'. And presumably they will continue to survive even if they have gone through the cataclysmic experience of participating in the birth.

While there has been a revolution in the family hierarchy throughout the world, in many Western countries we have seen a drastic change in the dynamics of family life over the past forty years and this has directly affected the father's role.

After World War Two, there was a rise in the birth-rate of the middle classes and there evolved in the 1960s the natural childbirth movement. There was a dedication to motherhood, and heightened awareness of the benefits of breastfeeding. A 'good husband and father' would go to classes, 'coach' his wife at the birth and care for the newborn. It was a sort of 'rite of passage'.

In many cases the nuclear family has turned in on itself and the extended family network has become smaller and less involved. The family is on the move, often living far away from the grand-mothers, aunts and childhood friends who in former days were the source of support for the new mother.

Mothers themselves have changing attitudes to parenthood and with more and more women returning to work after giving birth, many welcome the modern approach that children benefit from an active, interested father who shares the chores and the responsi-bility, together with the fun.

The emergence of the 'new father' is actually less apparent in Britain than in the United States. This may be because distances are shorter and an increasing number of families own cars and telephones, making kinship networks stronger than previously, says Dr Richards who quotes a survey in which it was found that after the mother, a grandmother was most likely to be the care-giver, followed by the father.

Women who return to work, either for economic reasons or to advance their career, will where possible utilize family childcare rather than pay out a hefty percentage of their salary to a stranger whom they cannot trust as much as a family member.

However, while there is much to be said for the extended family, studies show that the more active involvement of fathers in childcare and family activity is a very healthy development and that the child is enriched by the closer ties with his father.

Before looking at men's reactions to fatherhood, let us first discuss the decision-making process. There has indeed been very little research into what makes a man decide to become a father.

In K. A. May's study,[11] thirty-four men over the age of thirty were interviewed. The group was divided into two and were similar in demography, number of years together with partner, educational level, religious affiliation, marital history, income and, interestingly, pet ownership. They were interviewed in the third trimester using the Pie method devised by Cown and Coile in 1978, whereby the total self is divided up and personality traits including achievement, impulsiveness, autonomy, dominance and nurturance are analysed.

It appeared that three factors were important to signify readiness for fatherhood: 1) stability in couple's relationships; 2) relative financial security; 3) sense of closure to childless period. The third factor was often dependent on the reasons for having waited. For example, a man who was now facing fatherhood after fifteen years of infertility felt trapped and ambivalent about the 'success' of all the treatment undergone by his wife and himself.

Most of the interviews expressed ambivalence. 'I really didn't feel ready,' but when interviewed after the birth, 'The moment I saw the baby, I felt deep emotional bonding'.

Illogically, fathers who were unemployed were less willing to assume responsibility for infant care than those working fulltime.

David Owen writes in *The Father Figure*[12] that 'men look forward to having children and anticipate enjoying their activities when they are older'. For this reason there is a preference that there will be at least one son in the family to play rugby and go fishing, although many fathers expressed the desire to have a daughter as a companion for the wife.

In today's educational climate, this companionship can be enjoyed between mothers and sons and fathers and daughters. When my own daughter Sara, the fourth child but only girl in the family, was three years old, she would spend fifteen minutes every morning choosing her clothes for nursery school. 'Not this one, not this one, not this one,' the princess would reject each item for some unfathomable reason. My husband was amused by this, but he could not really connect with this phase in her development.

Now that she studies biology and chemistry at university, they sit together for hours while he helps her prepare for examinations and he obviously enjoys this interaction.

Dr Richards points out that fathers' reactions to pregnancy may be influenced by the sex of the child. The father may see the woman as an incubator for a dream baby. In some cultures, a male heir is essential for the continuation of the family, clan or tribe, and a father may well lose his enthusiasm if one female after another fills the nest. On the other hand, the birth of a boy may cause conflicts of ideology, a sort of reliving of his own infancy and a desire that things will be better for his son.

Continuing on the theme of the dream baby, it was found by E. D'Arcy[13] that fathers were more distraught than mothers if the baby was abnormal, particularly if the infant was a boy.

An investigation of reactions to the birth of babies with Down's syndrome by Gumz and Gubrium[14] found that mothers were more concerned about the emotional strain, physical care and reorientation of family routines. The fathers focused on the practical problems, cost of additional care and concern about the infant's ability to cope.

FATHERS IN THE PERINATAL PERIOD

In order to understand the changing role of fathers in society, it is important to discuss the impact of pregnancy and of their partici-pation in the birth itself. In the same way as the birth experience influences women's adjustment after birth, so men too are pro-foundly affected by this transition, perhaps even more so because they do actually have the choice of whether or not to go into the labour ward.

During today's pregnancies, men have an opportunity to work through fantasies and establish a paternal-foetal bonding, either by attending antenatal examinations with their partner, listening to the Doppler recording the foetal heart or by monitoring the baby's development on the ultrasound screen. Or he can simply tune in to his baby's movements by laying his head on his partner's abdomen when she is resting.

It is understandable that a study done by R. Weaver and M. Cranley[15] shows a correlation between this foetal attachment and the strength of the marital relationship. It goes without saying that if a man is insecure in his marriage, he may be reluctant to relate so permanently with his baby.

Joel Richman[16] discusses Biller and Meredith's[17] description of prevalent categories of fathers' attitudes towards marriage and pregnancy:

1. Eagerly accepts reponsibility of being family man and considers pregnancy a gift; becomes close to wife;
2. Regards fatherhood as a burden, reaffirms old habits, denies need for change;

3. Emotionally immature, frightened of prospect of supporting wife and child, faces problem of transition from carefree former existence.

'Fatherhood is a dynamic process with changes swinging between the poles,' write Richman and Goldthorp.[18] Therefore attitudes can change back and forth from time to time:

1. Denies existence of pregnancy, looks for escape, works overtime or away from home;
2. Adopts attitude that pregnancy is 'nothing unusual' and is wife's responsibility;
3. Wishes to share pregnancy, develops bonds with foetus, offers increased emotional and practical help;
4. Claims total identification with foetus, attempts to socially sterilize the mother.

When a man learns that he is to become a father, there are many conflicting reactions, many of them dependent on his age, his economic situation, his desire for a baby, his relationship with his wife, his own parents.

He may be proud that the family line will be continued and he fantasizes that he will be as good or a better parent than were his own. At the same time he may be fearful that the new responsibilities will curtail his growth and freedom. His wife is getting all the attention and he is bewildered by her body and personality changes.

How many men experience a lower sexual drive during pregnancy? His partner was his girlfriend, his woman, and now she is in transition, going into the mysterious world of motherhood.

The three phases of pregnancy for fathers are described rather like three trimesters by Katharyn May.[19] These stages are:

1. Awareness – announcement;
2. Moratorium – a time when he can forget, particularly when he is busy at work or out of the house;
3. Focusing – waiting for the birth.

It is during the second phase, the moratorium, that it is appropriate to begin the childbirth course so that he can reconnect with the pregnancy and tune in to his partner and the baby.

Some men empathize with the pregnancy by suffering similar discomforts such as tiredness, weight gain, backache, even nausea.

The anthropological literature discusses the *couvade* syndrome where the father lies in the family hut, suffering and crying out, while his wife quietly gets on with the job of giving birth. Most known primitive cultures had some sort of ritual couvade – a term taken from *couver*, to hatch.

Research done by Liebenberg in 1973[20] showed that 11–65% of men experienced weight gain, food cravings, backache and fatigue. This is not to be confused with a condition called pseudocyesis in which the man experiences these symptoms because he actually believes he is pregnant. There is, however, a danger that a man will not seek medical advice on the assumption that all these symptoms are psychosomatic and in fact he may fear being teased by his health care provider.

It has been noted by R. Munroe[21] that ritual couvade enables men to enact the female role symbolically in a culturally approved way.

The researchers observe that couvade and male initiation rites at puberty rarely occur in the same culture, which suggests that both couvade and initiation rites have evolved for the same reason; to acknowledge and resolve conflicts between sexual roles.

A doctor in the British Army in India during the Second World War recorded that one of his soldiers reported to his clinic with severe abdominal pains. The doctor could not find anything wrong and it did not seem to be symptomatic of appendicitis or a stomach upset. The next morning, the soldier received a telegram that his wife had given birth, the labour having progressed exactly during those hours that he had experienced the pain. Was this a totally unconscious involvement – or was it telepathy – for he did not know exactly when his wife was due to give birth?

But in a situation where the couple are together during the pregnancy and the period after the birth, the father may indeed resent the surfeit of attention being given to his partner and even be resentful that he cannot himself give birth. He may also worry that he will take second place with his partner and that they will no longer be a couple.

Many of the available pregnancy books and childbirth courses discuss the father's role in terms of what he contributes to his partner. There is not nearly enough attention paid to what the father actually needs for himself during this life change.

Going back to early twentieth century literature, it was perhaps beneficial for a man to sit in the pub drinking with his friends while his wife gave birth. It established his manliness, his virility, his achievement.

It might therefore be a good thing if a man, after attending his wife in labour, did not go home to an empty house. He too could go and have a drink with his friends or a meal with his family so that at least for those two or three days before his wife comes home, he is the centre of attention.

In hospitals where I have worked in Israel, the entire extended family may sit in the waiting room during labour. This is some-what hard on the father who is torn between supporting his wife and reporting to the family. But it does mean that when it is all over, and his wife is resting, the family take him home for chicken soup and glory.

ATTENDANCE AT THE BIRTH

Although it has never been proved that participation at the birth increases paternal/infant bonding, it does seem that the prepara-tion process as well as the attendance at the birth enhances a father's view of childbirth and intensifies his wellbeing and affection.

Greenberg and Morris[22] concluded that fathers who attended the birth could more easily distinguish their babies from others, while Cronenwett and Newmark[23] found that their overall child-birth experience and marital relationships were more positive.

Some studies have shown that men who attended the birth were more attuned to the mother's needs in the weeks following the birth. At Charing Cross Hospital, London, 99.6% of the 730 men interviewed who participated in the birth were satisfied that they had done so. They reported that they recognized the definitive roles of the father and knew what to do and how to help.

By participating in decision-making in the alien environment of the hospital, the father is empowered to take a more active role in nurturing his wife and baby when they return home. If he does not get pushed out by too much interference from female relatives who do not appreciate his role, he will establish his place as an equal partner in childcare oriented tasks.

The challenge of supporting women in labour is daunting to many men. There are age-old taboos and fears about childbirth, about witnessing women during this overwhelming life experi-ence, about destroying the mystery of the woman's body.

Some men sail quite happily into childbirth classes declaring: 'No way will anyone keep me out of this. We made this child together and we are going to give birth together, all the way'. Nevertheless, very few men are prepared for the earth-shattering emotions of those few hours, and in the many births I have attended, I have often been moved to tears to see how the father feels the very pain experienced by his partner and how, in his relief after the birth, he often breaks down weeping. It is as if he himself gave birth, and on more than one occasion I have walked into the delivery room within half an hour of a birth to be greeted by a father who has kissed me ecstatically and cried out in delight, 'Do you know what I did, I gave birth to a baby'.

Although it is not possible to anticipate fully the experience of this momentous life event, without doubt the antenatal preparation course will provide the tools and very often the motivation for the father to go into the labour ward.

Over a period of time I have seen a swing in awareness and popularity of these courses. They used to be labelled as suitable for the middle-class well-educated, the ones who read all the books and come to the first lesson with lists of questions and challenges for the unsuspecting instructor.

My own courses reach out to many levels of society, to the Students Union of a science and technology university, to the multi-ethnic population who have registered at a city hospital, to younger-than-usual couples living in a new lower income development area, to those who manage to find my own private studio. In all these groups I see an emergence of awareness on the part of the father, that moment when he takes his wife's hand and connects with her and the development and growth of his baby.

'Without doubt, the father's own emotional health is a significant factor in this issue, not only as to how it affects his own reaction but also how the woman herself experiences the birth and the overall quality of the parent-infant relationship', write Grossman, Eichler and Winichoff.[24]

In Britain, where home birth is still possible, the participation of the father seems more natural. He is the host, the householder, and he receives the doctor and midwife, makes them comfortable, supports his wife, gives everyone a cup of tea.

Dr Richards comments that in fact the man's presence in the hospital, a relatively recent innovation, has increased from 5% in 1960 to 80% in the early 1980s, with lower figures for the second birth. This may be due as much to the acceptance and encouragement of hospital management as to the increased willingness of the father to participate.

Expanding on his comments, Dr Richards observes that in most cultures, birth has always been a matter for women from which men are excluded. The changes in Europe, Britain and elsewhere are very recent.

> It is very culturally abnormal for men to be present at delivery and perhaps we should expect difficulties. My own view is that presence at birth grew up with a very particular kind of marriage, with the expectation that everything should be shared. One of the difficulties for men is that birth demonstrates that there are things which cannot be shared. It reinforces the separate roles of men and women which can be submerged in the early and childless years of marriage but cannot be sustained once the children arrive. A second important difficulty is that men may feel powerless to help at birth and this can make them feel very uncomfortable. It is other women (midwives) who seem to be most helpful.

This last statement is true in traditional or intimate birthing rooms. But my experience of busy city hospitals is that if the partner was not present, the labouring woman could be left alone for hours with nobody to give her the comfort, the extra pillows, the sips of water and the massage which are essential if non-nursing tasks during that stressful time.

In fact, most women facing their first birth in hospital express a dependence on their partners as the only stable and familiar person on the scene. Home births by their nature are attended by family doctors and the domiciliary midwife, both of whom have been meeting with the childbearing woman throughout her pregnancy.

If we read the older literature about births at home, the man was often shooed out to the pub as we discussed earlier, and after a message was sent to him that the birth was over, he celebrated with his friends until he came home at closing time to find mother and new baby peacefully sleeping.

In upper-class homes, the expectant father was graphically depicted pacing the floor of the dining room, whisky in hand, while the cries of the labouring woman echoed through the house.

D. H. Lawrence, however, describes the beautiful relationship between Lydia and Thomas in his book *The Rainbow*.[25] He sits by her side throughout the labour, expressing deep tenderness, and 'she looked at him as only a woman looks at the man who begot her child'.

In *Maternity – Letters from Working Women*,[26] a collection of letters first published in 1915 by the Womens Cooperative Guild, it was possible to capture the varied attitudes of the fathers. First of all, women had been conditioned to believe that, even during pregnancy, their needs were last on the family list. 'Father had the meat, the children had the gravy, and I got the bread and dripping,' reported one mother who perhaps began to associate her weariness and discomforts with her impoverished diet.

'My husband stayed with me during labour – he was like a nurse and mother to me,' reports one woman, while another writes, 'The doctor gave my husband a sleeping pill so that he could rest undisturbed in the next room'.

That it might be a natural desire to be left in peace during labour is borne out when many modern men ask, albeit in jest, if they can also have a dose of nitrous oxide, or laughing gas as it is known.

Assuming that the couple have an open supportive relationship and that the father is really convinced that it takes two to birth a baby, men sometimes have to overcome inner resistance and perhaps previous traumas in order to attend the birth. It is only their own conviction that they need to be there for reasons we have discussed that pulls them through.

Ronnie had been injured in a car crash, and was hospitalized for several months with severe burns. His memories of hospital, the same one where his wife was due to give birth, were very negative. He confessed that it was a tremendous effort even to attend the childbirth course in the hospital, but his wife was very frightened and declared that she needed him during the course even if he did not stay through the birth.

Ronnie was relieved that there were other men in the group who felt ambivalent about attending the birth, although none of them had such traumatic associations with hospitals. The group and the instructor helped him take each stage step by step, with the option to leave when he felt he could not go any further. He completed the course, accompanied his wife to the hospital, stayed with her during labour and supported her throughout the birth.

Ronnie emerged triumphant. He had achieved so much. He had worked through his own hospital trauma and could put behind him the painful experiences of his own injury.

Most men, even without Ronnie's previous trauma, fear that they will not be able to keep pace with the birth, that they will faint or make a fool of themselves. Michael went with his wife to a childbirth course feeing very positive and optimistic. However, he noticed that every time there was a discussion about intravenous drips or injections, he felt nauseous and dizzy. He and his wife discussed this with the instructor who suggested that they sit together for a few private sessions without the group. At one point, the instructor described the epidural anaesthetic and Michael went pale and asked to lie down.

However, by meeting privately without the fear of making a fool of himself in front of the group, Michael gradually absorbed the material, helped his wife do the exercises, until finally he confronted the two sessions which he feared most, the birth slides and the tour of the labour ward.

He chose to see the slides first, and as he watched the sequence of first stage of labour, the methods for supporting his wife, breathing techniques, helping her to move around, rubbing her back, the more disturbing aspects such as medical intervention and hospital atmosphere fell into sequence.

In fact he coped throughout the birth, helped the midwife adjust the monitor, held his wife's hand while she received an epidural anaesthetic and practically caught the baby who sped out into the world after a very fast second stage of labour. 'I was just too busy to faint,' he admitted half an hour later, flopped down in a chair drinking a strong cup of tea.

Without doubt, participation at the birth gives the father the opportunity for establishing a relationship with his baby from the moment of birth. He may have been aware of foetal movements during the pregnancy if his partner lay next to him with her abdomen against him; he may have talked to the baby and sang songs while he cuddled his partner. But that moment of birth, when he sees the transition of the foetus to baby, when the infant emerges covered with vernix, maybe mauve or grey in colour, squashed with a head like a rugby ball, and the transformation to a healthy plump human being, that is the moment of realization for him that he participated in the creation of a new life.

This continuum flows smoothly and logically if one witnesses a father at the birth of his child. He holds the baby close to his face, examines him, touches him, smiles, makes eye contact; in other words, he is taking on a parental role. He knows his baby from that moment.

This is very different from the traditional system of viewing a baby through a window for a few moments each day until the baby comes home, a stranger who has experienced his first days of life without knowing his father.

'When my first baby was born, the hospitals did not allow fathers to be present,' reports David. 'I went home, paced the floor all night, then fell into a heavy sleep and woke up in the middle of the morning. I phoned the hospital and was told that I had been a father for the past six hours!' The next birth was at home and David did not leave his wife for a moment.

Greenberg and Morris[27] describe the first interaction of father and baby as a peak experience, listing the processes observed:

Absorption
Preoccupation
Visual awareness
Tactile stimulation
Perception of baby as perfect
Attraction
Elation
Self-esteem

Danny had twin daughters in their teens when his wife's next pregnancy started. It had not occurred to him to be present at the birth but this time all his friends told him that it was the thing to do. His wife had had a very difficult first birth and it had taken many years to start another pregnancy. She very much wanted him to be there. 'It's always better to agree with one's wife,' he quipped. He attended the childbirth course with much scepticism, was the clown of the group, and declared that he couldn't see himself in that situation.

He emerged from the birth experience with awe and wonder. 'The baby was born with an erection – a real man!' He was obviously happy to have an ally in this house of women.

Danny is a well-known artist and he invited me to an exhibition of his new work a year after the birth of his son. All his new pictures were of creation, of forests with women's bodies emerging from the trees, he was greatly acclaimed for this development in his work.

Later I met him at his home, and while he painted, his son came to him with an offering in his potty. Danny was enthralled and so proud of his son's achievements.

ATTITUDES TO FATHERHOOD

It is indeed a fact that fatherhood does not begin the moment the baby is born, and it is therefore obvious that when a man does prepare together with his wife, he is more ready to take on this new role, not just that of supporting his partner but one which will enrich his own self-image.

At one time a father would feel remote from the babies in the family, declaring that he would feel like a father when he bought the first football for his son, but today's fathers balance babies in front-carriers while doing the weekly shop at the supermarket.

At my end-of-course parties when couples return with their babies, I often hear the fathers sitting in a group discussing the colour of the baby's stools, how much weight was gained that week, and the merits of certain brands of nappies, dummies and other baby paraphernalia.

The women, who are still on maternity leave and spend all their daytime hours at home with the baby, enjoy the party, freely chatting, holding a drink, while it is the men who are cuddling the babies and making the best of those precious hours.

For many fathers, the homecoming is a conflict of emotions. He has cleaned the house, cooked a meal, put flowers on the table and he looks forward to a sort of second honeymoon. He fetches his partner from the hospital and proudly they show the baby to all the neighbours who happen to be hanging around the front door.

And then the action starts. He has taken a few days off work to help the mother and baby get into a routine, but very often he is glad to get back to work, haggard and bleary-eyed. All those books and courses and theories just do not apply to this new baby, and day and night are indistinguishable as the parents try to understand what is happening.

Being left alone with a new baby is hard enough, but it is sometimes even more difficult when the emerging routine is disrupted by well-meaning relatives and friends giving advice and the doubtful benefits of their experience.

It is assumed that, because the father returns to his normal work routine, he will not be so sensitive to changes in the family. But apart from sleep starvation, he comes home after work to a changed environment. Instead of a quiet evening eating dinner and watching TV or going out with his partner to play tennis or to see a film, he may find a bedraggled, exhausted woman who needs comfort and support – and no sign of dinner!

He picks up his baby, the child of his dreams, and wonders why the world has turned upside down for this three or four kilos of humanity.

Many fathers, however, report a development in the relationship with their babies when the child begins to respond or to smile in recognition. 'We have our bath together – he lies on my chest and pulls at the hair – he loves it,' said one father who enjoyed this 'locker-room intimacy'.

Just as there have been countless studies and research theses on motherhood, so much of the professional literature has analysed fatherhood over the past few years.

In *Transition to Fatherhood*, a paper written by Karin Larson Hangsleben, fifty first-time fathers were interviewed three weeks before the birth and again between three to five weeks afterwards. She examined attitudes to childcare tasks and reported on lifestyle changes.

Continuing her study of marital adjustment and history of activities with their own fathers, it emerged that while there are many irrational episodes of depression or difficulties in adjustment for fathers, there was a link between healthy mental state and stable marital relationships, and positive memories of activities with their own fathers.

There were certainly negative effects as a result of drastic changes, economic hardship, worries about work permanency, the wear and tear of sleepless nights and taking the greater share of domestic responsibilities. Without doubt, the mature, older and economically more established father suffered less from the physical restrictions, but for them the change in lifestyle was more drastic.

These reactions are parallel to those of women whose adjustment to motherhood is so tangibly influenced by these same factors. A study by E. LeMasters[28] compared reaction and adjustment to the first baby in forty-six couples. Both parents felt a loss of social contact and difficulty in providing continuous and prolonged infant care. The fathers were more concerned by their partners' declining sexual responsiveness and change in social life.

Another study by D. Hobbs[29] concludes that while there were few differences in reactions, the fathers' overall adjustment score was lower than that of the mothers. He describes fatherhood as 'a normative developmental event involving some transitional difficulties'.

Interestingly, fathers' attitudes to breastfeeding expressed during the pregnancy did not always match up to the depth of their support after the birth.

Many studies describe the reasons given against encouraging breastfeeding, which were honest jealousy, less involvement with the baby if the father cannot give bottles, a desire to see the woman return to normal weight and energy, revulsion at leaking and heavy breasts.

It would be interesting to know if those men had attended courses where breastfeeding was discussed during pregnancy. My own field experience is very different. The majority of couples who attend the reunion party, which can be from three weeks to three months after the birth, are still enthusiastic about breastfeeding, and it is obvious that the men are still supportive and positive about the experience.

Psychoanalyst Joan Raphael-Leff[30] categorizes fathers as Participators or Renouncers (Table 5) and obviously most men are a mixture of both.

Table 5. Early paternal orientations

Participators	*Renouncers*
Involved in pregnancy	Verbalizes male/female differences
Reads, goes to course	Activation of his mother's control
Views process as miracle	Identification with father (non-supportive)
Frustrated by his limits	
'Couvade' – shares symptoms	Proud of virility but unable to empathize
Goes to ultrasound	
Wants to care for baby	Embarrassed
Jealous of mother/baby relationship	Goes to ultrasound and course if coerced
Positive about touch, massage during labour	
	Prefers not to attend birth
	Fears blood and gore
	Association of birth and death
	Role of father – get to know baby when he is older
	Feels out of place

We saw in Chapter 3 Joan Raphael-Leff's analysis of women's attitudes within categories of Regulator and Facilitator. In this study of fatherhood, she adds that if the woman is a Regulator and routine is very important to her, the father in our second category above of Renouncer may feel compelled to share more than he would wish, or if their income is sufficient, to get paid help. In the same way, a man who really wishes to be involved and is prepared to change his working hours to take equal shares in parenthood may be ousted if his partner is a Facilitator and cannot 'let go' of the parenting tasks.

Of course there are surprises. Doris and her husband Norman were living abroad while Norman was building up an overseas branch of a large company. They were both in their thirties and this pregnancy was unplanned and less than wanted by Norman. He expressed anxiety during the pregnancy, claiming that he could never change nappies or deal with the messy side of parenthood. The birth was straightforward and Norman did participate because he knew that in a strange country with a foreign language, it would be very difficult for Doris on her own. The next day when I visited, Doris was resting in bed and Norman was pacing the room, earnestly and expertly trying to burp the baby.

'Men may be predisposed to adjustment difficulties after the birth because of unfilled dependency needs and missing links in their own family structure,' observes H. J. Osofsky.[31]

Denis came from a broken home and did not even know his mother. He loved children and was very eager to have a large family and make up for all the deprivations of his childhood. But Denis experienced such serious difficulties in adjusting to fatherhood that his own marriage nearly broke up. He was devoted to his wife and children but it took a lot of patience and many crises before he accepted the joys and limitations of fatherhood.

Bill, on the other hand, did accept fatherhood unconditionally. His own mother died when he was born and he grew up with all the cousins and aunts, all of whom were kind and caring, but this did not replace the intimacy of the nuclear family. He married young and his life focuses primarily on his three young children. It is he who checks what they eat, if they do their homework, if they are healthy, and if he is separated from them for more than a day he is fretful and unhappy. Because his own mother had died indirectly as a result of childbirth, he experienced severe anxiety during his wife's pregnancies but once he was reassured that she was alive and well, he enjoyed his family and his entire life centred around the home.

Dr Osofsky lists the positive and negative reactions to fatherhood:

Positive	*Negative*
Excitement	Feels forced into marriage or
Pride	relationship
Symbol of virility	Rivalry
Potency	Concern about birth outcome
Hope for heir	Fear for wife's safety

Enjoyment of woman's body changes	Isolation
Warmth	Envy
Comfort	Fears of inadequacy as father
Tenderness	Resents partner's body/mood changes
	Escapes to work
	Fantasizes about other women
	Compares partner to own mother, resulting in sexual problems

Whether the conflicts be physical or emotional, it is very evident that fathers do suffer postpartum disturbance even in the most normal of circumstances.

The role of antenatal education and postnatal support groups was discussed by Dr Andy McCafferty of Glasgow College at a seminar organized by the NCT.[32] 'The causes are not hormonal as they are in the woman after birth, but men are nevertheless vulnerable to the effects of personality and levels of adjustment, expectations and stress points such as fatigue, isolation.'

But whereas society will sympathize with a woman suffering from PND, it is much more difficult for a man to admit this problem. Instead he will often escape, stay late at work, go to the pub until all hours, retreat into his computer game, things that actually distance him from the root cause rather than confronting it. Encounter groups in women's organizations are recognized as being supportive and empowering. Men too need to understand that they are not alone with their ambivalence and that all around them, in the workplace, the neighbourhood, the swimming club, are other men with similar emotional needs.

6 Mothers and Fathers

'WANTED: Administrator with following skills – teacher, counsellor, psychologist, friend, confidant, nurse, doctor, chauffeur, maid, cook, home economist, plumber, advisor, coach, comforter, confessor, assistant company director, peacemaker, playmate, protector, prophet, judge.'

This is a parent, according to Kate Clancy Shales, writing in the *International Childbirth Education Association Journal*.[1]

With all these qualifications needed for one job, it is hardly surprising that there is something called 'parent burn-out'. Procacinni and Kiefaber,[2] writing on this phenomenon report that specifically at risk are families with severe economic problems or an overactive, difficult or handicapped child. This causes a build-up of fatigue, seeming lack of reward and overwhelming responsibility for what seems an indeterminate period.

Becoming a parent in normal circumstances requires a lot of adjustment and flexibility, even when the baby is easy and contented. Sometimes, life events make the job even more difficult.

Stanley is a radiographer working in a hospital, a very confident and assured young man from a secure family background. Maureen, who was born in Australia and was separated from her own family, was working as a schoolteacher during her pregnancy. As the pregnancy progressed, she felt more insecure and isolated but Stanley was always there to support her and reassure her and she appreciated that he was always attuned to her mood if she was worried or unhappy.

Both their first and second babies were born very prematurely, and the solidarity of their relationship was indeed tested. With two small vulnerable children, the couple had little time and energy for themselves. Maureen felt even more isolated without her family because she had no time for outside activity. Stanley's tenderness and sensitivity continued throughout this difficult period, but Maureen realized that it was at some cost to himself, both in terms of advancement in his career and his own social needs.

At the time of the first pregnancy, Stanley had been accepted for a doctorate but he postponed this heavy study programme until the second baby was stronger and better developed. 'This was priority number one, to nurture these two fragile babies and get them to a stage of development where Maureen and I could relax and take up our lives again.' Stanley noted that this period of dependency seemed long at the time, but now three years after the birth of the second child, he is well into his dissertation and even finds time to play football, a hobby which had also been pushed aside during that stressful time.

There is something mystical about the concept of twins in every society, and every culture abounds with superstitions concerning them. But there was nothing mystical about the sheer exhaustion of the 24-hour, round-the-clock routine shared by Marcello and Françoise, coping alone without family in a strange country.

They had met at university in London and when Marcello got a good job in the north of England, they bought a small flat and settled there. They were very happy during the pregnancy because they had both travelled a great deal and felt the need to put down roots. But they did feel some apprehension when twin foetuses were seen on the ultrasound. Françoise accepted it more easily: 'It seemed like a bonus. I was thrilled. But I was also scared because I didn't have a clue what was involved. I am an only child'.

As is usual with twin pregnancies, Françoise was advised to rest from the twenty-eighth week to the thirty-sixth in order to prevent premature birth. They did not yet have a network of friends to support them through this and both parents felt the isolation of this enforced confinement to the house.

After the birth of two healthy babies, there was not a moment to spare. 'If one slept, the other cried,' said Françoise, who did not even have time to join a support group. The twins were very different in personality and appearance and had very different needs and routines.

'I felt that I was living a totally divided life,' admitted Marcello. 'I was very busy at work and enjoying the demands of each day, dealing with people and problems. And then I came home to a house which was like a cocoon of steaming laundry and babies' baths.'

'I was feeling more and more isolated,' says Françoise, 'and I began to resent the freedom which my husband enjoyed. It did not occur to me that it was also very demanding on his time and energy.'

When the twins were eight months old, Françoise decided to go back to work part-time and put the babies into a crèche. At first she felt a sense of release because she could use her brain again and start to meet people. However, one of the children caught a succession of infections and eventually the parents decided that she was too vulnerable in the crèche. Marcello unfortunately was made redundant, but while he looked for another job, he cared for the babies and Françoise continued working. 'In a way it came at a good time because it only took me a couple of months to find a job and it gave my wife an opportunity to be out of the house. At the same time, we needed her salary.'

When Françoise changed places again with her husband, she realized that during the period she had worked, she had managed to get the house and childcare into some sort of routine. So at that point she joined a support group, made friends, did some time-sharing childcare so that she could go out sometimes. At the same time, her sick child regained her strength and life took on some degree of normalcy.

PREVENTING BURNOUT

Since most parents are not facing such extremes in difficult conditions, it might be worth discussing some guidelines to prevent this burnout.

However much one enjoys one's profession, one needs time out, and parenthood is no exception. During the first two or three months it may be very difficult to find enough time between feeds to go out for an entire evening, but there might nevertheless be an opportunity to get to a keep fit class or even just to browse around the shops or meet a friend for a cup of coffee, while the father is at the ready with a bottle of expressed breast milk.

Social support, for fathers as well as mothers, is important and it is amazing that as soon as one has a baby, one does meet up with neighbours and colleagues who share the same anxieties and concerns.

For some couples, this is a difficult transition. They may be the first in their social circle to have a baby and they then feel very cut off from their previous life. The friends who do not yet have children are not aware of the limitations of time and may get quite glassy-eyed with boredom when the parents go on and on about their baby's brilliant achievements.

If one has family available for reliable babysitting, or friends who can sometimes take the baby for short periods on a reciprocal basis, it becomes more and more possible to again take up hobbies or interests, things that can be done together as a couple or separately.

Because these occasions are rare, they become very precious. Our own four children were born when we were living in Hampshire, with our families based in London and the north of England. Through my local support group I made friends who eventually were as close to me as my family. The children all grew up together sharing holidays and outings, picnics and theatres, while we as mothers helped each other during illness or if one wanted a day out.

These days stand out like an oasis, and I will never forget one special day my husband and I spent at the Chichester Festival. We left the children early in the morning with one of our friends, dressed in elegant clothes for a change, knowing that no small child was going to be carsick over us. We browsed around the antique market at Chichester, had a leisurely lunch and went to a performance of Peer Gynt. It was an enchanting day and driving home through the sunset, we didn't want it to end. We stopped the car in the heart of the countryside and strolled hand in hand through a field, not wanting to curtail our freedom.

The following months until we could again have such a day to ourselves were much easier and of course we in turn looked after our friends' children while they went off for a day's leisure.

A parent needs decompression time on a regular basis, a period of quiet, just to think or listen to music, or have a bubble bath. Barbara leads a busy life. She has three lively children and works part-time as an occupational therapist in a children's hospital. At 5.30 in the morning, Barbara sits in her garden with a cup of coffee, listening to the birds and watching the dawn. In winter, she still enjoys that early hour sitting by a window looking out onto her garden. This is her quiet time before the noise and bustle of the day begins.

My decompression time is midnight, and when my children

were small, however tired I was after a busy day of work and parenting, I very often sat late at night after everyone was asleep, listening to quiet music and writing poems.

PARENTHOOD AND MARITAL RELATIONSHIPS

What is the effect of parenthood on the marriage relationship? A report from the Thomas Coran Research Institute[3] on 'marriage and the transition to parenthood' states that only one in ten marriages is weakened by parenthood. It was added that the age and length of the marriage was relevant, with more problems experienced in very young newly-weds.

E. LeMasters and E. D. Dyer[4] call the birth of a first child a crisis event.

F. Grossman[5] reports that women showed decreased marital satisfaction with the birth of the first child ... but couples also reported enrichment and enhanced meaning in the relationship, while at the same time acknowledging the effects of increased stress and conflict.

Eighty-five mothers in Grossman's study were interviewed at sixteen weeks and thirty-four weeks of pregnancy and again at seven weeks, six months and twelve months after the birth. The fathers were interviewed once during pregnancy and at seven weeks and twelve months after the birth. In analysing the sexual relationship, women seemed to show a decline in satisfaction during that time.

Only 49% of mothers felt that husbands understood what life was like at home with a baby while 73% of husbands acknowledged that their wives appreciated employment commitments and did not make unrealistic demands on their work hours.

In *The First Birth*, Drs D. R. Entwistle and S. G. Doering[6] studied the family life cycle of 120 women and sixty husbands after the birth of their first child, with ten to twenty hours of interviews from the sixth month of pregnancy to six months after the birth. The interviews explored the family formation, self-concepts, attitudes towards each other, sex roles and behaviour, financial situation, and linked circumstances and events during pregnancy and the postpartum period.

They found that preparation in pregnancy produced more realistic expectations, and social support from friends, family and the community significantly improved adjustment to the role of parenthood.

Table 6. Marital satisfaction scores – individual items and total score – for men and women (%) (reproduced with permission from P. Moss, G. Bollard, R. Foxman and C. Owen, 'Transition to parenthood', *Journal of Reproductive and Infant Psychology*, 1986)

		Marital satisfaction items:														Total score 30 or less		Mean	
		Decision-making		Time together		Sharing affection		Confiding		Sexual relations		Rows		Amount in common					
Contact†		1	5	1	5	1	5	1	5	1	5	1	5	1	5	1	5	1	5
Wives	1	82	55	48	28	92	57	39	67	75	48	59	52	71	55	20	46	33.4	30.2
	2	15	45	50	47	8	43	11	29	22	40	33	38	28	40				
	3	2	2	2	25	—	1	—	4	2	12	9	11	1	5				
Husbands	1	84	68	48	35	87	59	85	72	69	55	68	57	64	56	19	41	33.2	30.8
	2	16	30	32	37	13	32	12	24	26	32	30	36	34	41				
	3	—	3	20	28	—	9	2	4	5	17	3	7	1	3				

* 1, item rated 'perfect' or 'very happy'; 2, item rated 'fairly happy' or 'neither happy or unhappy'; 3, item rated 'a little unhappy', 'fairly unhappy' or 'extremely unhappy'.
† Contact 1, interview in early pregnancy. Contact 5, interview 12 months after birth.

Table 7. Communication questions for men and women (reproduced with permission from Moss et al.)

Contact*	Time together: not satisfied		Amount talk together				Spouse's understanding				Confiding			
			Positive with qualifications		Negative		Positive with qualifications		Negative		Spouse closest confidant		Does not confide all matters to spouse	
	1	5	1	5	1	5	1	5	1	5	1	5	1	5
Wives	51%	54%	12%	8%	16%	23%	35%	30%	8%	17%	90%	93%	18%	16%
Husbands	49%	51%	7%	7%	17%	25%	44%	25%	3%	7%	92%	93%	40%	25%

* Contact 1, interview in early pregnancy. Contact 5, interview 12 months after birth.

ADJUSTING TO PARENTHOOD

When couples start a family at a young age, they are sometimes overwhelmed by the changes and limitations. When parents are more mature they may anticipate them although it is no less difficult.

Yvonne and Harry were both working as advertising executives when they met on a market research project. They married and opened their own agency as equal partners.

They had been married for four years and saved up enough to buy a house when they decided that this was an appropriate time to start a family. They were both then aged thirty, and were relieved that their first pregnancy started without any problems. Throughout the pregnancy, Yvonne worked and felt well. She was enthusiastic about the birth and had decided to take some time off afterwards to establish breastfeeding and focus on the baby.

It was only four weeks before the due date that Yvonne suddenly felt apprehensive, rather like Patricia in a previous case history. 'We have had such a good time together, enjoy our work and spend our weekends relaxing, staying in bed late on Sunday mornings, going to concerts, reading. How is a baby going to fit into all this, or should I ask how I am going to change my lifestyle to suit the baby's needs?'

Yvonne was expressing very real and honest doubts, but she felt guilty about these issues because she had very genuinely wanted this pregnancy.

With this foresight, Yvonne and Harry sat down together and worked out a programme for time-sharing. Yvonne would be able to attend an international conference in the United States when the baby would be four months old if she and Harry took turns to attend sessions and exchanged notes. The couple equipped the home with easily transportable equipment to make it possible to be continually on the move with a small baby.

In fact for Yvonne, the mothering hormone prolactin was working fulltime and she thoroughly enjoyed the first months at home with the baby. She fully breastfed for six months and then managed to start working again, taking the baby with her, with a babysitter to stand by when she had important meetings.

There are fathers who are so deeply convinced that their role is equal to that of mothers that they take an extended leave from work. Sometimes this is for practical reasons, because the mother's salary is higher, or because the father is in an easier position to take a break from his work.

Eric is a schoolteacher and he was due for a sabbatical year at the time of the birth of their first child. His wife is a social worker and although she didn't want to return to work full time, she did have the opportunity to work three days a week.

This was a perfect arrangement for this couple because Eric very happily coped with the home and baby during those three days each week. On other days he was free to get on with his projects and research. This was Eric's second marriage, and he reported that he had never had such a close relationship with his two older children.

As this arrangement becomes more acceptable, fathers are expressing specific needs in coping with being at home. Richard Seel, coordinator of fathers groups for the National Childbirth Trust and author of *Uncertain Father*,[7] states that men can also be lonely at home and need emotional and practical support.

Graeme Russell writes in *Reassessing Fatherhood*:[8] 'Few fathers anticipate difficulties in staying at home and caring for children. They imagine that they will have so much free time, but in fact get bored by repetitious routines and lack of adult company'.

Richard Seel continues: 'Fathers need to campaign for changes on a practical level. There are no serious men's magazines for example which focus on the problems of fathering.'

A survey once carried out in a women's magazine on facilities for babies in shopping centres led to an improvement in the provision of changing rooms, high chairs in restaurants, ramps for prams and crèches. No such survey has been done for fathers and apart from a unisex changing room for babies at Heathrow Airport, one rarely finds hotels or restaurants equipped with a playpen or changing table, nor are there crèches in men's sports clubs.

During the Gulf War in Israel, at the height of the Scud missile attacks, kindergartens and daycare centres for babies were closed. In general, it was the mothers, not the fathers, who were expected to stay at home with the children. This is surprising in a country where the majority of women return to work after childbirth because few families can manage financially on one salary.

Interestingly, one network of daycare centres was sharply criticized because when they opened again with a reduced staff working restricted hours at the tail-end of the war, they gave priority to working mothers, *not* fathers.

Because of the lack of a forum to discuss these issues, many men feel very isolated with their conflicting emotions. One of the goals of the NCT fathers groups was to provide an opportunity for men to sit together and see that they are not alone in their reactions. Issues such as resentment of reduced freedom, disappointment about the sex of the baby, ambivalence about breastfeeding, anxiety relating to sexual relations after the birth, can be shared on a peer support basis so that at the end of the day, there also emerges a sharing in the joy and wonder of fatherhood.

Men also need the support services such as daycare centres at the workplace and consideration for time taken off during children's illnesses.

This is even more relevant if the father is coping alone after the death of a partner or if he is among the less than 5% who have children living with them after divorce. Geoffrey Greif writes in *Single Fathers*[9] that in the USA, between 1970 and 1983 there was an increase of 180% in single fathers caring for children under eighteen.

There are, of course, varying stages of adjustment for both partners, and this goes hand in hand with recognizing their own emotional needs.

Richard Seel continues: 'It was easier once upon a time. Father was the breadwinner and the link between the cosy life of the home and the dangerous world outside. It was the mother who nurtured the family. To the children he was firm but fair, distant but not unloving, the ultimate source of authority.' One often heard in not so distant days, 'You wait till your father comes home,' as the frantic mother tried to find the ultimate threat for the unruly child.

On the breadwinner theme, Dr Barbara Ehrenreich[10] reports: 'Men have for generations accepted the breadwinner ethic. Marriage used to provide men with guaranteed sex, emotional security and laundry service. With the liberation of women, men need to worry about their own laundry, so who needs marriage?' But Dr Jill Scheppler[11] of the University of Florida observed in her research that males aged twenty-eight to thirty-two were happier married than not.

The women's movement opened the gates to the outside world but for many working mothers life is actually harder, particularly if their partners are still attuned to a previous age. Many men are overprotected by their own parents and even today consider that the home and the children are 'women's work'. For these men eventually to understand that modern parenthood is a partnership, there has to be rethinking about roles and expectations.

If the father feels that he is doing women's work and has to be coerced into doing these tasks, he will not derive satisfaction from his role even if he does feel rather self-righteous about it.

The ideas of cooperation and time-sharing work very well when both partners are equally enthusiastic about their parenthood. But there are undoubtedly situations where the father opts out, claiming that he cannot make any concessions in his workplace, that only his job is of importance, and that even if he is in the house with the baby, he does not know what to do with it.

And behind every parent is an extended family network with parents who may be supportive, encouraging and loving, or overprotective, obsessive, possessive or simply uncaring or cruel.

Michael was very much influenced by his own father, a successful businessman. While respecting his father, the relationship during childhood had been distant because the father was always busy at the office or away on work projects. However, his mother had been able to afford live-in help and not all the tasks of household and childcare had been handled by her alone.

When Michael married, he had just graduated and was starting his career in the academic world. There certainly was not enough money for domestic help for even a couple of mornings a week and when their first baby was born, Michael's wife Vera coped singlehanded.

Michael's childhood had prepared him for certain expectations which were totally incompatible with their own situation. His reluctance to do anything for the baby or help with household chores imposed tremendous burdens and isolation on his wife.

Sometimes he enjoyed playing with the baby, but the moment he detected a dirty nappy, he handed the baby back to Vera, even if she was busy or resting at that moment. 'My father never messed around with smelly nappies and I can't either.' Michael seemed to fear that his father would ridicule him if he was caught doing such a basic job for his child. It went even deeper than this because he could not even share in the concerns and normal worries about his child.

Decision-making such as when to call the doctor or take the child to a hospital if he was ill became conflicts for disagreement and issues of inconsistency. Vera did not drive and on one snowy morning when she was concerned that the baby had an ear infection, she asked Michael to take him to the doctor. Michael claimed that he had no time and told her to ask for a home visit. Vera was a very unassertive person and lacking in confidence and she did not feel that she could ask the doctor to call for something that could be treated at the surgery. Once before, the doctor had reprimanded her when he thought she was wasting his time.

When the baby needed emergency care late that night, both Michael and his parents blamed Vera for not taking sufficient care of the baby and for not calling the doctor. The marriage nearly ended in disaster for as Vera felt more and more victimized, she suffered from severe depression and withdrew totally for a couple of months, unable to relate to her husband or the baby.

Michael's parents paid for the young couple to have a holiday together, and it is a matter of conjecture whether they spent some of the time during that holiday on some mental stock-taking and setting down of priorities.

GENDER ROLES

Richard Seel links the spontaneous way in which many men share in the care of the infant with participation at the birth. 'This is a potent symbol for the way the modern father is able to become deeply involved with his family.'

We have discussed in other chapters the impact of birth on the father and the element of jealousy he may feel when his wife and baby get all the attention. Even after she is home, on the one hand, he wants to get the home routine back to normal, but he needs to protect his wife from negative interference, make sure she rests and eats enough. He also gets to know his baby by being around at that critical time.

He may face more problems when he goes back to work because he is tired after a long day and he may not feel so tolerant of a house that is a mess and a wife who is too exhausted to listen to him.

It is easier for men to face these conflicts if society will allow him some emotional outlet. Ruth Forbes, writing on this subject in *New Generation*,[12] discusses new roles in a changing society. 'We have to reverse the old saying – men must work and women may weep. Women who work are applauded but a man who allows himself to be seen weeping or expressing emotion is treated differently.'

When Harriet and Edward's youngest child died of a brain

tumour at the age of two, all mourners at the funeral empathized with their distress. When Harriet broke down, weeping, her family and friends immediately gathered round her, consoling and comforting her, while Edward stood stoically, his arms around her.

At the end of thirty days, they again gathered at the cemetery and this time it was Edward, overcome by the sight of the tiny grave, who wept, his shoulders heaving. It took a few moments for the mourners to respond to his cries and to reach out to him and give him comfort.

In *Reassessing Fatherhood*, Drs Lewis and O'Brien[13] write: 'The recent ideology of "the new father" is one that is highly nurturant towards his children and increasingly involved in their care and work in the house.'

The editors of *The Father Figure*[14] state that their work is aimed at correcting research which has emphasized the mother–child bond and neglected the role of the male parent.

However, research studies are sometimes misleading. 'Much of the data about fathers' involvement was more than likely collected by researchers interviewing mothers – because the fathers were out at work at the time,' Dr Martin Richards[15] criticizes research methods on this subject.

As mentioned in Chapter 5, Dr Richards quotes studies that show that in Britain, the maternal grandmother rather than the father is more likely to care for the child in addition to the mother.

In *The Father Figure*, Dr Richards[16] writes, 'Very little study has been done on the connection between men's feelings as a father and his experience of his relationships with his own father.' N. Biller's[17] postwar interviews with families where fathers had been absent compared to those where the fathers were present on a regular basis examined male gender identity of their sons in terms of aggressiveness and pursuit of stereotype male activities and did not focus on such issues as development of attitudes to father-hood.

The Newson study[18] recorded interviews where fathers expressed the expectation that they would be more involved when the child was more 'sociable' and starting to walk and talk.

Sometimes when women complain that men will never accept parenthood and housework as an equal partner, we have to remember how drastically attitudes have changed in only this century. Historically, agricultural societies have separated male and female activities and this is reinforced by Judaeo-Christian ideology. Let us look at these bipolar categories.

Men	*Women*
Strong	Physically weak
Intelligent	Fearful
Brave	Unreliable
Reliable	Look after others
Responsible	
Breadwinner	

We have only in recent years seen a change in these traditional attitudes in the male/female roles. The women's movements have improved conditions not only for women who want to be liberated in their working and political lives but also for those who combine family life with careers.

There is still a long way to go, but if one compares the conditions for women today with those at the beginning of the century, one realizes that much has been achieved.

In speculations on English middle-class families, Dr Richards[19] compares mid-nineteenth century marriage and parenthood with post-World War One. He describes a patriarchal double standard in which women were the property of men, from father to husband. Divorce was rare because men could have sexual relationships outside the marriage and women were not in a position to make demands. If women had adulterous relationships, however, they were severely sanctioned to the extent of losing their children to the custody of the father.

'Even in the home, rooms were separated,' wrote Girouard in *The Victorian Country House*.[20] 'The men kept to the smoking room, the study, and even had a separate bedroom, while the women had their own boudoir, dressing room or morning room.'

Children of course were kept even more separate, with nurseries, schoolrooms, nannies and governesses.

Women were not expected to enjoy sex and William Acton, genito-urinary surgeon, wrote in 1857, 'The majority of women (happily for them) are not very much troubled with sexual feeling of any kind ... what men are habitually, women are only exceptionally'.

The distance between fathers and children were often consistent with the husband/wife relationship, with many couples living quite separate lives characterized by distance and undemonstrativeness.

In the 1920s with the emergence of the behaviourists, Watson and Truby King, [21] fathers were seen as responsible for discipline and keeping the family going literally like clockwork. Fathers played very little part in the household, but Dr Richard's paper includes an essay written by Mrs C. Gasgoine Hartley in 1924:

> The mother is of supreme importance, but the father comes as interrupter and friend in this mother–child cycle . . . he plays with the children and opens up new delightful ways of interest . . . but he is also a disturbance . . . at a very early age, jealousy of the father begins to show.

While sexual liberation and legitimization of birth control emerged in post-World War One Britain, it took many years, until after World War Two, for this to affect the dynamic of family life noticeably.

The birth-rate between the Wars continued to fall and households became smaller, with servants going into jobs with better pay and conditions. Women then bore the brunt of domestic work in the home and this opened up a new world of priorities and sharing of parenthood.

Women always worked outside their own kitchen, whether it was in the family farmyard, factories or mills or other female-orientated jobs. Women also worked in offices, wrote books, nursed in hospitals, sang in operas and acted on the stage but it is only in later years that these professions have become more respected. While women were working as engineers and railway porters in Russia from the time of the Revolution, it is only in the past fifty years in Western Europe that professions such as law and medicine and science have become so popular and acceptable for women.

When the Womens Cooperative Guild published *Maternity – Letters from Working Women* in 1915[22] there was uncovered a scandalous neglect of concern for mothers both in the home and workplace. With no Social Services or supplementary benefits available, women were poorly nourished, deprived of maternity care and totally without rights as mothers and wives.

When Herbert Samuel read these letters, which were presented to him during demonstrations by the Womens Cooperative Guild, he was appalled on humanitarian grounds. But the social reforms were introduced by convincing Parliament that in order to breed healthy soldiers and workers of the future, their mothers must be given better care. And for this dubious reason, conditions were improved.

From that time when children were indeed distant from their fathers, there has been a revolution in family behaviour. As the nuclear family becomes smaller and the extended family less available in many societies, as more and more women train to join the workforce, fathers are becoming more and more essential in the home. And perhaps as a bonus for this, many of them are deriving great satisfaction from the closer relationship that they have with their babies.

Perhaps the education authorities are at last waking up to the emancipation of fathers. More attention is now paid in schools to this issue and fathers as well as mothers are invited to come with their babies so that children can ask questions about babycare and parenting. In this way, boys can also identify with the problems and challenges which arise when they become fathers.

When my own children were in their early teens, I gave occasional workshops to their classes on preparing to be healthy parents. We worked through the subjects of nutrition and avoiding drugs and smoking and how this affected future pregnancies. The boys in the groups were also surprised to realize that they shared in this responsibility because of the effects of lifestyle on sperm quality.

They had up to that point distanced themselves from their own role as future fathers, so it is obvious that the issues of adjustment to fatherhood are at that age even more remote and can be made more tangible by focusing on them in the curriculum.

Some parents are caught in the middle of the generations. They are still the children of their own parents, or the young brother or sister, but they are now parents themselves. For this reason many couples complain that their homes are never private. Their families walk in unannounced, criticize the untidy kitchen, or start every sentence with: 'If I were you ...' or in the case of unamicable relationships with inlaws, there is always a veiled or less than hidden hostility and implied criticism.

This can indeed reinforce negative feelings that a young parent has about his or her new role. 'You never had to wash dishes in my house,' says the mother-in-law to her son who is automatically clearing the table while his wife breastfeeds. 'You could afford better clothes when you were single,' the wife's mother comments as her daughter walks around in a comfortable smock. They can either laugh it off, ignore it, answer back or smoulder.

SEX AFTER BIRTH

Breastfeeding can arouse sexual jealousy – after all the breast is part of love-play. Husbands too go through a personal growth and development when they become fathers and handling this conflict is part of the process.

In *Breast is Best*,[23] the authors write, 'If a woman gets pleasure from having her baby stimulate and feed from her breasts, her husband may well resent this relationship. Until now, his wife's breasts have "belonged" to him'. They conclude, 'However, sexual arousal from breastfeeding can be a positive asset to the couple's adjustment after the birth'.

There have not been many separate studies on the actual impact of birth and parenthood on sexual satisfaction alone, but it is obvious that the cycle of childbearing with its physical changes will affect, albeit temporarily, the sexual behaviour of the couple.

During the last stages of pregnancy, most women feel heavy and tired and it may take some ingenuity to find comfortable positions for lovemaking.

The pregnancy hormones can swing either way as far as sexual feeling is concerned. Some women report that they need their partner to hold them close, but do not feel like full sexual intercourse. Others say that they feel very sexy and have much more frequent sexual desires than usual. Many men are rather wary of sex during pregnancy, partly because they fear that it might induce labour or harm the baby, and sometimes because of deep-rooted fears that their partner has changed both in body and personality.

If the couple went through a period of infertility and sex became a ritual to be practised at optimum times of ovulation according to the thermometer, the man may feel that he is used and have a cooling-off period.

After the birth, with the upheaval and separation while the woman is in hospital, the man may have an urgent need to get his partner back home and to resume a normal sexual life. But it may take a woman much longer before she feels her sexual needs returning. While she has lochia discharge and discomfort from stitches and her breasts are heavy and leaking, she may really fear any physical contact. After that, sheer tiredness and precious intervals between feeds may cause her to feel that sleep is more urgent than sex. Some women may fear becoming pregnant before they can organize effective contraception.

There may be some sense in the various religious rituals which forbid sex after childbirth for a prescribed period. For example, Jewish women are in a condition called *niddah*[24] during and for seven days after menstruation and from the first sign of bleeding in labour until a full seven days after the bleeding completely stops. During this time, orthdox women sleep in a separate bed and have no physical contact with their husbands. They then go to the ritual bath for a spiritual cleansing and are then ready to resume normal marital relations.

Ethiopian Jewish women move into a separate building for these periods of *niddah* and do not even handle food that is eaten by the man.

Although the idea that a woman is 'unclean' during this period is offensive to many modern women, and indeed it is difficult not to be able to even cuddle one's partner, it does give the woman time for recovery without her feeling guilty that she is depriving her man of her attentions.

However, even after these prescribed ritual separations, there may be some difficulties in returning to normal sexual activity. During the months following the birth, the hormonal changes cause a decrease in the secretions in the vagina, and this relative dryness may cause discomfort.

If the perineum is still sore when the woman is ready to resume sex, it will be helped with frequent compresses of camomile tea or witch-hazel. As in pregnancy, different positions, with a cushion under the hips or the woman on top or man kneeling will be more comfortable. A gel or oil can be used for lubrication.

The Kegel exercise learned in pregnancy to strengthen the pelvic floor will also help these muscles and tissues return to normal.

Babies have no sense of timing and the most passionate interlude between a couple may be interrupted by cries for food. It may sound contrived but it is worth feeding the baby before turning attention to sex, also because sexual arousal stimulates the flow of milk. While some men may find it interesting, others may have their ardour reduced when they receive a shower of milk in bed.

In *Women's Experiences of Sex*,[25] Sheila Kitzinger's psychosexual approach relates the experiences of labour to the woman's sexuality and how she feels about her baby. The place of birth and the technology used today often confuse women's sexual roles.

During the postpartum period, a woman feels tired and often

'leaky' or a 'mess'. This self-image may destroy her fantasies of being a 'radiant new mother' and she feels ugly and unattractive.

Continuing the theme of the influence of the birth experience, women often do feel fulfilled and radiant, thrilled with the miracle of birth and so sexy that they can't wait to get home.

In Derrick Dodshon's lecture to the Nursing Mothers of Australia,[26] he attributed loss of libido to exhaustion, fatigue and depression. He quoted studies in which it was quite normal for frequency of sexual activity at seven months after the birth to be lower than that even during pregnancy. Dr Dodshon also discussed breastfeeding as a way of arousal and that it is quite common for a woman to have an orgasm during feeding. He quoted Masters and Johnson as observing that this lack of libido is not connected to the hormone changes because this would negate the evidence that breastfeeding women generally are aroused more easily.

Dr Dodshon was more concerned about the psychological causes. 'Women's image of themselves is changed,' he said. 'They think of themselves as mothers, not women. One woman called herself a "milk factory".' He reminds us that in some cultures, a man calls his wife 'Ma' or 'Mother' instead of the usual terms of endearment.

A NEW NORMALITY

But all in all, do any parents expect to return to normal if the word normal indicates life as it was? Nobody returns to the point from which they came. If pregnancy and birth is a journey and every man and woman starts from a different railway station, we could talk of this in terms of a one-way and not a return ticket.

Or one can look at it like a road map. Each parent may come from a different side road, meet at the crossroads which is marriage, continue on bypasses and meet up again at another junction which is childbirth, and then go on in whichever direction choice or circumstance takes them.

Dr Osofsky, writing on transition to parenthood[27] declares: 'It takes time for parents to realize that the old sense of what was normal will not return but that a different kind of normalcy will occur'.

Many couples mourn the loss of that spontaneity or romance with which they started the relationship. Remember when the

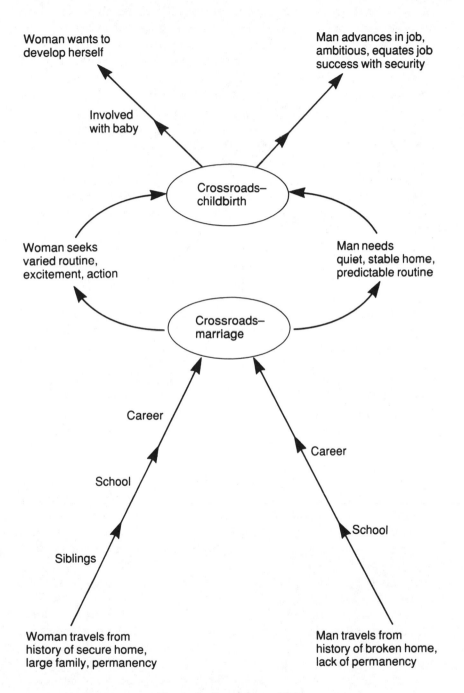

Woman wants to develop herself

Man advances in job, ambitious, equates job success with security

Involved with baby

Crossroads–childbirth

Woman seeks varied routine, excitement, action

Man needs quiet, stable home, predictable routine

Crossroads–marriage

Career

Career

School

School

Siblings

Woman travels from history of secure home, large family, permanency

Man travels from history of broken home, lack of permanency

Figure 3. Road map of life

chicken burnt to a cinder because you couldn't wait to get into bed together and forgot to turn the oven low? Most of us go through the highs and lows of romantic love at some time or other and in regretting its passing, we sometimes forget just how exhausting it could be. I remember throwing the telephone directory at my brother because he wouldn't finish his phone call and I was desperately and hopefully waiting for a call from a boyfriend.

As one matures, these relationships become more familiar, more comfortable and with that, some of the romance is lost. Most couples relate that transition to the birth of the first baby when plans have to be made and spontaneity is a thing of the past.

Take, for example, a journey to visit the grandparents who live forty miles away. At one time, you got in the car or travelled by train at the last moment and arrived there. When you had had enough, you moved on, agreeing that you wanted to see a film or play, go out with friends and finish the evening at the pub. Nobody interfered with your plans and providing the two of you agreed what you wanted to do, nothing else mattered.

Now, with a small baby, one has to make sure he is fed and washed, with fresh clothes before the journey starts. You load the car with the carrycot and wheels and pack bags with nappies, spare clothes, and all the toiletries needed to keep the baby sweet-smelling for the day. At the point of securing him in his car seat, the baby burps and dribbles all over the clean white suit which had been given by the grandmother you are visiting. You start again, select another suit, but just as you are going out of the door, the baby produces a giant bowel movement which leaks out of his nappy, over his suit and onto your clean clothes.

At this point the car won't start because you couldn't afford to change the battery and were hoping that it would be a warm day and that the car would start without difficulty. By the time you borrow the neighbour's battery charger and the car springs to life, the baby has again possetted over all his clothes and needs feeding again.

When I was a very little girl, my parents brought me a doll's pram. This was very precious because it was the end of the War and toys were scarce. I had owned a little wooden pram and didn't like the way it rattled and shook when I wheeled it along the road. My mother went shopping one dark winter's day just before my birthday and, during a power cut, in Hamleys by candlelight, she saw the perfect pram, a real high-sprung chariot. I remember to this very day the ecstatic excitement of receiving this pram.

My grandfather gave me a large china doll to put in my pram. It had flaxen curly hair, a great delight to me because my own hair was straight dark brown. The doll had a rosebud open mouth and I discovered that when I gave her a drink of water, she immediately wet her pants. This was no deliberate design of the toy company but merely because the doll was hollow and she leaked through the joints. I was so proud, I ran down the street showing my doll to the neighbours: 'Look what my doll did'.

As they grow up, girls believe that they are going to have little real-life dolls to play with and smart chariots to wheel them along the road, and we are even ready for the wet pants. However, the game doesn't end at tea-time and we have to keep on changing those nappies, mopping up puddles, feeding one end and cleaning up the other, however tired we are and however much we would now like to play another game.

So perhaps the most important thing is to learn to be comfortable, to decide together what is good for each other and for oneself and for the child who is dependent on both of his parents. We try to drive ourselves to achieve unrealistic goals which exhaust us and often are not satisfying when actually achieved. We need be less responsive to criticism which drives us to demand too much of ourselves and of others.

'Isn't he talking yet . . . or walking . . . or sitting on the pot?' one gets asked and anxiously looks at one's child to see if he is normal. Parents know only too well the criticism of society when they or their children don't conform but, if they feel comfortable with each other, they should be able to ignore this or give a rebuff.

As Dr Dodshon concluded in his lecture, 'When we neglect the relationship between husband and wife, we forget that this intense stage of parenthood is temporary. There will come the day when the children will be, although still members of the family, less demanding, and eventually leave home'. He discusses the marriages which break up after the children leave home because the couple no longer have a focus of communication, and mothers may feel that they are no longer needed.

As a mother of four grown-up children, I think that Dr Dodshon's fears of parents' redundancy are premature. My children still feed on demand, helping themselves to whatever is in the fridge the moment they walk through the door, and come home frequently to do their laundry, borrow the car, use my computer just when I am struggling to finish a chapter. Family celebrations get even bigger and more complicated to organize as each year adds a daugher-in-law or close friend. And each of these additional family members also needs time and attention, support in their studies and decision-making.

But with this growing up it is true that one can start to look outwards again and develop one's skills and talents, go away for the weekend or even out for the evening without making complicated arrangements. It is perhaps therefore not such an unrealistic idea to sit down in pregnancy and work out a list of priorities and goals so that both parents can enjoy the real-life game of mothers and fathers.

SINGLE PARENTS

Parenthood, like the refugees in Noak's Ark, usually goes two by two, and indeed the focus of childbirth education and literature on parenthood is on the role of the father as an equal partner.

Therefore the single mother is a living paradox. In this era, it is quite common for women to choose to have a baby outside the marriage partnership. And yet they need to cope with parenthood without the support of a partner, the extended family or sometimes even a close female friend.[28,29,30,31]

With abortion so readily available, it is often forgotten that a single woman may actually want to have a baby and that her pregnancy is by choice and not accident. Support and information given at the right time may help these women cope with a difficult situation, while those who were considering abortion at an early stage of pregnancy might actually decide against it if they thought that society would be more sympathetic to their needs.

Ada is a biologist, 'passionate about growing things'. She had always wanted to marry and have a large family, but did not find a man with whom she wanted to spend her life. From the age of thirty, she played with the idea of having a baby, but it took several years before she felt sufficiently convinced and motivated to face the battles of a single parent.

'One day I met an old school friend who was a single mother – she seemed to cope,' said Ada. 'Suddenly the idea seemed practical and possible.' Ada was involved in a relationship at that time, but neither of them intended marriage. However, her friend was her ideal as her child's father. After many sleepless nights, the clarity of the decision was a relief. 'It was like a miracle, I suddenly knew what I wanted.'

There was no ambivalence, the pregnancy was very precious to her, but external events took a downward turn. She lost her job and her family were very angry with her. 'That was the only time I thought about abortion,' she said. Then her father changed his attitude and became very supportive. He longed for grandchildren although he would have preferred it if Ada was married or at least had a permanent relationship with the baby's father.

Then Ada's fighting spirit returned. She got her job back and resumed her working life. 'I was really not yet emotionally involved with the baby and it was important to work again. And of course I needed the salary.'

During the first weeks after the birth, Ada experienced almost every possible breastfeeding problem written in the books. But when they were solved, she enjoyed breastfeeding so much that she kept on postponing returning to work. 'When the feeding was so problematic, I just wanted to get back to work to escape. The baby was fretful and tense and I thought he would be better off with a professional childminder. As time passed and it was such a pleasure to be with the baby, my whole world revolved around him.'

I last saw Ada just after her child's first birthday. He was busy playing on the floor, building bricks and looking at his picture book. He started to concentrate for a moment or two, clambered to his feet, climbed up on his mother's knee and, pulling up her shirt, started suckling. He stopped every few moments to chuckle and pull at her hair but soon resumed sucking at the breast.

Ada did not understate the difficulties of coping alone. 'It is lonely being a single mother, but I'm so crazy about this child, he's enough for me right now.'

Ada was rich in resources but Mary was only twenty, living with her boyfriend, when they decided to get married and start a family. The pregnancy happened before the marriage and when Mary was in the seventh month, her boyfriend left her, totally unable to support herself. She had been at art school but could not continue to pay the fees, so she took a temporary office job.

She moved into a one-room bedsitter and found herself unable to buy enough food to eat or the basic requirements for the baby. Her friends rallied round and managed to borrow for her some baby clothes and an old pram. They were even considering demonstrating outside the boyfriend's workplace to publicize the injustice of the situation.

The existence of a permanent partner is not always a guarantee of support. Carol had been married for two years and the relationship had been fairly rocky all the way. But when the pregnancy began, her husband began abusing her. He drank heavily when depressed, and when sufficiently intoxicated, he started throwing bottles at her or hitting her with a strap. She was so terrified that the baby would be harmed that she moved into a shelter for battered wives, to which she returned from the hospital.

She was visited by her husband who begged her to return. Carol was so anxious to regain some normalcy in her life that she went back to live with him, started another pregnancy, and the cycle of violence began again. Again she returned to the shelter and began to try and put her life together, this time with two small infants.

At one time she returned to her parents' home and indeed they were anxious to help her. But her husband broke into their house and tore everything apart. Carol only felt safe in the shelter but gradually, as she regained her confidence, she transferred to another part of the country where the social worker helped her find a small flat and start life over again.

'It was even more difficult leaving my home town because my parents and brothers really wanted to help. But I couldn't expose them to the constant danger. My husband was arrested after he wrecked their house, but well-meaning social workers suggested that he be rehabilitated so he was soon free again to abuse us.'

Carol is very lonely at times, away from her family and friends. The children are so vulnerable that she does not want to leave them in a daycare centre and work full time. 'They go to a playgroup for a few hours each week and I do cleaning jobs while they are there.'

So there are many ways in which single mothers cope alone. There are various stages of acceptance and even those who really planned to have children alone experience ambivalence and even panic. Some even consider adoption and if pressured while still in the hospital may actually give their children away, perhaps to regret it deeply much later on.

But among those who decide to keep their babies and set their goals of bringing them up alone, there is a vast difference between those who enjoy family support and are economically comfortable, and those who are deserted by the child's father or who are without means of support.

7   *A Baby in The House – Time and Motion*

T HROUGHOUT history, there has been an aura of mystery about motherhood. The Biblical stories of Leah's passion for Jacob, Sara's longing for a child and her anguish when Abraham took Isaac away, as she thought, to be sacrificed, Hannah's bargain with God that if she could bear a child after years of infertility, she would leave him with the priests as a servant of the Temple, the efforts of Moses' mother and sister to protect him from the Pharaoh's decree that all male babies be slain, show motherhood in all its joys and pain. Art galleries exhibit many paintings of the Madonna and Child, most of them with a look of tranquillity and serenity on the face of the mother.

These ideological images fade into reality when the harassed mother on return from hospital finds herself in a haze of confusion between day and night, with little time to shower or comb her hair, still walking around in a bathrobe at lunchtime. Feeding, bathing, changing nappies seem to be the focal point of the daily routine, and many women feel that they will never have enough sleep or get the house into any semblance of order again.

Some books on infant care optimistically propose timetables and schedules which can cause a great deal of frustration. Until babies get into some sort of routine, their mothers need to sleep and eat when there is a gap in the baby's demands. This may mean going back to bed at eleven o'clock in the morning, closing the curtains, unplugging the telephone and trying to catch up on a lost night. If the woman has therefore set herself a goal of having the kitchen floor washed and the laundry hanging out to dry by mid-morning, she may find herself way out of schedule if she is out there in the garden with the clothes-pegs at eight o'clock in the evening.

In Chapter 9 we shall discuss coping with siblings, and without doubt when there are other children in the family, some sort of routine has to be kept in order to get them clothed, fed and off to kindergarten or school in time. Amazing as it is, most mothers claim that another baby fitting into the family is not nearly as difficult as that first baby which completely changes the family structure.

But in the case of a first baby, the mother can be much more flexible, and just concentrate on the need to keep afloat during that period of tiredness and adjustment.

The first baby is totally dependent on his parents for food, warmth, love and social interaction, and does not have the distraction and noise of a family of siblings to keep him amused. Therefore the baby who is happily cooing at three o'clock in the morning may not actually be hungry but is only asking to be talked to or cuddled. One cannot explain to a small baby that his mother and father would rather sleep right now and that playtime is preferably after 7 am.

So, while the father goes off bleary-eyed to work, perhaps snatching a few moments of sleep on the commuter train, the mother could in fact try to catch up on some rest during the day.

Again, we come back to the question of personality. A woman who has always managed to combine work and a clean shining home by being well organized and disciplined will find it almost impossible to go back to bed or put her feet up with a good book and relaxing drink if the house is in chaos around her.

It could be that one of the couple is an enthusiastic gardener and the sight of an immaculate lawn and blooming borders is so satisfying that that takes priority over elaborate cooking, in which case the couple could agree on take-away or convenience foods.

The husband may work in a job which demands that he is always dressed neatly and formally, so one of the couple has to make it a priority to iron shirts or send the suits to the cleaners. If the income is sufficient to use paid help, many of the essential chores can be delegated, but many couples are actually coping on a smaller joint income after the birth of a child and may have to save on outside help.

However, if a couple receive a generous cheque as a baby present, it might be worthwhile investing in temporary house-hold help, or a microwave or labour-saving appliances to cut down time on those endless repetitive chores. Find out about your local services, use home deliveries, cook double quantities when there is time so that half can be frozen for another occasion, organize a shopping pool with neighbours. All these ideas can save time and energy which are needed so badly when there is a new baby in the house.

Babies do not need regular times for bathing. It may be easier to bath the baby in the evening when his father is home so that he too can share in what could be a relaxed family experience. Some men like to take the baby into the bath with them and enjoy splashing together.

We hear so much in the media today about child abuse that we must be careful not to inhibit completely our natural instincts to touch and cuddle our children. The sensuous satisfaction of skin-to-skin contact when parents and children bath together is a precious part of the child's emotional development and crystallizes the parents' love for the child.

A baby needs to relax after what is for him a hard day of feeding, filling his nappies, being taken for walks, sitting in a baby chair, coping with colic. So when it seems that the baby is tense or upset or angry, try a soothing bath. Let him relax and splash in the water, wrap him up tightly in a soft warm towel and sing to him while you dry him well. Then gently massage his limbs and body and you will feel the tension easing out of his body. When babies are tense, they clench their fists and frown. During this massage, one can see the hands unclench and the facial expression clears.

Dr Frederick Leboyer, who wrote *Birth without Violence*,[1] writes of this bathing and massage immediately following the birth.

> It is through our hands that we speak to the child, that we communicate. Touching is the primary language. To calm the impact of this strange incomprehensible world, the hands holding him should speak in the language of the womb, remember the slowness, the continuous movement, the waves of the uterine environment ... the hands supporting the child in the bath soon feel the little body relax in complete abandon. Everything that was fear, stiffness, tension now melts like snow in the sun. Everything in the infant's body that was still anxious, frozen, blocked, begins to live, to dance.

ORGANIZING THE BABY'S ROOM

One cannot have a relaxed baby if the parents are tense, and it is worth planning in advance in order to avoid some of the confusion of the first weeks at home.

One way of simplifying the routine is by organizing the baby's room in such a way that everything is within reach and at a convenient height.

In the unreliable European climate, it is important to make sure that there is background heating, such as a thermostat radiator if there is no central heating or if it is not kept on at night. Avoid gas heaters, electric fires with open elements or kerosene because, apart from fire hazard, the heat is very drying. Even with thermostat heaters, it is important to check that the baby is not overheated or feeling the cold. Very small babies cannot control their temperatures in the same way as adults and severe temperature changes can be dangerous for them. It is possible, by feeling the nape of the neck, to check whether a baby is perspiring because he is wrapped up in too many layers in an overheated room, or whether he is suffering from cold.

When the weather is cold, keep the baby's head covered. In infancy the skin area of the head is relatively large, and since many small babies are almost bald, they lose heat this way.

The baby's cot should be placed by an inside wall, which keeps heat better than the external walls of a building.

Life will be easier if some thought is given beforehand to setting up the baby's room. This does not mean having to rob a bank to pay for expensive and sometimes superfluous equipment. The shops are full of tempting furniture, clothing and a variety of soaps, shampoos and creams, but in fact, babies need very little at the beginning. A nursery can be very romantic with matching curtains, rugs, quilts and wallpaper, with frilly rocking cradle and elegant nursery furniture, but it is possible to improvise a beautiful peaceful environment for the parent and baby on a budget.

Until one can take stock of presents, it is a good idea to buy the minimum. A strong pram and a firm cot mattress are essential, but all other furniture can be bought secondhand or borrowed from family and friends. It is advisable to strip off old paint because many family nursery items were made before the days when the British Standards Institute ruled that materials must be lead-free. Lead paints can be very dangerous because small children chew on the bars of cots or legs of tables and chairs, and accumulation of lead in the child's blood could cause poisoning or brain damage.

An old cot may not have a reliable safety catch which secures the folding side. A baby can catch his fingers, or release the lock and fall out of the cot. It is recommended to change mattresses with each baby because they contain synthetic materials which are suspected of giving off fumes when they deteriorate. The entire issue of these synthetic materials is now under fire and when buying a new mattress it is important to read all the consumer research on the subject.

A changing table is better for washing and dressing the baby than a bed or one's knees. Women after childbirth really need to look after their backs, because the pelvis is still contracting and the changing hormones are still causing muscle weakness. Ideally, if there is a basin in the baby's room, one can lift the baby straight from bath onto table, with all the clothing, towels and toiletries to hand on shelves or in drawers under the table.

If this is beyond the budget, a wide shelf can be fitted onto the wall and covered with quilted sticky-back plastic fabric. A basic kitchen trolley is useful for wheeling around with nappies, towels and toiletries, while other clothing and bedding can be kept on shelves below the table.

Until presents have been counted up, the very basic needs are bedlinen, warm quilt (*no pillow*, of course), a carrycot, pram and clothing to suit the season. If the baby is going to travel in a car, he must have a safety seat, starting from the journey home from hospital. These are adjustable for all ages or some firms rent out the seats for tiny babies, the cost of which is credited to the purchase of the longer-lasting infant seat from the age of six months.

Do not economize on these safety items because a faulty car seat or a pram with an insecure brake can cause a disaster.

If there is a cat in the house, or the baby will be left in his pram in the garden, buy a net which can be used also on his cot in the bedroom. The family cat may be very jealous and jump on the baby, or it may just be that the baby and his cot are nice, warm, cosy places for a catnap. In areas where there are wasps or mosquitoes, a finer net is needed to keep out insects.

It is a good idea to look around the house for the danger points. The baby at this stage seems a long way from crawling and climbing, but that comes only too quickly.

For this reason, the baby should never be left on the bed, settee or changing table and of course *never* in the bath. Windows on even the first floor can be a dangerous height and it is a good idea to secure them with bars. People with open balconies and french doors above ground height should pay special attention to this.

Even ground floor windows can be hazardous if there is a concrete path or rockery underneath.

Cleaning materials should not be stored in the cupboard under the kitchen sink, but kept high up in a locked place. The medicine cupboard should also be locked and out of reach. Put a guard round the cooker and make sure that the controls of oven, washing machine and microwave are out of reach. Electricity and gas points should be locked and a gate fitted on the stairs.

Make sure there is no peeling paint or wallpaper because the baby can put this in his mouth and, in the case of old houses, may get lead poisoning. Beware of loose carpets, polished floors, sharp table corners and overhanging table cloths.

Home seems a hazardous place after that long list but in fact one needs to be constantly on the alert with infants in the house and it is safer and easier to practise prevention.

THE NAPPY DEBATE

There is some controversy currently about the use of disposable nappies. Penny Stanway, in her book on environmental issues in infant care, *Green Babies*,[2] writes that three trees are destroyed to make 1500 nappies, and that in the USA, Canada and Britain, 23.2 billion nappies are used in one year! This destroys 2200 sq km or 850 sq miles of forest and produces 80 tons of non-biodegradable polyethylene.

Some parents for this reason are returning to the use of cloth nappies and nappy services may once again be in business. However, in some countries where there is a water shortage, one has to weigh up the balance of protecting the environment by using cloth nappies with over-using water and electricity resources for laundry.

An innovative idea has been developed by Yaron Cina of Kibbutz Afikim in Israel, who has received an international prize for a household device which breaks down dirty disposable nappies into components that can be recycled.[3] Several companies have expressed interest in his patent, so hopefully within a year or two, this problem may be partially solved.

If one lives in a very warm climate and the baby is out of doors a lot, it is possible to mop him up as you go along and not use nappies at all. But for most of us living an urban indoor lifestyle, this would be most inconvenient.

SLEEPING

The impact of a new baby in the family is directly influenced by the behaviour of the baby himself. A contented baby who seems to have read all the books, feeds well, gains weight and sleeps for a few hours during the night is a success symbol to the parents. They themselves are refreshed by longer periods of sleep and even when the baby is awake, they are not totally distracted by crying and demands for attention.

The baby who lies gurgling on a rug on the floor or is happy sitting in a baby chair gazing at the lamp or a picture gives the parents a feeling that they are going in the right direction. The more a baby reacts positively, with regular sleep patterns, healthy development and that breathtaking lopsided smile, the more positive the parent feels in his or her reaction.

It is, however, no fault of the parents that some babies are just not so easy. They suffer from colic which is painful when they feed and makes them wakeful after feeds.

Some babies are very sensitive to change in the environment, temperature, noise, light, and wake at the tiniest disturbance. Others only sleep when they are being rocked, sung to or if the stereo is at full volume. My eldest child, Jonathan, only fell asleep if I switched on the washing machine to the spinning cycle because the noise and vibration quietened him down. Some parents embark on nightly journeys in the car because only the vehicle's movement sends the baby off to sleep.

These babies are often restless and colicky, do not gain weight so quickly and take a long time to know the difference between night and day. It is not surprising that the parents may feel rather less confident about this angry little redfaced infant.

It is worth investigating first if there is any physical reason for the baby's difficulties. He may have allergies which cause him stomach disturbance or breathing difficulties, and he may not gain weight because he simply is not fed enough even though it seems that there is plenty of milk and he is always demanding more.

More temporary discomforts which make babies cry for help are cold or overheating, and of course a wet and dirty nappy. Some babies will communicate very clearly what they want.

Some babies are very fastidious and do not like to experience a wet or dirty nappy even for a short while. Others revel in it and enjoy their own body functions.

Babies make it very clear when they are uncomfortable and this brings us to the controversy about positions for sleeping. For the past twenty-five years, it was recommended that babies sleep on their stomachs so that if they posset food, it will dribble away and not pass back into the throat, causing them to choke.

In recent months, at the time of writing this book, news is coming from New Zealand of studies on cot deaths or SIDS (sudden infant death syndrome).[4]

New Zealand had one of the highest statistics for this tragic event but in the last six months they have seen a reduction in the number of cases after instructing parents not to place babies on their stomachs. Since lying flat on the back may be uncomfortable, it seems more logical to place a baby on his side, but in such a way that if he rolls over, it will be to his back and not to his front. This is totally contradictory to earlier advice on infant care and it would be a good idea to discuss this with your own doctor or health visitor. In fact, they will have received directives from the Department of Health on the subject.

FEEDING THE BABY

Having discussed many of the important issues of coping with a baby in the house, we now come to the most controversial subject of all and that is how to feed the infant.

Feeding one's child is traditionally a symbol of mother love throughout the world. Researchers have found that baby monkeys become attached even to a wire surrogate if it is holding a feeding bottle.

In most cultures, food is the balm for hasty tempers, the panacea for all ills. When a mother gives a tasty morsel to a child who has fallen over and hurt himself, the food is associated with the sympathy and concern that the child needs when he is hurt.

This does not end with childhood. My own family are now grown up and during the week we are all busy with our varied jobs and studies. My children and my husband are in fact all good cooks and cope very well when I am working or out of town. However, at the weekend, when all the family gravitate to the home, they especially enjoy the dishes which I have cooked with love and attention to their own individual tastes.

When the children were still very young, we lived for a year in a kibbutz where the food was prepared in the communal kitchen. I noted a definite decrease in their enjoyment and appetite because those meatballs churned out of the machines were not made with the love with which I prepare food made in my own kitchen.

Demanding food is a basic survival instinct. This instinct may be thwarted, resulting in deprivation to the infant, and not only because food may not be available, such as in the Third World areas of famine. It can happen because parents keep a rigid schedule and force a child to wait specified periods. This is sometimes reinforced in hospital maternity wards and in the advice given to 'teach the baby' a routine.

A baby under six months of age has no perception of the future. If he has a cold, empty feeling in his stomach, it is right now and he doesn't believe in future promises of help. Half an hour crying in a darkened quiet room can be an eternity for a hungry baby who only wants his mother's warm soft breast.

An older baby can be calmed even by hearing his parent's voice calling from another room. But the very young baby is not perceptive to outside stimuli and as far as he is concerned: 'If my mother is not with me, she doesn't exist'.

There are reams of studies and papers about the problems of infant feeding but most psychologists and child development experts agree that food is equated with love. Dr Donald Winnicott, in his book *The Child, The Family and the Outside World,*[5] gives a simple example of the changes in a mother's attitude towards feeding her child when he is sick. She feels that he is rejecting her, interpreting his illness as being caused by her 'poor milk'. Likewise, a mother whose child has colic or vomits after every feed will soon lose confidence in herself.

The mother and baby who are in complete harmony with each other at feeding times form a strong emotional bond that is the foundation of a lifetime's love.

No topic is as emotionally charged as that of infant feeding because of the constant changes in approach, new scientific information and the total involvement of society with the subject. This causes many parents to experience feelings of inadequacy and guilt.

When discussing breastfeeding in a group of pregnant women or postpartum mothers still in the maternity ward, there are expressed many myths, superstitions, old wives' tales and misinformation.

Attitudes to breastfeeding depend very much on background and the mothering experiences of one's own mother, mother-in-law and other women in the family, as well as friends, neighbours and the health professionals. And they all have something to say.

At this very vulnerable time, the mother needs the most diplomatic help and sympathetic support. Unfortunately it is often just at this period that she is confused by conflicting advice from well-meaning but uninformed neighbours and relatives.

There is a renaissance today in breastfeeding in the Western world. No parent exposed to the communications media can fail to be affected by the disasters of malnutrition in the Third World. Not only do those underdeveloped countries suffer from a chronic shortage of food, but aggressive sales campaigns by manufacturers of formula foods had a negative influence on mothers whose only hope of rearing healthy babies was to maintain breastfeeding.

That is not to say that a woman who cannot or definitely does not want to breastfeed should be wracked with guilt. There is a vast difference between preparing bottles in an African village, with possibly contaminated water, and the careful measuring and mixing of formula in the aseptic conditions of a modern kitchen.

Women who are dependent on certain medications which are contraindicated for breastfeeding or women who have a chronic illness and are unable to breastfeed need to come to terms with the fact that they can be good mothers with a bottle too. It is possible to hold a baby closely and cuddle him while bottlefeeding and to provide him with just as much love and devotion as the woman who is breastfeeding. But for the woman who wants to breast-feed, the benefits and advantages are clearly documented in all the professional literature.

Short-term illness such as flu or an infection are not contra-indications for breastfeeding. On the contrary, the baby will receive antibodies to the illness through the milk.

Refugees from areas of famine may suffer from deficient milk until they are better nourished. It was found that some of the Ethiopian women who were rescued in the airlift to Israel were suffering from tuberculosis, a disease almost unknown now in the West. Both the disease and the medication used to treat it rule out breastfeeding for these women, a tragedy for them because they have a strong tradition of breastfeeding.

Chloe Fisher, community midwife from Oxford, writes in *Bestfeeding*[6] of AIDS transmission through the breast milk of HIV positive women. 'A small number of babies may have been infected from the milk of their mothers who had received a trans-fusion after birth with blood which had not been tested, or who had been breastfed by wet nurses who were ill with AIDS.' Because of this possibility, the milk banks which had so success-fully organized donations from women with a plentiful supply of milk to babies in need have had to stop functioning.

However, the authors of *Bestfeeding* point out that many babies have been fed by infected but symptom-free mothers and have not themselves become infected. In countries where the alternatives to breastfeeding are not safe, it was thought that the risk of being infected was outweighed by the nutritional and immunological benefits of breastfeeding. The most common way in which babies become infected is if the mother passes on the virus during pregnancy.

Women who have undergone breast surgery which has reduced the number of milk glands may not be able to breastfeed.

And then there are women who just cannot stand the thought and breastfeeding disgusts them. Nobody should force a woman who feels so negative about it to do something which is so repellent to her, but it may be that correct therapy and counselling will help her get to the root of why she feels like this.

Drs Penny and Andrew Stanway, in their book *Breast is Best*,[7] point out that breastfeeding is often associated with sexual arousal, and some women feel very guilty about this. 'Since sex hormones affect a woman's response to love-making as well as her body's functions during pregnancy, birth and lactation, it is logical that some women experience a strong sexual pleasure, even orgasm, when breastfeeding,' they write. 'Sexuality is part of motherliness and acceptance or rejection of one's womanhood affects attitudes to this very basic primitive sensation in breastfeeding.'

But so often a woman does not breastfeed or stops at an early stage simply because she did not receive enough information or support.

A couple need to examine attitudes and analyse how much they are influenced by families and friends so that they have sufficient time before the birth to work through their problems and seek advice. A woman may be afraid that she will not live up to the Mother Earth image expected of her. She may be afraid of the dependency, knowing that nobody can share with her the task of feeding her baby. But if the parents are confident in their knowledge and are convinced that breastfeeding presents long-term benefits in terms of the health of the infant and enhancement of parent−child relationships, they will seek the right sources of support.

The Mother's Attitude

John Bowlby, in his work on mother–infant bonding, *Child Care and the Growth of Love*,[8] discusses how a mother's attitudes to feeding affect the attachment. 'A loving giving attitude without demands for return, guilt and anger if food is rejected will set up a pattern for a food–love cycle.' Relaxed feeding in those early months will set a pattern for battle-free meal times. Toddlers often use refusal to eat as a weapon, but if from the start they consider feeding as a warm happy experience, they will be less likely to use this ammunition as they grow older.

A survey done in the middle 1960s in the north of England by John and Elizabeth Newson,[9] when breastfeeding was at a low ebb, showed that while at one month after birth, 54% were still breastfeeding, at three months only 29% were still persevering. The reasons given for stopping breastfeeding showed that basic lack of knowledge was the root cause.

> I had plenty of milk but it wasn't any good.
> My milk all went to water.
> My milk was too rich/thin/sour.

There is no such thing as milk being too weak or rich or sour although it does look quite different from cows' milk.

'He lost weight in the first two days so I gave him a bottle.' All babies lose weight, often up to 10%, as they lose fluid in the first few days, and it can take more than a week to replace birth weight. Those two days are not sufficient to establish the milk supply and the bottle will only upset the balance of the baby's needs and the mother's supply. Babies are born with a reserve of nutrients for the first forty-eight hours so will not go hungry if they receive nothing except the enriched first milk, the colostrum.

Since 1970, there has been a significant return to breastfeeding but one third stop at four to eight weeks.

Examining attitudes,[10] 62% of those who breastfed were happy with the demand feeding and 31% would allow supplementary bottles. Eighty-three per cent found breastfeeding enjoyable and 95% were prepared to feed in front of people, although in most cases that included family only.

Of the 66% who had gone to antenatal classes, thirty-four of them had received information on breastfeeding but only twenty considered this adequate.

In Chapter 5 on fatherhood, we discussed the reactions of the woman's partner to the idea of breastfeeding. Without doubt, if the father has an opportunity to express his possible ambivalence during pregnancy, he will be better equipped to handle his emotional reaction when the situation actually arises.

It is significant that even in a recent study, only 13% of mothers were encouraged to put the baby to the breast in the first hour after birth and three quarters of babies were given glucose water.

Of course, adequate preparation in pregnancy will provide the basis for a positive early breastfeeding experience. However tired a mother is after the birth, she usually does have the energy and the desire to hold her baby and put him to the breast. Even if the baby sucks for only a few minutes, this will reinforce the sucking instinct, help the milk to start flowing and of course effect the contractions of the uterus.

Colostrum

During pregnancy, many women leak a watery or yellowish discharge from the nipples. This is the colostrum which flows more copiously immediately after the birth, when the pregnancy hormones start on the down-swing and there is a release of the lactation hormones, prolactin and oxytocin.

Calves cannot survive without colostrum because it lines the gut. Baby humans, too, benefit from this enriched food source which provides valuable antibodies and prevents the leaking of protein into the intestines which in turn can precipitate allergies.

Colostrum is also a laxative and helps the baby expel the meconium, the first bowel movements, which are black and sticky in texture; getting rid of this helps prevent neonatal jaundice.

During the next seventy-two hours, the colostrum will continue and is then replaced by the regular milk which flows in greater quantities. The colostrum is sufficient for these first days, but very tiny or very large babies whose blood sugar may not be stable may need extra fluids.

Demand Feeding

It is better to be available for the baby night and day in order to build up the milk supply and use the minimum of bottles. Babies get used to bottles very quickly because it is far easier to suck from a bottle than the more strenuous action of jaw and tongue which is involved in breastfeeding.

One of the criteria for choosing a hospital, if there is a choice, should be the flexibility of routine and encouragement of breast-feeding. Rooming-in is definitely an advantage because the mother tunes in to her baby's needs from the beginning and does not have to rely on the nursery staff to bring the baby when he cries. In many hospitals, rooming-in is available only during the daytime and the baby is returned to the nursery at night.

Whatever the situation, if the baby spends time away from the mother it is worth attaching a note to the cot: 'I am a breastfed baby – please do *not* give me bottles. Call my mother . . . Room no . . .'. It may seem cruel to wake a sleeping mother, and indeed if she is exhausted the first night or two, it is not the end of the world to give a bottle of expressed breast milk or even formula. But if the baby is given too many bottles in those first days he will start to prefer the ease of bottlefeeding. Also the mother's milk supply will not be stimulated, and the baby will not benefit from the antibodies provided by the colostrum.

The spontaneity of demand feeding may be disrupted if the baby is kept in the nursery either because this is the normal routine of the hospital or because the baby suffers from jaundice and needs to spend time under a lamp. Physiological jaundice occurs in a high percentage of babies (perhaps too high a percentage because it has been linked with pitocin which is used to induce labour). The baby's liver is less mature in the first days and does not always break down the red blood cells effectively. This causes a build-up of bilirubin which makes the baby look yellow, particularly in the whites of the eyes. This is not a pathological condition caused by any disease but it must be treated in order not to cause any lasting damage. A day or two under the ultraviolet light usually breaks down the residue of bilirubin, but sometimes the baby has to be kept in the hospital for an extra period of time. Babies with jaundice need lots of fluids so they should be breastfed very frequently.

Occasionally, although it is very rare, the jaundice is connected to the breastfeeding hormones and women may have to interrupt feeding for a few days. The baby can be taken out of the light for feeding and in fact they are often quite lethargic after this treat-ment and feed very slowly.

Once the baby is back home, it is easier to feed the baby on demand and if there is still an elevated bilirubin count the baby should be put in sunlight next to an open window. If the weather is hot, expose his body to the sunlight but make sure that he is never left out of doors in strong sun.

After caesarean births, women may have more limited access to their babies because their own recovery period demands more rest. Where epidural anaesthetic is given for a caesarean birth, it is still possible to breastfeed on the operating table and to be given the baby regularly on the same day. However, the mother is less able to lift the baby and wheel him herself to and from the nursery. She needs to recruit the help of nurses or family to get the baby as much as possible.

The lactation hormones are released in exactly the same way as after a vaginal birth, but the body has after all experienced the trauma of surgery and it might take a few extra days for the milk to come in. Again, maximum stimulation and access to the baby will help the milk flow, and often the caesarean mother will need the satisfaction of breastfeeding even more in order to counteract some of the disappointment of missing out on a vaginal birth.

Positioning is very important after a caesarean. The baby should be held with the head to the breast and feet *away* from the body to avoid pressure on the scar. When the mother can sit in a chair to feed, she should put a pillow on her stomach so that if the baby suddenly kicks or moves it will not be painful for her.

Breastfeeding twins, triplets or quads works in exactly the same way as for one baby. The more the babies demand, the more milk is produced. Although one cannot minimize the amount of work involved after multiple births, breastfeeding does reduce the kitchen chores.

If twins wake at the same time they can be fed together, in the posture described for caesareans, with the support of pillows.

If the babies wake up at different times, it is perhaps an opportunity to get to know each baby as an individual and give each their own special attention. Greta and Robert had twins when their two other children were only four and two, so that for the first few months life was very hectic. Fortunately both sets of grandparents lived nearby and they all made careful plans to keep the household ticking over and to make sure that the older children were happy and stimulated. Greta could then concentrate on breastfeeding the twins, while at the same time giving the other children sufficient love and attention.

Human females, perhaps unfortunately, are not equipped for

feeding triplets or quads simultaneously and a mother who does want to provide breast milk for so many babies does need the maximum of practical assistance and support.

Premature Babies

Premature babies require specific skills in breastfeeding. They are at special risk in the early weeks and for this reason, mother's milk is more protective in terms of antibodies and immunization as well as ease of digestion.

Most premature baby units encourage parents to spend the maximum time with the baby, so as to provide the emotional bonding, touching and love that these babies need so badly. It is often very painful for parents to see their infants in this situation, dependent on life-support systems for their survival.

The milk of a mother who has given birth prematurely is particularly suited to her own baby and is especially rich in the nutrients and antibodies needed by the infant whose system is not yet matured. In the same way, the milk of a mother who gives birth at full term suits her fully developed baby. The milk changes to suit the baby's development up to about six months of age.

Very premature babies are not able to suck. The mother can use an electric breast pump in the hospital, and when she is at home can continue expressing so that her supply is built up. Her milk can then be given in a bottle or, for very tiny babies, through a feeding tube. Of course, there is a big difference between a baby born at twenty-seven weeks and one at thirty-four weeks in terms of the maturity of their digestive system. The tiniest babies may need extra fluids and glucose, but in most cases breast milk can partially be used.

The advantage to the baby is obvious but there are also more subtle advantages to the parents. Sometimes close contact with the premature baby is feared because the parents feel that the loss will be unbearable if the baby dies. Research shows that touching and holding are as important for the survival of the baby as the best medical expertise and equipment. In one Third World hospital where incubators were not available, mothers kept their premature babies strapped to their chest night and day, and subsequent studies showed that the survival rate compared favourably with those who were cared for in high-tech neonatology units.

By spending time with the baby and expressing milk, the parents also know that they have a very active role to play in the care of their infant. This also eases the homecoming, and the baby seems less of a stranger if the emotional bonding has already been established.

Breast versus Bottle

Both the handling of problems and analysing of attitudes are facilitated if the mother is convinced of the advantages of breast-feeding. And indeed, in this age of manufactured formula food and ease of sterilizing bottles, what are the advantages of a system which is neither regular or measurable? Why do all the researchers agree that breast is best?

Apart from the joy and emotional satisfaction of this intimate relationship, the actual composition of human milk is precisely attuned to the baby's needs. Cows' milk is suitable for baby cows whose physical development is much faster than that of a human baby. A calf doubles his birth weight in ten weeks, where a baby takes twenty-four weeks. For this reason, the milk of a primate is lower in fat, solute and protein.

The human brain develops with special growth in the frontal lobes, and mother's milk adjusts with the needs of this development. Using other milks with higher fat, mineral or protein levels can upset this balance.

Breast milk is a complete diet for a baby up to six months of age or to the equivalent weight. Its composition aids the absorption of iron and the liberation of fatty acids, and provides antibodies and a balance of vitamins. Digestion is aided and gastric disorders prevented by the balance of 'curds and whey' which produce acid stools which in turn discourage bacteria.

Studies done on adults show a lower incidence of coronary disease and diabetes in those who are breastfed as infants. Breast milk contains cholesterol and it is thought that this gives the body the potential to cope with it in later life, thus reducing the risk of heart disease.

The latest news from the Cambridge Nutrition Centre is that breastfed premature babies may rate an extra eight points on the IQ scale.[11]

The World Health Organization took action in 1979, when the Third World was threatened by aggressive advertising of formula foods.[12] Their *Code for Marketing of Infant Foods*, which is regularly updated, forbids any advertising which suggests that any supplementary food is as good as or better than human milk.

Bonnie Worthington-Roberts' book *Nutrition in Pregnancy and Lactation*[13] contains vital information about the differences between human and cows' milk. Cows' milk is richer in protein and poorer in carbohydrate. Why is this a disadvantage? Think of how a baby calf develops, with the concentration on body growth. A calf at six months is fully developed, while it takes more than two years for a baby to attain complete motor ability and more than sixteen years to reach full growth. The carbohydrate in breast milk, lactose, develops the central nervous system, provides extra energy, facilitates calcium absorption and aids brain growth. This lactose is a natural sugar, which is non-addictive and will not affect the child's teeth or cause obesity, whereas the sugar used in formula is metabolized.

Although bottlefed babies are usually more colicky than those who are fed breast milk, there is a rare condition called lactose intolerance which can affect breastfed babies, causing gas pains and stomach discomfort. True lactose intolerance is very rare in babies under a year. This is because during the period that babies depend on breast milk, the body manufactures the enzyme lactase which breaks down the lactose in breast milk into a form that the body can absorb. However, all symptoms of stomach upsets, dehydration and slow weight gain should be investigated thoroughly. It may just be a matter of something in the mother's diet disagreeing with the baby or that the baby is feeding so quickly that he is getting filled with wind. But a consultation with a paediatrician or good family doctor is essential in order to rule out more serious problems which could lead to malnutrition or insufficient weight gain.

Sometimes medication such as antibiotics given to a sick baby can temporarily cause an imbalance of lactase, leading to lactose intolerance. In these situations, changing over to formula food will often aggravate this condition. If the baby is sensitive to foods taken by the mother, he may be even more disturbed by the cows' milk base of formula foods. If formula is essential, it might be worthwhile giving soya-based milk.

Very small babies, up to two or three months of age, sometimes suffer from 'transient' lactose intolerance. In other words, their bodies are perfectly equipped to cope with it, but the lactase enzyme supply has not yet sufficiently established itself to cope with an overload. That is why some babies have a colicky crying period, often at the end of the day when their tiny stomachs are too full. The highest concentration of lactose in breast milk is present after a long interval between feeds, for example if the baby has slept for an extended period.

In this situation expressing the first flow of milk will reduce the concentration of lactose passing to the baby. Once the baby's stomach is larger, he will be able to tolerate this. Usually it is not recommended to express part of the flow because there are very important nutritional properties in each phase of the flow.

It may be clear why breastfeeding mothers sometimes envy their bottlefeeding friends whose babies sleep for longer periods after feeds of sweetened formula, maybe with a spoonful or two of cornflour thrown in to 'get him through the night'. It does indeed take the baby all night to metabolize this difficult food and what may in the short term appear to be an easier way of rearing an infant may turn out to be more costly in terms of long-term digestive and respiratory health and development.

The excess of minerals in cows' milk makes it hard work for the baby's immature kidneys to excrete these salts. This is why gastric upsets are more common in bottlefed babies. Severe overdose of minerals which may occur if, for example, one underdilutes the formula can cause kidney and brain damage. Preparing baby feeds in a bottle is not like making tea. 'One for the pot' is not applicable here and the instructions on the packaging should be very carefully noted.

While the fat content in both milks is similar, cows' milk contains less polyunsaturated fatty acids and is therefore more difficult to digest.

Add to all this the convenience of mother's milk being ready-to-serve and preheated – all of which enables the mother to be much more mobile.

Quantity and Quality

'Do I have enough milk?' is a question most asked in a society which is used to measuring and weighing everything. Because of the delicate nutritional balance of breast milk, the baby does not need to consume the same quantity gram for gram as cows' milk. The milk may look rather watery, even bluish in colour, which prompts well-meaning relatives to suggest that it is too weak or sour. But the mother's milk will almost always suit her baby, unless she is taking specific medication contraindicated in breast-feeding, or eating certain foods to which she and/or the baby are allergic.

The baby's weight gains are less dramatic with breastfeeding because the body is not creating superfluous fat cells and body tissues are not swollen with excess fluid. The baby is getting enough to eat if (a) weight gains are regular; (b) without extra water, the baby urinates six to eight times daily; (c) he has a good, firm skin; and (d) stools resemble the colour of mustard.

Breastfed babies produce less waste so do not be misled into thinking the baby is constipated if he does not have a bowel motion for a few days, provided he is not in pain. A well-fed baby is usually fairly content although there can be many reasons for crying apart from hunger.

Babies who demand to be fed every couple of hours are not eating frequently because they are getting too little milk. During the first few weeks the digestion is not fully developed and the baby's stomach is too small to absorb large meals. The finely balanced composition of the milk is rapidly metabolized, and it may seem as if the baby is constantly hungry. This is perfectly normal. In fact, the clock should be totally disregarded, both in terms of length of feeding and the intervals between feeds. This is very different from the digestive process of a baby who is stocked full of cows' milk and cereals and will need several hours to sleep it off!

The Milk Supply

Some women may have plenty of milk for the first couple of weeks and then feel that their supply is diminishing. Worried about the baby's weight, they may be tempted to give supplementary bottles.

When lactation is established and the mother is still enjoying comparative rest, the milk may be plentiful. However, on returning home to a hectic routine, the milk can be affected. It is important to rest and eat adequately.

Fluid intake is also important. A breastfeeding mother is usually very thirsty and should drink as much as she wants without worrying about weight gain. Avoid coffee, tea, Coke and cocoa because they do not contain any nutrients but are high in caffeine. Water, natural juice, herb tea and non-alcoholic black beer which contains brewers yeast, a very helpful ingredient for increasing milk supply, provide more healthy fluids.

The return of menstruation, an attack of flu, excessive fatigue, depression or stress can temporarily reduce the milk supply. A sick baby whose appetite has abated will also provide less stimulation and it may take a couple of days to balance this again.

Of course, the breastfeeding woman is using an extra 500 calories a day which leads to the myth that it is less exhausting to bottlefeed a baby. But in fact the physiological recovery of the woman after birth is in itself tiring, with possible anaemia caused by the demands of birth and the loss of lochia in the weeks that the uterus contracts. Women need to continue their iron supplements at this time and make sure that they eat nutritious and healthy food. Garlic is another aid for lactation.

The uterus involutes more effectively with breastfeeding, but there will naturally be extra weight caused by the extra fluids needed for lactation. If, therefore, the mother undertakes a strict diet to get her figure back, she will not only reduce her milk supply but will herself feel weak and lacking in energy. It is possible to get rid of excess weight by eating healthily and adequately and avoiding junk food, including chips, cakes and other fatty and sugary foods which do not provide basic nutrients.

Each feeding time should be a rest time for the mother if she lies on the bed or props herself up with plenty of pillows, listens to music and keeps a long drink and a bowl of nuts and fruit next to her. Even while breastfeeding, talking to the baby and listening to music, there is a hand free, so the mother whose time is even more limited because there are other children in the house can cuddle the toddler or read to him.

It is important to avoid deadlines. The day that you plan a special dinner party and you want to clean the house and cook something interesting will be the day that the baby demands extra attention or brings up all his food after every meal.

Sometimes there has been insufficient stimulation of the breasts because of jaundice. Babies with jaundice are often very sleepy and lethargic following their treatment under the lamp and this can also cause a temporary reduction in milk.

If the supply diminishes a few weeks later, it could be that the baby has had a growth spurt and is dissatisfied with the existing supply. If the mother concentrates on demand feeding, she will recharge her batteries and within a few days be making enough milk for the baby's needs.

If a baby really does not get enough to eat and either is not gaining or is actually losing weight, supplementary feeds may be recommended. It is a good idea to give the breast first and only add the bottle afterwards. In this way, the supply is maintained and increased. As the baby gains weight he will suck more vigorously and cause more milk to be produced so that eventually the bottles may be discarded.

It may be worthwhile for a tired or anxious mother to go to bed for several hours and either keep the baby with her for frequent feedings or, if she wants to sleep for an extended period, leave a bottle of either her expressed milk or formula for her partner to give to the baby. A good night's sleep can do wonders and may contribute greatly to a subsequent increase in supply.

While some women are concerned that their milk is not sufficient for their growing baby, others may experience real problems because the milk is spurting out all the time, leaking through clothes and almost drowning the baby when he starts to feed. There is no connection between size of breast and volume of milk and some thin, small women are very surprised by the amount of milk they produce.

For the first few weeks, as the baby's sucking gets stronger, the breast will produce more and more milk to suit the demand. Sometimes, the hormones work so well that there is indeed too much milk. If this happens, the baby should be fed according to demand but the mother should not overdo her own fluid intake. This is difficult advice to accept, especially in hot weather when it is very important to drink enough fluids. Women are often advised to drink more when they are breastfeeding, but of course, if they do have an abundant supply they can worry less about their fluids. Parsley is a natural diuretic and a green salad or sandwich including this herb will sometimes control the milk supply.

It is better to avoid expressing milk and just give the baby the milk which flows spontaneously and easily, unless of course the mother has to leave the baby for a few hours and wishes to leave expressed breast milk for him. However, it does seem a pity to waste all this excess milk, so if the milk is really flowing copiously and meanwhile the baby is fast asleep, it is possible to catch it in a sterile cup and freeze it in sterile bags. Milk can be stored in the freezer for three weeks or in the refrigerator for twenty hours.

At the beginning of lactation, milk leaks more because the little 'storehouses' underneath the nipple are not stretched and milk released from the alveoli spurts straight out of the breast. After a few weeks, these ducts underneath the nipple stretch enough to store some of the milk and this controls the leaking to some extent. Splashing cold water on the breasts and nipples will restrict leakage and, during the feed, place the heel of the hand on the side of the breast not being used.

If the baby is spluttering and choking because the flow is too fast, place him in an 'uphill' position with his legs under your arm and face towards the breast. This slows down the flow because it is harder work for the baby.

In those first days of breastfeeding, the nipples may become quite sore. The duration of feeds should not be timed because babies feed at different rates and he should be allowed to finish as much as he wants. It is a good idea, after ten minutes on one breast, to release the suction with the little finger and start on the other side, in order to reduce tenderness and to stimulate the milk flow in both breasts and also to make sure that the baby gets the richer hindmilk as well as the foremilk from both breasts.

The authors of *Bestfeeding* describe these different stages of milk flow. The first milk, or foremilk, is high in volume and low in fat. Although this milk is low in calories it is high in protein and essential for growth and resistance of infection. This is followed by the hindmilk which flows more slowly and is lower in quantity but higher in calories. This is why sometimes when babies fall asleep after only a few minutes on the breast, they wake up soon after to finish the feed because they simply did not get enough volume.

It is therefore better to leave the baby for longer on one side rather than change frequently from breast to breast. If he falls asleep after a shorter period on one breast, he should start on that side at the next feed.

Care of Nipples

Nipples can be prepared in pregnancy by gentle massage with wheatgerm oil (vitamin E). Do not use soap or 'toughen' the nipples with a rough towel as is sometimes recommended. The nipples are very delicate tissue and need very gentle handling.

After breastfeeding the baby, a little of the milk can be expressed and left to dry on the nipple. This is sterile and also keeps the nipple lubricated. Occasional use of wheatgerm oil is also effective and the nipples should only be wiped clean and not rigorously washed. Again, soaps should not be used when feeding because they dry out the nipples. Lanolin is now not recommended because it is made from sheepskin and most farm animals today are treated with pesticides which can cause a great deal of harm if ingested with the lanolin.

It is very important to check the breast pads carefully because those with plastic backing will cause the nipple to be moist all the time, leading to soreness. The brassiere should be well-fitting and comfortable. Whatever the budgetary restrictions, a good bra is essential, preferably made of cotton.

One of the points of emphasis of Chloe Fisher's work, both in her book and in her counselling, is that the root cause of sore nipples is incorrect positioning or latching on. 'Good positioning means getting yourself and your baby into comfortable effective body positions. When you learn to drive a car, you need to be sitting comfortably in the driver's seat, hands on the wheel and feet on the pedals. If the seat was too far back from the pedals and wheel, it would not be comfortable or safe. Like learning to dance, breastfeeding takes practice and rhythm because there are two of you doing it together.'

The mother should sit comfortably in a low chair with feet well supported and a pillow on her lap. This brings the baby to the level of the breast without the need to bend her back or for the baby to pull on the nipple. Alternatively she can lie on her side supported with pillows with the baby's mouth directly under the breast.

The baby should take not only the centre of the nipple but as much as possible of the areola, the brown area around the nipple, in his mouth so that he does not chew just on the nipple itself. Milk also comes out of the Montgomery tubercles in the areola.

Engorgement

'I feel like a cow before milking time' is the comment of many women suffering the discomfort of engorgement in the first days or weeks.

The breasts are normally enlarged when the milk starts flowing but are softer and more comfortable after feeds. However, occasionally, if the baby does not empty the breast, residue milk dries up in the milk glands or ducts and this causes a blockage This can also happen if the milk flow is impeded, perhaps because the bra is not well fitted or even if there is pressure on the breasts during feeding from, for example, the arm of a chair.

The signs are sore, lumpy breasts and the first aid treatment for this is a long hot shower and gentle massage of the lumpy areas. Sometimes this releases the blockage and milk will spurt out of the nipple. Lying down with a hot water bottle or hot towel will also ease the discomfort.

After feeding, cold compresses can be used to help the glands and ducts to contract. Cold cabbage leaves which have been stored in the refrigerator can be placed around the breasts to absorb some of the heat.

Frequent feeding will gradually solve the problem and keep the milk flowing. While heat is effective *before* feeds, ice packs will help the ducts contract *after* feeding.

If the mother herself feels fluey and finds that she has a fever, or there are red patches on the breast, she should consult her doctor because the area may be infected and require antibiotics. The worst action at that point is to stop breastfeeding. If this is done, the milk will build up inside the breast and can lead to a serious abscess.

When there is a breast infection of this type, the inflammation is of the actual breast tissue. The milk itself is not contaminated and there is no danger in letting the baby feed. If an abscess does form and it is thought that the milk is not clean, it should still be pumped, even if it is thrown away, so that the milk does not dry up inside the breasts, and in order to maintain the flow and supply so that breastfeeding can continue afterwards.

The antibiotics prescribed for this condition are usually in the penicillin group and not contraindicated for breastfeeding unless of course the mother is allergic to this medication.

It is sometimes difficult to sleep on one's side or stomach when the breasts are so heavy and tender. But arranging a pillow under the stomach as well as under the head makes a sort of 'hollow' for the enlarged breasts.

Babies too have problems with engorged breasts because the nipple sometimes does not protrude sufficiently to suck easily. If this happens, splash some hot water on the breasts and express a few drops of the milk before feeding the baby and this will soften the breast and help the nipple protrude.

Make sure the baby's airways are clear because the heaviness of the breast may obstruct his nose.

During this engorged period, breasts feel lumpy, but one

should note that this condition changes in intensity before and after feeding and disappears within a couple of days. Women should be aware that any specific lump which does not change in this way and disappear in a short time should be investigated. Cysts and fibrous tissues can form during breastfeeding as at any other time and any lump should be checked.

Refusal to Feed

Baby 'strike' or fighting at the breast may be caused by various factors. It is always upsetting for the mother that the baby is not contentedly feeding and she may feel quite insulted that he is constantly spitting out the nipple, crying or even refusing the breast.

Check first that the baby's nose is not blocked, either by an overfull breast or because he has a cold. The baby may have got used to bottles if he was getting supplementary feeds and be protesting at the extra effort of breastfeeding.

Some babies prefer one breast to the other, either because of the position or milk flow, so the mother's position and posture should be adjusted. Occasionally a breast infection can cause this so if it persists, she should check with her doctor.

Sometimes the taste of the milk is affected by medication or specific foods. Medication should only be prescribed by a doctor who is aware that the mother is breastfeeding, but occasionally even if the medicine is safe, it affects the taste.

Naomi called me one day four months after the birth of her daughter. She had enjoyed feeding and the baby was doing well. Suddenly at midnight, the baby went on strike, crying for food, but spluttering and spitting out the milk when she fed. This continued all night and it was now midday. Both Naomi and her baby were frantic, one with hunger, the other with anxiety.

We worked through all the reasons: change in soap or deodorant, unusual food, medication, a period. There seemed to be no significant change in Naomi's habits. I asked Naomi to express milk into a bottle because sometimes it is not the milk but the breast which the baby is rejecting. This can happen if there is a breast infection. The baby tasted the milk from the bottle, and again spluttered and spat it out.

The only change in Naomi's routine was that she had been to the dentist the previous day and received a local anaesthetic for filling a cavity. I had never heard of this affecting the milk but suggested that if this was the reason, the taste should go back to normal within twenty-four hours of the injection. Sure enough at 3 pm, exactly twenty-four hours after Naomi had been at the dentist, the baby started feeding from the breast and sucked energetically and enjoyably as if nothing had happened.

Babies sometimes react to certain foods eaten by the mother. She may have a dormant allergy which is only apparent when the baby suffers from colic or produces green loose stools. It is popularly thought that spicy foods, beans or cauliflower cause this problem, but it can just as easily be milk products, chocolate or strawberries. It is therefore worth keeping a chart of daily intake of foods if the baby does have periods of stomach discomfort and it is then possible to correlate the attacks of colic or diarrhoea with the foods responsible.

Weaning

While breastfeeding supplies full nutrition for the first five or six months, it is the first three months which are critical as far as development and protection are concerned. For this reason, many working mothers aim to take time off work for those three months in order to concentrate on fully breastfeeding.

When lactation is well established and both mother and baby are enjoying the experience, many mothers are reluctant to wean when they return to work. They may therefore either fully or partially breastfeed according to their working conditions and timetable.

If the working mother does not have suitable conditions at her workplace or finds it too demanding to pump milk, she can still partially breastfeed. But it is important to note that if she is giving fewer feeds each day, she should reduce these feeds very gradually in order to prevent engorgement.

In the same way as the milk supply builds up according to the baby's demand, so the milk is reduced if she gives fewer feeds. If she allows a few days for each meal which is to be replaced, her supply will gradually decrease without painful engorgement. If, for example, she knows that she will be out of the house for eight out of twenty-four hours when the baby is aged three months, she needs to replace two feeds with formula. She should therefore cut down one of the feeds almost two weeks before the deadline, and a week later reduce the second feed. When the baby is older she may wish to replace those feeds with fruit or soup, with the formula milk simply given as a drink to finish the meal.

Babies who are fully breastfed only need a supplement of vitamins A and D in the first six months. They are born with a reserve of iron and breast milk contains all the necessary nutrients for that period of time.

Breastfeeding can of course continue for as long as both the mother and baby are content, and in some societies babies are fed till the age of three. After six months it is important to start introducing a variety of other foods.

Meat, chicken, egg yolk and cows' milk are absolutely contra-indicated up to the age of one year, and so is honey which is found to contain bacteria which affect small babies.

The first foods should be fruit and vegetables, blended until the baby is old enough to chew and eat with his fingers. Certain fruits do not mix well together and it was found that bananas and oranges eaten together reduce the metabolization of the vitamin C in the fruit. Drinks should not be sweetened. Plain boiled water or pure fruit juices can be given as a supplement if the baby is being weaned. Camomile tea is very helpful for stomach discomfort but regular tea is not recommended because apart from the caffeine and tannin, its action on other foods causes problems in the absorption of iron. Cocoa should not be regularly added to milk drinks or desserts, even for older children, because it reacts to negate the benefits of the calcium in the milk.

A baby who is showing signs of needing more carbohydrates can be given enriched cereals. However, while many of the prepared baby foods are nourishing and convenient, it is important to check the ingredients very carefully for added sugar. Babies do not need sugar added to their foods and even the sometimes recommended grape sugar can be addictive and harmful.

Conclusion

It is established that breastfeeding is best for babies. Many studies have shown that it is also beneficial for the mother. It is the natural conclusion to the childbearing year, brings the hormones round full circle and helps the uterus contract more effectively after the birth.

Whatever the rationale, women who enjoy breastfeeding derive great satisfaction from the experience and feel very close to babies who are nourished from their own bodies. It is indeed a wonderful feeling to pick up a baby who is red-faced, angry and hungry, and watch him calm down and relax as he grasps the breast and starts feeding, until finally, satiated, he gives a thankful burp and a wobbly smile and settles down to sleep.

8 *Ways of Recovery: Sources of Support*

DURING pregnancy, the woman and the foetus are cherished and nurtured. Medical care and the concern of society provide the pregnant woman with a special status. It can be quite difficult to climb down from that pedestal after the birth.

It is rather like preparing for a wedding. Great plans are made for the party, menus, printing of invitations, ordering of flowers and as the day approaches and tension rises, the couple just want it to be over. But this is just the beginning. The couple then have to get down to the task of knowing each other more intimately and coping with the everyday problems of working, running a home and managing the bank balance.

So it is with birth. Everybody is excited about the great day and not many people think ahead to the period of adjustment afterwards. It is perhaps a comfort, therefore, to know that there is a network of support agencies and, for some parents, the extra help of the extended family.

Women sometimes feel very vulnerable coming home from hospital and there may be various questions and causes for concern. In the last chapter, the problems and issues which may arise as far as the baby is concerned were discussed. In this chapter we shall concentrate on the needs of the mother and how she herself copes with the physical and emotional recovery after the birth.

CARE OF THE PERINEUM

The recovery period varies with each individual, but without doubt there is more discomfort and difficulty in moving around when there has been an episiotomy. The stitches given are soluble, but during the few days that they take to dissolve, the area may be very tender.

Frequent showers are essential, keeping the area especially clean after urinating or defaecating. Cold compresses of camomile tea are very effective because this herb is soothing and the compress reduces the swelling of bruised tissue. The tea should be prepared beforehand, because it will infuse better if made with boiling water, then cooled and kept in the ice tray or in ice lolly moulds. The iced tea cube can then be wrapped in a pad and placed on the perineum, particularly after the effort of a bowel movement which may have caused extra tenderness.

Witchhazel pads are effective for stitches and also for haemorrhoids. At night, when more time is spent in bed, aloe vera gel can be carefully applied to the area.

Warm baths are very comforting and luxurious for a woman after birth, or one could take a long hot shower. To prevent dizziness, it might be worth putting a low chair or stool in the shower so that one can be seated. It is advisable, during the first week or so, only to take a bath or shower when there is somebody else in the house so that help is at hand if one falls or feels dizzy.

Stitches may make walking difficult but a conscious effort should be made to stand straight because walking bent over may cause backache and strain on the stomach muscles.

The pelvic floor exercise should be done from day one, and when sitting down, the pelvic floor should be contracted as one sits and then released as the weight is put fully on the rear end.

When sitting up in bed, either to feed the baby or to read, one leg should be kept straight and the other tucked up with the sole of the foot towards the opposite thigh. This will take the weight off the perineum.

It is also important to avoid constipation because this will aggravate the discomfort of the episiotomy as well as haemorrhoids. The intestinal muscles are often strained during labour and it can take a few days for full strength to return. Eating plenty of fibre foods, dried fruit and drinking lots of fluids will gradually train the intestines back to normal behaviour. Haemorrhoids can be particularly painful if the pushing stage of labour was strenuous.

BLOOD LOSS

There is an acceptable rate of blood loss in the days or even weeks following the birth. Light contractions will be felt for several days, particularly when breastfeeding, and the flow of lochia may be heavier at that time. Women having second babies onwards often complain that those contractions are not so minor and indeed they feel as if they are having a heavy period.

The blood lost in those first five to seven days is dark red and often contains clots. This is absolutely normal because the uterus is closing down after its hard work. After the placenta is expelled, the blood vessels which attached the placenta to the uterine wall shut off and the uterus begins to involute. The lining of the uterus which has provided a sort of nest for the baby during the pregnancy begins to disintegrate and because there has not been a menstrual period during the nine months of gestation, this process is really like a maxi-menstruation.

Within a week, the bleeding will phase out to a much slower discharge of darker colour and gradually in the next week or two will become a brownish-beige colour, until it stops. Breastfeeding speeds up this process and from time to time the midwife may measure the height of the uterus to see how it is contracting.

Sometimes, a week or two after the initial flow has subsided and the mother resumes looking after the household, she may be dismayed to see that the lochia has increased. It is important to speak to the doctor at that stage because it can either be caused by insufficient contraction of the uterus, overdoing the physical work or in rarer cases, it might be a sign of infection, particularly if the discharge has a bad odour. In any case, treatment is necessary and the mother will need to rest until the flow has eased up.

In the early weeks, it is important to avoid carrying heavy shopping bags, lifting and hanging out laundry and any household job which means lifting or pushing. This is not the time for springcleaning even if the house looks a mess after some time of neglect.

HEALTHCARE AFTER BIRTH

From the time that the midwife finishes her regular calls, the health visitor takes over. In some districts these jobs are one and the same. The health visitor will usually call at the home if needed, but is available at the mother and baby clinic. The family doctor works in cooperation with the health visitor and together they will give advice on when the baby should be immunized, check weight gains and answer questions on the care of the baby.

If the family doctor was the primary caregiver during pregnancy, an appointment should be made with him for the post-natal check-up. This is important even if the mother feels 100% well, because there are no external signs that the uterus has contracted to its previous size and position, or that the cervix is closed. Sometimes, minor technical problems can cause future fertility difficulties.

This is also an opportunity to discuss problems such as unhealed episiotomy or sexual difficulties. Sometimes the vagina is rather dry during this period and the first few times a couple have sex, it may be quite painful for the woman. She can use a lubricating gel, but it is worth discussing this with the doctor during that visit.

For many women, pregnancy may be the first time they experience a gynaecological examination, and this postpartum check-up six weeks after the birth should start a yearly routine. However young and healthy a woman is, it is worth the time and effort to make an annual appointment because it is only by pelvic and vaginal examination that such problems as fibroids or cysts can be detected. Although persistent backache, irregular bleeding and other changes in the menstrual cycle may be a warning that something is wrong, many small growths go undetected until a routine gynaecological examination.

While the majority of growths are benign and cause no trouble, it is important to diagnose them accurately so that if there are any suspicions of malignancy, treatment can be given quickly and more effectively. The Pap smear has long been recommended for the earliest possible detection of precancerous cells in the cervix, giving the maximum opportunity to prevent the development of cancer. In recent years, it has also been used extensively for diagnosing viral diseases or infections, which facilitates early treatment and prevents transmission through sexual intercourse by warning the couple at an early stage.

Breast examinations should be done after each menstrual period and a more thorough check-up asked for at a breast clinic or from the family doctor each year.

Women who are breastfeeding will not have the same timing as those who have regular menstruation. While it is rare for young women or those who are breastfeeding to develop malignancies in the breast, it can happen and women should be aware of changes in their bodies.

There are periods of lumpiness during breastfeeding, caused by engorgement. Usually these lumps disappear or get softer after a couple of days of hot compresses and massage, and indeed there is even a different feeling after the baby has fed. Any change in the breast which does not disappear within two or three days should be investigated. Here again the highest percentage of growths in the breasts are cystic or fibrous and sometimes disappear in the course of time. However, it is essential that it be checked and a correct diagnosis made.

At the risk of offending some health caregivers, I do warn women not to take it for granted that, when they are told, 'Leave it for three months and come back if it hasn't disappeared', the doctor or nurse knows that the growth is benign. An experienced practitioner can often guess by palpating the growth that it is almost certainly non-malignant. But there is absolutely no way of being absolutely sure of this without testing by mammography or fine needle aspiration, or preferably both tests done together.

In general, women who have given birth and breastfed have a lower incidence of malignant diseases of the breast and genital tract, but routine check-ups take little time and body awareness helps a woman to notice any suspicious changes.

Family doctors are in the closest proximity to the parents and it is usually possible within one group practice to establish a harmonious relationship with at least one of them. This can protect one from a lot of running around. In rural areas where the doctors are part of the community, this relationship can be of two-way enrichment.

So, at this point, the new parents will see that there are various sources of routine information and medical care, the family doctor and the health visitor being the central agencies.

FAMILY SUPPORT

One should not underestimate the potential support from the grandparents. For those who have good relationships with the extended family and who live within a reasonable distance, the pleasure is two-way. The grandparents, however busy with their own lives, will often be delighted to be involved again after those adolescent and student years when the children have drifted away or cut themselves off from their families.

And what is nicer for an exhausted mother than to sit down to a delicious meal cooked by her mother or mother-in-law and be spoiled and encouraged to rest?

The grandparent/grandchild relationship is very precious and children who are deprived of this because of death or distance do miss out on a very rich experience.

The attitude of the generations to each other is, however, an integral part of the in-law relationship. It is a sad fact that many marriages are doomed from the start by either the unwanted interference of the parent-in-law or the inability of the new son or daughter to relate to the established family unit.

The situation becomes more intense when a grandchild is born, and it is at this time that relationships can be strengthened, nurtured and cherished – or they can deteriorate into a complete breakdown of communication.

If the young couple are strong and secure with each other, they can set their own standards and resist interference while at the same time showing respect to the older generation.

This is often illustrated in pregnancy when a couple attend a childbirth preparation course. One example was Patrick who sat quietly without contributing to the discussion while all the men were talking about participating in the birth, being at one with their wives in labour.

In a private conversation later, Patrick confessed that every time the subject came up in the family, his father laughed at him. 'My mother had eleven children and he spent each of the labours in the pub waiting for the news.' Patrick said that his father was a wonderful family man and was trying to convince him that he would be no less of a father if he kept out of the labour ward. 'He makes me feel that I am abnormal for wanting to be with my wife.'

Eventually, his wife went into labour and Patrick found himself unable to tear himself away from her. I happened to meet him half-an-hour after the birth coming out of the labour ward where he ecstatically related the events to his extended family and was indeed treated like a hero.

There are different reactions to varied ethnic practices in the family. Bella lived in the north of England far from her English family and near to her Indian in-laws. She loved being part of this extended family. 'I didn't have to do a thing for a month after the birth. We moved in with my husband's family, his mother cooked wonderful meals and lots of eager aunts as well as my father-in-law were always ready to help with the baby. I really enjoyed being spoiled during that month and it set me up for the time when I eventually would be coping on my own.' Bella smiled. 'Not that I ever really had to cope by myself, there were always pots of food being sent over and willing babysitters.'

Bella was ready to accept the family's norms and values and she in turn fulfilled their expectations of a woman who needs family support after childbirth. It is not always so positive.

'I cannot stand those family meals,' said Laura who married into a large Italian family. 'They lapse into Italian when they are all together and I don't understand what is going on. And we all have to kiss and be kissed every time we meet which is at least three time a week.'

Men sometimes find it easier to adjust because for periods of the day they are out of the domestic scene. 'I adore my mother-in-law's couscous,' beamed big burly Andy who claims that this was the reason he married his tiny Moroccan wife.

The grandparents too go through an emotional transition when the first of the next generation is born. The idea of continuing the family line is important in most cultures, particularly where the family are migrants or have endured periods of war or persecution.

The grandfather who was busy and overstressed at the time of the birth of his own children may delight in the leisure time he can spend with the grandchildren.

Interviews with seventy pairs of middle-class grandfathers by Neugarten and Weinstein[1] revealed the following reactions:

23% experienced biological renewal, continuum
11% felt that their role was that of resource person
 4% viewed grandparenthood as an extension of self
29% felt remote
24% expressed their role as that of provider of fun
 6% as reservoir of wisdom

Most of these grandfathers, whose views were reflected to some extent by their wives, said that they felt young again and accepted responsibility as a surrogate parent.

There may be a difference between maternal and paternal grandparents, depending on the relationships between the in-laws, claims the Kahana study.[2] They listed the positive response to grandparenthood as giving fun and treats without the constraints of discipline, passing on skills, giving advice and participating in childcare. On the negative side, grandparents reported that their status makes them feel old, the children are too noisy and that this added to their expenses and responsibilities.

My own mother died during my second pregnancy and my father lived with us for some time. Completely uprooted, bereft, grieving, he took great comfort and consolation from his relationship with my little boys.

Where family ties are strong, the benefits go in both directions. At a recent Jewish barmitzvah service I saw an old man sitting at the front in a wheelchair while his great-grandson read the Torah. When the boy finished, the old man was called to recite blessings. Two strong hefty grandsons lifted him to his feet and held him while he read. They guided his shaking hand to kiss the Torah Scroll. The old man wept, as did almost every congregant in the synagogue that morning.

Nevertheless, grandparents are getting younger, if not in chronological age then in attitudes and physical strength, and they may not always have that leisure time to spare. When the first grandchild is born, the grandparents may only be in their early fifties and they do not cease to have their individual needs and identities just because they have gone up one rung on the ladder of the family dynasty.

Many women are at the peak of their careers at this time, happy at last to be able to concentrate on their professions. They are not always so ready to become an emergency centre for every crisis. When grandmother walked out of the nursery and took up painting or went back to work, a generation of new mothers were left stranded and with this went a whole tradition of pampering and coddling.

The grandfather may be nowhere near retirement and also may be under tremendous pressure in his job.

But certainly even busy grandparents can give a young couple a break. Overtired parents can benefit tremendously from a weekend on their own or with friends, catching up on their interests, camping, skiing, diving, pottering around museums, an occasional theatre or concert, or just staying in bed.

While the proximity of in-laws can make this participation possible, conflicts too are exacerbated by this nearness.

The grandmother may see that the parents are doing things very differently from her day. It may take a lot of patience for a young mother to listen to the repetitive accounts of how babies were fed on routine, put to bed at six o'clock and given syrup of figs once a week!

This patience might be rewarded if the grandmother is prepared to read a few books and to understand that there are a lot of changes in the techniques and attitudes of modern infant care.

There are sometimes deep roots to these conflicts. A grandmother who found childbirth or breastfeeding unpleasant may adversely influence the younger woman. Maybe she in fact resents the pleasure the young woman derives from this behaviour which she considers as 'animal'. Overdressing, overfeeding, wrapping a baby in cotton wool may be seen as genuine concern for the baby but can also undermine the confidence of the parents.

In the chapter on grandparenthood in *Reassessing Fatherhood*,[3] Sarah Cunningham Berkley reports on interviews with eighteen couples in Aberdeen, two of them middle-class, the rest working-class. They were aged between forty-two and fifty-five, and one couple were in their early sixties. All the grandfathers were employed, as were all the grandmothers except one.

The interviews examined the attitudes to new methods of childcare, and while many of them were critical of the relative lack of discipline, they were reluctant to go against the wishes of the parents. Some of them had less than positive memories of interference from their own parents and did not want to repeat the mistakes.

While enjoying the fact that most of them had more money and time to spend on their grandchildren than they had had when their own children were small, they did appreciate that they didn't have to pace the floor all night.

The grandmothers were particularly appreciative of the more active role of the fathers in today's childcare. 'You see young fathers walking out with the pram – you never would have seen that in my time.'

Issues that may lead to conflict need to be settled in the first months after the birth. Ground rules need to be established so that the parents make it clear that they make the decisions about their child but that the wisdom and proximity of the grandparents is cherished.

A grandparent may legitimately spoil a child provided that the parents' principles are not violated. Battles at mealtime or bedtime should not be reinforced by grandparents, but an extra cuddle or storyreading given to the child will nevertheless reassure him that the grandparents still love him.

The young couple visiting with their baby should also respect the fact that the home of an older family is not childproof and take precautions so that the baby does not wet the best carpet or throw his toys at the china cabinet.

This extra dimension of the grandparents' relationship can be very valuable in family life, releasing the parents from being constantly on duty and giving the older couple new interests.

Sometimes when grandparents are not available, elderly neighbours are glad to be surrogates. My children remember to this day Mrs Parker who lived next door. We had moved from our first house, a semi-detached, when our fourth child was due, partly because it was too small and partly because our neighbours were always complaining about the noise and driving me to distraction. We soon discovered that our new neighbour, a childless widow, loved small children, and if she did not hear any noise, she came to enquire if everybody was well!

She loved to babysit for us and refused to take any money. The only way we could repay her was by fixing things in the house and mowing her lawn. But she claimed that babysitting was as much a pleasure for her as a release for us.

Sometimes, after a high-risk birth, the support of grandparents reduces the isolation and fear. Danny is a journalist and he and his wife Ena were looking forward to the birth of their first child. The labour started three weeks early and although the weight was not abnormally low, the birth was long and the baby was kept under observation for a few days.

When they came home they felt like the babes in the wood. 'We just didn't know what to do with this baby. He seemed so tiny and fragile.'

The couple were born and brought up in the same area and fortunately for them, both sets of grandparents live nearby and they all took turns to be with the young couple. The relationships were very harmonious and a few months later when Danny had an assignment abroad, Ena was able to join him for a short relaxing holiday, while the baby was looked after by all the adoring family.

EXTERNAL SOURCES OF SUPPORT

Another source of support is the childbirth educator or postnatal support group in the area. Parents who attend courses given by the National Childbirth Trust are encouraged to keep in contact with their instructor who is either a qualified breastfeeding counsellor or can refer the mother to one in the area. She can be a good resource person because apart from giving help on individual questions, she can direct the parent to the right address for further support.

On an individual basis, the counsellor is there to listen, open options, encourage the mother to express her fears, or suggest practical help on the basis of what the woman herself wants to do. If a woman talks to someone who has been there before, the barriers are lifted.

In some countries, such as Belgium, the social services provide postpartum support and there are automatic home visits after leaving hospital from social workers specially trained in this field.

However, a mother would usually prefer to talk to somebody she already knows and her NCT counsellor or health visitor is the nearest at hand.

Dr Desmond Bardon writes in *New Generation*,[4] 'If to a certain extent social and vulnerability factors play a large part in causation of depression, then it is unrealistic to expect that doctors can cure or prevent all such cases.

'It is the trained counsellor who will help women over crises, and without this help mothers could move into long drawnout suffering and disability.

'Support is not solely concerned with women with difficulties, but it is in a sense a significant social celebration of a highly important event, of a woman becoming a mother.'

The NCT has a network of peer support groups, usually organized in the home of one of the members. In some areas these groups are expanded to meet the individual needs of parents of twins, handicapped mothers and parents of children with special needs. At the back of this book can be found lists of other useful organizations.

The principles of these peer groups are clearly defined, in that they are non-judgemental, open to all mothers (there are fathers' groups too, or groups open to both parents) whether the mother is breastfeeding or bottlefeeding.

The group provides an opportunity to meet other parents in an atmosphere where nobody criticizes the way you change your baby's nappy or feed him. The meetings are usually in the daytime when new mothers can feel very isolated in a neighbourhood where fathers and female friends may be at work.

The groups can be structured if the majority agree and each

meeting can focus on an activity or subject of discussion, or they can be informal with the conversation going in whichever direction is found useful on that particular day.

Although members take turns to host the meeting, they are encouraged not to prepare elaborate food or feel compelled to springclean beforehand. On the contrary, if the other members arrive to find the hostess in chaos, they will set to, wash the dishes from last night's dinner and sit the harassed mother down with a long relaxing drink.

The National Housewives Register is also organized in small groups and if an activity is planned one of the members takes responsibility for all the babies so that the group can concentrate on a lecture or topic of discussion.

Many mothers feel very comfortable in these groups. For the first time, they can let their hair down. Lesley commented with relief how she felt that she could say anything in the group. She looks forward to the meeting each week and takes her small baby and eighteen month old toddler.

'When I had my first baby, my neighbour used to invite me in for a cup of coffee. Then when my daughter started toddling, it was made very clear, "Don't come with the baby, I've finished with sticky fingers."

'The first time I phoned the coordinator, I apologized for bringing two small children. She just laughed and said everybody came with children and it didn't matter how much noise or mess they made.

'She even arranged a lift for me. That really helped because the morning of the first meeting I was very nervous and if I had not been picked up from the house I think I would have had cold feet about going there.'

'I made friends for life at the group,' said Gwendoline who years later moved abroad but kept contact with her group and visited them every time she came back to Britain for a holiday.

'I felt for the first time that I was normal, and that all those media images of immaculate well-groomed mums with sparkling kitchens were just fantasy.'

'It felt so good to be in a non-threatening group situation. We suddenly realized that all our ambivalences and love–hate feelings about our babies and our husbands were common and that we were not monsters because there were times when we wished we could be a hundred miles away,' said Shirley.

Sometimes the group meeting can be used to give specific support to one member who is going through a bad time.

Elizabeth lives near her parents and she herself is an only child. At first she was glad of their help but now they are becoming too domineering. If they do not see her and the baby on one particular day, they phone to see where she is and what she is doing. 'We find ourselves rushing home for the phone call,' says Elizabeth. 'If they get no reply they start making frantic enquiries among our friends.'

One morning Elizabeth came to the group feeling both guilty and defiant. Her mother had told her not to take the baby out in winter, but she had wanted to come to the group the previous week. The baby was well wrapped up and the meeting was held in a warm house. But the baby got a cold and she did not dare admit to her mother that she had taken the baby out. However if her mother phoned when she was out, she would know anyway.

The group helped her to come to terms with the ambivalent reaction. On one hand, she welcomed her parents' support and proximity but resented their inflexibility and assumption that they could tell her what to do with her life. Elizabeth realized that she was not alone because some of her peers were going through the same thing with their own families.

Many of these groups become very cohesive so that families join together for holidays and picnics, run babysitting cooperatives and help each other during illness or when another baby is born. The children grow up in an atmosphere of support and trust and where grandparents and other family are not available, these groups provide them also with a social framework.

GETTING BACK INTO SHAPE

Most women feel that they need to get their bodies back into shape after childbirth. It isn't only that they look flabby but the feeling of slack muscles is uncomfortable. It takes six weeks for the uterus to involute and during that time it is worthwhile doing some basic exercises, similar to those learned in pregnancy.

During pregnancy, the muscles and ligaments were relaxed, particular the recti (stomach muscles) and pelvic floor. This relaxation is caused by the hormone changes which are intended to keep the uterus calm and inactive. The uterine muscles are like any others in the body and contract continuously. We are not usually aware of this because the uterus is very small but in the last months of pregnancy women are often aware of these contractions. Those which do not activate labour are called practice or Braxton Hicks contractions.

Unfortunately, the relaxing influence of the hormones also affects the pelvic floor and the support of the intestines and bowel so that many women are constipated and some complain of diarrhoea.

At about twenty-six weeks of pregnancy, the pelvic ligaments are softened and stretched so that the pelvis increases in width. This is nature's clever way of preparing for the birth but at that time women may experience backache which stretches round the pelvic basin.

During the first weeks after the birth, this all goes into reverse. The hormones again change, this time to initiate lactation, and the uterus contracts back to its normal size. All the muscles and ligaments in the body tighten up and the pelvis returns to its normal width.

While the pelvic ligaments return to normal, a process which can take up to five months, there may again be back pain. It is important therefore to reduce all strain on the back. Make sure that breastfeeding is always in a comfortable position with support of chairback and cushions. Carrying the baby in a front-carrier is better for the mother's back than balancing him on the hip. It is, however, important to investigate which type of carrier is most suitable because they can cause strain on the baby's back if they are not sufficiently supporting, as well as affecting the mother's posture.

The pram and pushchair should be of correct height and it is better to change nappies and dress the baby on a table rather than on one's lap or by bending over the cot.

The pelvic floor too is very vulnerable at this stage and some women suffer from stress incontinence. Sudden action can cause a leak of urine when the pelvic floor is still recovering so remember *bend your knees when you laugh or sneeze* – in order to support the pelvic floor. If the Kegel exercise was learned in pregnancy, this is the best way of toning up those muscles. The Kegel exercise can be done in any position and can be practised in any spare moments. Simply pull in those muscles which control the urethra, as if you were trying to stop yourself urinating. Then let them go. Do this several times, but try to pull in slowly and gradually and then release slowly instead of an abrupt movement of tensing and relaxing.

The pelvic muscle is like a hammock which supports the three openings, the urethra, vagina and rectum, so its good tone is also important for sexual intercourse.

Good posture will prevent some of the aches and pains and is also important for keeping the shape of the breasts. Exercising the pectoral muscles improves circulation and therefore benefits lactation.

During the hospital stay, there may be instruction on the simplest exercises such as circling one's ankles to improve circulation, pulling in the pelvic floor and toning up the stomach muscles.

After a caesarean birth, the physiotherapist will usually make extra visits to teach how to handle walking, getting out of bed, coughing and exercises to improve circulation and breathing. The immediate post-operative recovery is obviously different according to whether the anaesthetic was general or epidural, but in each case it is important to learn comfortable positions for sleeping and feeding the baby.

In many neighbourhoods, there are postnatal exercise groups and not only does this discipline one to actually do the exercises, but it is also an ideal opportunity to meet other new mothers. Working in a group helps to avoid exercises which can be damaging at this vulnerable stage, for example sit-ups with straight legs or cycling movements from a lying position, or other movements which may overstrain tendons and ligaments. Very often these groups teach body movement and massage for babies too.

A progressive programme of exercises, *Postnatal Exercises*[5] written by obstetric physiotherapists Margie Polden and Barbara Whiteford, sets out three phases of work-out: birth to six weeks when exercises should be gentle and not overtire the new mother; six weeks to three months when swimming can be added to the exercises; and three months to six months. However, the authors warn, 'Get advice before doing any strenuous exercise, particularly if there is a previous history of back problems'.

Most mothers in the weeks following birth may find that their days and nights are so full that they don't manage to get out to a regular exercise group. However, the authors point out, 'So much has to be done for the baby, but you need to do something positive for yourself'.

In addition to the benefit of exercise to those muscles which

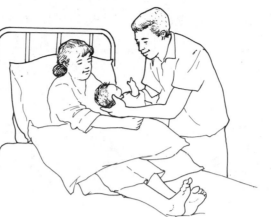

A pillow placed under your thighs will prevent you from slipping down the bed and another resting across your wound will help prevent too much pain as you feed your baby.

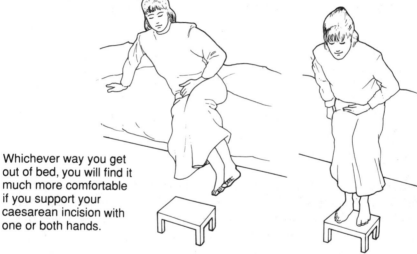

Whichever way you get out of bed, you will find it much more comfortable if you support your caesarean incision with one or both hands.

Figure 4. Post-caesarean mother (reproduced with permission from *Postnatal Exercises* by Margie Polden and Barbara Whiteford, published by Century, 1992)

have been involved in the long journey through pregnancy and birth, physical activity releases endorphins which add to one's sense of wellbeing.

The relaxation techniques taught during pregnancy are very important after the birth because they enable the body to function efficiently and recharge the energy resources.

Babies also enjoy touch and relaxation, so choose a time when both mother and baby are well fed, warm and comfortable, and do the exercises on a very wide bed or mattress or carpet where

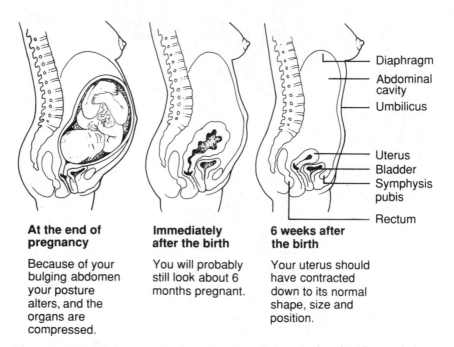

	— Diaphragm
	— Abdominal cavity
	— Umbilicus
	— Uterus
	— Bladder
	— Symphysis pubis
	— Rectum

At the end of pregnancy

Because of your bulging abdomen your posture alters, and the organs are compressed.

Immediately after the birth

You will probably still look about 6 months pregnant.

6 weeks after the birth

Your uterus should have contracted down to its normal shape, size and position.

Figure 5. The pelvic organs in the perinatal period (reproduced with permission from *Postnatal Exercises*)

there is no danger of the baby falling off. If the baby has just had a bath, massage his body so that he is already feeling relaxed. Better still, if the father is in the house, he can massage the mother after a bath so that she starts the exercise in a responsive frame of mind.

One of the easiest relaxation methods when time is precious is the Laura Mitchell reciprocal relaxation.[6] Working through the body, one checks all the tension points and simply does the opposite. For example, if shoulders are hunched, pull them down, if teeth are clenched, drop jaw. This should be done with deep breathing so that as all the tension points are relaxed, the body becomes heavy, warm and comfortable.

Margie Polden and Barbara Whiteford suggest another remedy for tension: sigh with relief even when everything is in chaos. This might be a good idea for all high-tension situations, when you are looking for the car keys or the baby is crying for food and the phone is ringing.

Very often, deep breathing or this sigh of relief actually helps one to think more clearly and work out the source of the chaos.

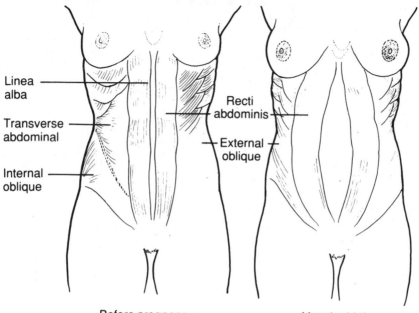

Figure 6. Changes in the abdominal muscles (reproduced with permission from *Postnatal Exercises*)

HEALTHY EATING DURING BREASTFEEDING

Although much of the weight gained in pregnancy goes with the baby, for example the amniotic fluid and placenta, it does take a few weeks to lose the fat reserve, particularly that which has concentrated round the thighs and buttocks.

By two months after the birth, much of the pregnancy weight has been lost, but breastfeeding women should be aware that there will still be extra fluid in the body which may account for another couple of kilos. And it will be to the detriment of the mother's health and her milk supply if she goes on a drastic diet. Breastfeeding women need 300–600 extra calories a day in their diet for breastfeeding but, as in pregnancy, these should be full calories. Junk food, especially caffeine, synthetic juices, fats and sugary foods, should be avoided.

In the book *Nutrition in Pregnancy and Lactation*[7] the recommendations on healthy eating while breastfeeding base this calorie estimate on the fact that 200–300 calories are provided a day from

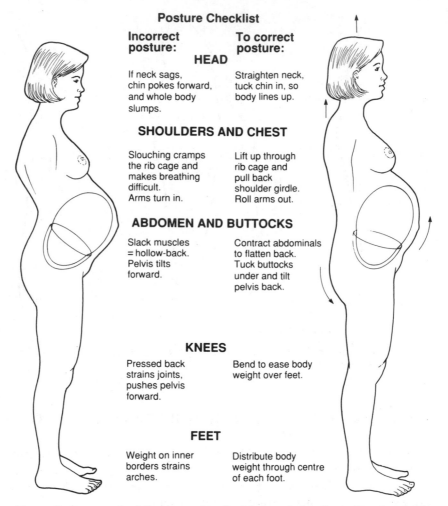

Posture Checklist

Incorrect posture:	To correct posture:

HEAD

If neck sags, chin pokes forward, and whole body slumps.	Straighten neck, tuck chin in, so body lines up.

SHOULDERS AND CHEST

Slouching cramps the rib cage and makes breathing difficult. Arms turn in.	Lift up through rib cage and pull back shoulder girdle. Roll arms out.

ABDOMEN AND BUTTOCKS

Slack muscles = hollow-back. Pelvis tilts forward.	Contract abdominals to flatten back. Tuck buttocks under and tilt pelvis back.

KNEES

Pressed back strains joints, pushes pelvis forward.	Bend to ease body weight over feet.

FEET

Weight on inner borders strains arches.	Distribute body weight through centre of each foot.

Figure 7. Posture checklist (reproduced with permission from *Exercises for the Childbearing Year* by Elizabeth Noble, published by John Murray, 1982)

the reserves of fat which were stored during pregnancy. The balance of 300–600 therefore has to be obtained in the diet. An additional daily twenty grams of protein is needed to cover the requirement for milk production together with an allowance of 70% efficiency of protein utilization. This extra need for energy and protein can be met by three extra cups a day of milk but this does not provide enough ascorbic acid, vitamin E and folic acid. It is therefore recommended that citrus fruits, vegetable oils and leafy green vegetables be increased in the diet.

Table 8. Recommended daily dietary allowances for lactation* (reproduced with permission from *Nutrition for Pregnancy and Lactation* by Bonnie Worthington-Roberts, published by C. V. Mosby, 1981)

	Age			
	11–14 years	15–18 years	19–22 years	23–50 years
Body size				
Weight (kg)	46	55	55	55
(lb)	101	120	120	120
Height (cm)	157	163	163	163
(in)	62	64	64	64
Nutrients				
Energy (kcal)	2700	2600	2600	2500
Protein (gm)	66	66	64	64
Vitamin A (RE†)	1200	1200	1200	1200
Vitamin D (μg)	15	15	12.5	10
Vitamin E activity (mg αTE)§	13	13	13	13
Ascorbic acid (mg)	90	100	100	100
Folacin (μg)	500	500	500	500
Niacin (mg‡)	20	19	19	1811
Riboflavin (mg)	1.8	1.8	1.8	1.7
Thiamine (mg)	1.6	1.6	1.6	1.5
Vitamin B_6 (mg)	2.3	2.5	2.5	2.5
Vitamin B_{12} (μg)	4.0	4.0	4.0	4.0
Calcium (mg)	1600	1600	1200	1200
Phosphorus (mg)	1600	1600	1200	1200
Iodine (μg)	200	200	200	200
Iron (mg)	1811	1811	1811	1811
Magnesium (mg)	450	450	450	450
Zinc (mg)	25	25	25	25

* Modified from Food and Nutrition Board, National Research Council, National Academy of Sciences: Recommended dietary allowances, ed. 9, Washington D.C., 1980, U.S. Government Printing Office.

† RE = Retinol equivalent.

‡ Although allowances are expressed as niacin, it is recognized that on the average, 1 mg of niacin is derived from each 60 mg of dietary tryptophan.

§ α-Tocopherol equivalents; 1 mg d-α-tocopherol = 1 αTE.

‖ Iron needs during lactation are not substantially different from those of non-pregnant women but continued supplementation of the mother for 2 to 3 months after parturition is advisable in order to replenish stores depleted by pregnancy.

Vegetarian women who nevertheless drink milk products can maintain the nutritional balance necessary during lactation. If dairy products are not eaten, this has to be compensated for with vegetables, nuts and grains which produce the necessary energy, while the calcium can be obtained from large quantities of leafy green vegetables.

Iron supplements are usually recommended for at least six

weeks after the birth, not because there is insufficient for lactation but because the reserve of iron is depleted during pregnancy and birth. The baby is born with a store of iron and there is after all a significant blood loss during the birth. When a mother is rushed for time, it is very difficult to plan meals and sometimes, when the hunger pangs start gnawing, it is easier just to spread jam on a roll. So it is a good idea to keep in stock more nutritious fillings of low fat cheese, tuna or sardines which, with a few slices of salad vegetables, will make that sandwich much more nutritious. When energy levels are low, there can be a craving for sweet things. Dried fruit and nuts can sometimes assuage that craving with food which is more healthy than a bar of chocolate. Desserts such as apple purée topped with a granola mixture, fresh fruit and yoghurt or baked apples stuffed with honey and raisins are much easier and more nutritious than heavy puddings and pastry dishes.

Many savoury dishes too can be made quickly, or prepared and frozen when there is time. Aubergine, for example, has a rich meaty taste if it is lightly fried with onions and seasoning, put through the food processor for a few seconds and served either hot or as a cold paté.

Fish grilled with mushrooms and tomatoes, jacket potatoes stuffed with cheese and mushrooms, baked beans and tomatoes on toast, all provide maximum nutrients and are quick to prepare. These dishes are healthier even if a little more time-consuming to cook than sausages and chips, both of which are over-rich in fat, while processed food such as manufactured sausages may contain harmful chemicals and food colouring.

Liquids too provide a source of nutrition. Herb tea, milk, natural fruit juices and an occasional black beer are preferable to coffee, tea, cola and synthetic soft drinks. The calcium in milk is more difficult to absorb if it is mixed with cocoa, so although it is very comforting on a cold evening to drink hot chocolate, one should be aware that it contains less calcium than a straight milk drink.

So it can be seen that with the appropriate support and information, it is possible to start out on the next phase of life with renewed energy, self-confidence and a healthy mental state.

9   *Looking Ahead*

ONE of the most overwhelming changes that a new mother experiences is that of identity and the paradox this presents.

On one hand, society exalts motherhood. From the Matriarchs onwards, every culture through history reveres the mother and even in modern society, most women believe that they are fulfilled by motherhood. So much so that the childless woman often suffers endless torments, not only because she herself may or may not yearn for a child, but because of the attitudes of the people around her.

Not so many years ago, even in the Western world, girls were discouraged from studying for a profession because it was assumed that whatever their brainpower, all would be submerged in the glorious roles of wife and mother. Today, when many women combine work and motherhood, these attitudes die hard and most working mothers still feel guilty if they have to leave their child when he is sick or during school holidays.

It is in those early months when most women do take time off to recover from the birth and give the maximum time to their babies that the changes can be quite overwhelming.

Looking back on this period of my life I recall that with four children born very close together, and living in a rural area, returning to work was a far-off vision. No babysitter could ever have coped with this. I must confess that it was enjoyable to set my own routine and not have to worry about organizing child-care. I really did enjoy participating in every stage of the children's development and being there when they needed me. Golden moments are imprinted on my memory: scrambling through

autumn forests with my four rosy-cheeked children, searching for
acorns, the leaves crunching beneath our feet; running along
windswept beaches trying to tire out the children and the dog;
smooth, sweet-smelling bodies after the evening bath; sharing
tea with the rabbits and the guinea pigs in the garden; the kisses
and cuddles. As they grew, there was a tremendous satisfaction
in taking them to plays, ballets, films and museums, the train
rides into town, browsing around the library, choosing books
together.

But I will never romanticize that time and forget what went
with it: the endless piles of nappies, the disturbed nights, scraping
plasticine off the walls and flour off the kitchen floor; the need to
provide continuous supplies of food, laundry and love; those
wailing afternoons when it was too wet to go outside and I
watched the clock turn so slowly towards bathtime and bed.

And my own utter exhaustion which left me fit for nothing but
bath and bed for myself by 9 pm every evening!

Somewhere along the line, a mother might find herself asking,
'Where am I going? What has happened to me as a woman – when
can I use my talents and skills again?'

In Chapter 6 I recommended making a list during pregnancy of
the activities enjoyed by the mother herself or the couple together.
If, after the birth, one refers to that list written optimistically
during pregnancy, the mother may find that she actually hasn't
gone out on her own or with friends, or even to get her hair cut.
An evening at the theatre with her husband or drinks with friends
at the pub seem a distant goal. It may be worth asking oneself: 'Do
I feel complete with this? How does my partner feel?'

SEPARATION

For many women there is no choice about returning to work.
There are women who cannot afford to stay at home even if they
want to, because the single salary of the partner is not sufficient for
the mortgage payments and other family expenses or because the
woman is the sole wage-earner and she has no partner to share in
the childcare.

A mother who has a very interesting job or fulfilling profession
and enjoys the social and intellectual interaction in her place of
work may view those months of domesticity as a prison sentence.
She in fact enjoys motherhood far more by combining it with her

job. The hours that she gives to her child, although more limited, are quality hours, richer and more relaxed.

Other women are amazed at their own capacity to spend hours with the baby without adult company, and are delighted to have a more flexible routine unrestricted by office hours. The walk in the park on a sunny day, cuddling up together in bed on a rainy afternoon, the quiet periods when the baby sleeps and one can actually read a book or write a letter or bake a cake. This is sometimes a period of tranquillity for mother and baby which discourages her from even considering returning to work.

Women can feel quite ambivalent about this because there are also the difficult days, colicky baby, bad weather, colds and coughs which keep mother and baby isolated in a small flat or house and then she feels that she is climbing the wall.

Every morning, thousands of mothers clock in to work in schools and factories, shops and offices, hospitals and universities. In every walk of life, women form a significant percentage of the work force.

Interestingly enough, Dr Martin Richards[1] points out that women's ability to return to work has an influence on the birth rate in countries where good childcare is available, such as Norway and Finland. At the same time in countries such as Spain, Italy and Greece, where traditionally families were large, the growing involvement of women in the work force and less developed public childcare has caused a downward trend in the birth rate.

Not every woman can start work secure in the knowledge that her children are safely occupied at school. Many have younger children and have to make complicated arrangements so that their babies and toddlers are cared for during those hours of work, and only too often there is a breakdown in the system.

When looking for the optimum time to begin separation from one's baby, it is worth studying the stages of child development during the first year.

Dr T. Berry Brazleton, an American paediatrician, developed a series of neonatal assessment tests to ascertain the stages of awareness and perception.[2]

From as little as ten to fourteen days old, the baby uses periods of alertness to relate to the parents and recognizes their faces and voices. Up to eight weeks is a period of nurturing, responding to stimulation. He communicates needs through body language and facial expression as well as crying. Parents can recognize attention span for talking and playing and know when to rest.

From ten weeks to four months, the infant can prolong interaction, produce smiles, gurgles, reach out for something offered.

By four months he learns about himself and his world. He will catch sight of his fingers and suddenly realize that this is part of himself. He learns signals and is distracted by outside stimulation.

By being available during those first months, the mother will establish the relationship. The strength of that relationship then makes it easier for the baby to separate from his mother later on. Of course it is vital that any childminder employed when the mother returns to work should care for the child in accordance with the parents' ideology and philosophy.

There are periods which are ideal or less than perfect for separation. Dr John Bowlby[3] advises against separation for the first two years. Dr Brazleton, however, perhaps taking a more realistic attitude, discusses coping with separation at an earlier age. He recommends as the optimum time seven to nine months when the baby has learned to relate to strangers and has achieved goals of sitting and crawling, or after eighteen months when he has weathered the ten to eighteen month peak of fear of separation and the unknown.

At this point, the childminder, or in some cases the staff of the daycare centre, becomes the new dimension in the family dynamic.

CHILDMINDING

For those who qualify for a daycare centre or who have a neighbour or friend who looks after a few babies in her home, this system can be more satisfactory because the mother does not have to worry each day if the babysitter will turn up.

Small babies do not relate to a peer group until they are over six months of age, but nevertheless a centre which is well equipped and heated, and open throughout the year for all the hours the parent is working should provide a social and warm environment for the baby. It is important to visit the centre frequently and watch the staff at work before making a commitment. If this is discouraged, it might be a warning sign that the centre is not run according to the child's interests.

Quite apart from the law which stipulates how many babies can be cared for in the available space and the ratio of staff to babies, there are many other variables which are important to the mother.

Will the staff cooperate and feed the baby your expressed milk, for example? When fruit juice is given, do they provide natural and healthy drinks or synthetic sweetened syrups? Is fruit available or are sweets and biscuits given freely to keep children quiet? Is there an outside area so that the baby can enjoy fresh air in good weather and later play with safe, well-maintained equipment?

Is there a flexible routine or does every baby have to eat, sleep and sit on the pot at fixed times? How well qualified are the staff? One does not need to have a doctorate in child psychology to be a loving and devoted caregiver but it is important that out-of-date and unsuitable theories are not imposed on your child. Is the staff permanent or are there frequent changes?

In all the research on child development, it is found that the child will not be harmed by separation provided that the childminder is permanent. Sudden changes of caregiver or environment can undermine the child's confidence and any inevitable transitions should be taken in easy stages. It has been established that from nine months to eighteen months is one of the most vulnerable times for change, but in fact for many small children this may be just the time that the mother returns to work and the baby is in the care of a new person in his life. At this age it is very difficult for a child to understand rational explanations and he can interpret change as rejection.

When we lived on a kibbutz, I worked in the babies' house and looked after a group of babies aged from three months. As in most kibbutzim today, the children spent only the working hours in the crèche and were brought in the morning at 7 am and picked up by their parents at 4 pm. Up to three months of age, the babies were at home with their mothers also during the daytime and were only brought to the central house when the mother needed guidance or supplies.

During that time, my mornings were lit up in particular by one little boy aged six months called Or, a very appropriate name because this is the Hebrew word for light. We established a beautiful relationship and Or's mother was very relieved that he was so pleased to see me each morning. He leaped from her arms into mine and she went to work knowing that he was happy. He was a very alert and affectionate little boy, and already at that age was outgoing and mischievous. Everyone adored him.

As I worked he followed me around, first crawling and then when he took his first steps, he staggered along the floor into my arms.

If I met Or and his family outside the babies' house, he immediately related to me. His perception was advanced for his age, because for him I existed even if we met at the pool or in the dining room.

When Or was fourteen months old, he and two other babies of that age were transferred to the playgroup. Amid celebrations with cakes and balloons the children were moved with their belongings to another building. I asked to move with them for a few days to help them adjust but the request was refused.

Or's mother reported that in fact he settled very well with her help and was enjoying the new house and the new toys. But whenever I met Or, he turned his head and would not look me in the eye. He was angry that *I* had abandoned *him*. At fourteen months of age he had experienced rejection and lost confidence in his caregiver.

Sometimes it is not possible to find a suitable daycare centre and the baby is looked after in his own home by a paid childminder. This can be a more vulnerable situation because there is no supervision or anyone to watch what is going on. It is worth working together with the childminder for the first couple of weeks and one can soon pick up vibrations which may be positive or otherwise.

Babies need more than feeding and having their nappies changed. The childminder who comes with a large bag of knitting may be suspected of dumping the child in a playpen for hours while she finishes her family's winter woollens. For the same reason it is worth doing a spot check occasionally, to see for example what she does when she takes the baby to the park. If the baby is still small, does she take routine precautions to make sure he is dressed appropriately and protected from the weather? If he is older, does she play with him in the sandbox or keep him strapped in the push-chair while she reads her book? In the house, does she keep him close at hand where she can see him all the time or, if he is older, does she put him in front of the television for all the hours she is there?

From birth, a child needs stimulation, conversation, kind words, familiar songs and stories, a walk in the park and lots of cuddling.

A child's development of language depends on the adults who look after him.

Ann returned to work when Benny was eight months old. She employed Sally, a middle-aged woman who had been recommended by friends, to look after Benny each morning.

Very soon, all Ann's fears were calmed as one after the other, all the neighbours reported on Sally's activities. Nobody could fail to notice Sally's walks with Benny. She started off by counting out loud all the steps to the street, then named every tree, every flower, the colours of cars, the shapes and sizes of every object in the street. In the playground, she sang songs, clapped hands and Benny's eyes were always wide open as he listened and participated. The delight with which he greeted Sally each morning proved that, for him, his childminder was a friend to be welcomed rather than a stranger who separated him from his mother.

These are obviously issues which need to be discussed in advance, together with the very basic principles of feeding and other routines. For example, if the parents do not believe in toilet training until the child is two years old, make sure that the childminder does not force the child to sit on the pot for long periods of time.

Sometimes the most devoted and reliable babysitter is a member of the family. While grandmothers get younger and are often at the peak of their own careers, some will take a year off to look after the baby so that the mother can go back to work.

Dr Richards' field work on working women showed surprisingly that contacts within kinship networks are greater than they used to be, helped by rising car ownership and telephones. A recent survey of childcare for preschool children showed that after the mother, the maternal grandmother was the most likely person to take care of the child, followed by the father.

In the USA where families have migrated greater distances or where there is a large immigrant population, this help may not be so easily available, but within the United Kingdom, many families still have an easily available grandparent. However, although the parents do not have to worry whether the baby is kept warm, fed and happy, there can also be conflicts of opinions about suitable foods, routines and other issues, and approaches to childcare which have changed over the years.

Time-sharing is another option. If it is possible to return to work on a part-time basis, childcare can be shared with another mother. This not only saves the expense of a childminder but each mother gets to know the other and the other's baby intimately so that it can soon be seen whether they share each other's principles of childcare.

There are also many jobs which can be shared and it might be worth suggesting to one's employer that two women work half-time each in a job which is usually for one full-timer. There are advantages to the employer, too, for this covers time off for sickness, holidays and other inevitable absences.

As babies grow into toddlerhood, a cooperative playgroup is feasible with a group of four to six babies, each mother taking her turn one day a week to take care of the children. To provide some sort of permanence for the child who is still vulnerable to change at that time, one room or a church hall with outdoor space should be used all the time, equipped with familiar toys and furniture.

While the end of the symbiotic period is very hard to accept, it is easier to put one's life together again if one is reassured that children are coping with whatever stage they are in.

While many parents dread the idea of the emptying nest, it is perhaps a consolation to know that children who have always had a deep, loving relationship with their families will return. The adolescent needs unlimited support and encouragement when studying for exams or applying for a job or university or coping with the first love affair. Even the married sons and daughters touch base as often as possible, to get some spoiling and home cooking.

After all, we are all dependent on interpersonal relationships; the child, the family and the outside world.

RETURNING TO WORK

We have considered the needs of the child when the mother returns to work, but she herself also experiences quite an upheaval in her life. She is coping with the demands of her job together with broken nights and the never-ending domestic chores as well as trying to spend quality time with her baby.

If the father gets home from work at a reasonable time, division of labour can be devised so that he shares in the cleaning and cooking, walking the baby and giving him his bath. But often, just at that stage of life, he is working extra hours to earn more, or studying for exams.

Gillian worked full-time to support her husband through his second degree at university. She was very efficient, working in a busy office where tactful contact with the public was as necessary as typing skills.

They were both overjoyed when their daughter was born, but Gillian was overwhelmed by fatigue when she returned to work.

At 6.30 am every day, she hastily fed and dressed the baby, ran along the road to leave her with the childminder, and caught two buses in order to be in her office by 9 o'clock.

In the winter, she felt very ambivalent about taking the baby out of the warm, dry house into the early morning frost and rain. Her boss, although a woman, was not very sympathetic if Gillian was late.

At the end of the day, she rushed home to collect the baby, bath her, feed her and try and compensate for the hours of separation. During the evening, the baby's crying disturbed her husband who was studying for his final examinations and who additionally was teaching private lessons for extra income.

When her husband finished his courses, he took some time off to look after the baby and the house, and Gillian began at last to enjoy her job. However, when he started working again, Gillian decided to stay at home until the child was old enough for nursery school.

'I resented splitting myself into little compartments,' said Gillian. 'I feel very vague sometimes and would rather concentrate on my baby right now.'

Where there is shared labour in the house, the hours with the child can be very precious. Adam and Mary are both doctors in a nearby hospital. They work long and irregular hours, and their six month old baby is looked after in the hospital crèche. Whoever finishes work first picks up the baby, goes home, tidies the house and starts the dinner. At whichever stage of this the partner gets home, he or she continues until they are finished and can sit down together, eat their meal and enjoy their baby. This pattern was established before the baby was born, when they were still students and there is no argument about any particular job being the task of only one partner.

In this way the child grows up knowing that making a family is a joint enterprise. If there are no clean shirts to wear or the refrigerator is empty, it is not just one person's responsibility after a long day's work to do the washing or go to the shops.

While the child's needs are very egocentric for the first two years, he soon learns by example and the behaviour of the adults around him that every individual has needs, and that his mother was not put on this earth solely to clean up after him.

When my second son, Daniel, was just three, one of the guinea pigs got stuck down a drainpipe. Daniel stood frowning, trying to work out how to release it. Seeing my concern, he said, 'Don't worry mummy, I'll sort it out,' and indeed since that time he has been sorting everything out with imagination and resourcefulness.

It is delightful to see children progress from the dependency of the symbiotic period to awareness, the withered bunch of flowers picked on the way home and saved for his mother, the undrinkable cup of tea, the grey gluey biscuits baked for his father.

Encouraged by the gratitude and appreciation for these gestures, he will advance until he is an indispensable and very essential part of the household, sharing the dishwashing and the rubbish disposal, so that all the family has more leisure time together.

CONTRACEPTION

While the size of family is not always one of choice, there is usually a time when a couple make a conscious decision on the number of children they would like to have in their family.

In Chapter 7, we discussed the effects of the lactation hormone prolactin on ovulation, but the truth is that if contraception is of vital importance at this stage of life, the inhibiting factors of prolactin are not always sufficient to prevent pregnancy.

Since women during the year after birth are in an unstable hormonal situation and do not usually want to use a contraceptive which will adversely affect breastfeeding or future fertility, the choices are not so wide as for woman who are not lactating.

Throughout the centuries, women have been aware of the influence of their biological cycles on fertility, and with the controversy surrounding the various mechanical and chemical contraceptives, many women are again seeking nature's remedies.

Theoretically, once menstruation has resumed, there is each month a 'safe period' between the end of the menstrual period and the few days prior to ovulation. Women can measure their temperature each day to find out just when ovulation is due and then avoid intercourse at that time and for the few days following, during which the ova can survive and be fertilized.

Another natural way of tuning in with one's fertile periods is the Billings method, which can be used together with BBT (checking basal body temperature).[4] The Billings method focuses on the changes in the cervical mucus at different stages in the menstrual cycle and the woman herself checks these changes simply by using a swab. Once she recognizes the cervical mucus at various stages in the month, she can avoid intercourse during the period around ovulation.

Until menstruation resumes, it is difficult for the postparturient woman to estimate her state of ovulation. And ovulation occurs before menstruation so in theory she could become pregnant again and believe that her periods have not started again because of breastfeeding, when in fact she did ovulate and conceive. This is unlikely but does occur, particularly in women who have a very irregular menstrual cycle.

Up to the six week postnatal check-up it is not possible to use a diaphragm, cervical cap or intrauterine device (IUD) because the cervix may not have completely closed, the uterus is still englarged and the vagina may still be stretched. The condom, which has become more popular in recent years, mainly as a safeguard against AIDS and other sexually transmitted diseases, is the only device which can be used at that time.

After that period, the barrier methods can be reconsidered and if the couple were satisfied with whichever method they used before the previous pregnancy, this can be continued. However, it is essential that diaphragms and caps be fitted correctly and it is most likely that a different size will be needed after childbirth.

The IUD is not recommended during the lactation period because the hormonal changes during breastfeeding cause a thinning out of the uterine wall which could increase the existing risks of perforation by the IUD.

Some women cannot tolerate the IUD at any time because it can cause heavy periods and uterine contractions.

The first IUD was made of silkworm gut and invented by a German doctor, Richter. Nowadays they are usually made of plastic. A copper loop which released hormones was very popular in the 1970s but has since been taken off the market because of the hazards of the copper and hormone secretions.

Although it is considered 94% reliable, the modern IUD can also cause anaemia because of the heavy periods, inflammation and infection. Even with the newest innovations, the IUD is still associated with ectopic pregnancies (in the Fallopian tube), and if a pregnancy does occur it can cause abortion, premature birth, heavy bleeding throughout the pregnancy and separated placenta.

The most effective but invasive method is the contraceptive pill. Each year, there is new information about its effects on women of all ages or on pregnancies conceived while using it, and it is strongly recommended that its use is stopped at least six months before starting the next pregnancy.

This is not only because of its hormonal effect but also because of the effect on the woman's nutritional balance. Drs Barbara and Gideon Seaman[5] make it clear in their work that not one organ or tissue in the body remains unchanged during the use of birth control hormones. Although there have been many improvements in the combinations of hormones since they wrote about this in 1981, there nevertheless does exist an increased risk of circulatory diseases, high blood pressure, liver and breast diseases together with fluid retention, hair loss, oedema and depression.

The nutritional balance is affected because the absorption of vitamin B_6, folic acid, vitamin C, zinc, magnesium and vitamin E is reduced by the high-oestrogen pill.

New research and development is carried out continuously on hormone therapies, but one has to remember that very often it is only time – and human use – which determines whether a medication is safe and effective, or disastrous.

The politics of drug companies are determined by financial profits and it is amazing that very often trials of new chemicals are conducted by laboratories which are funded by the drug companies.

At the end of the 1950s, thalidomide was developed to ease pregnancy nausea and sleeplessness. At that time, medication was given quite freely to pregnant women in the naive belief that the placenta was a 'barrier' which did not allow *most* chemicals to cross into the baby's bloodstream.

Thalidomide was prescribed in Europe for two or three years until it was linked with multiple limb defects in the newborn babies and was withdrawn from the market. The impact was immediate but the tragedy remains for those children and their families.

In the USA, an alert sales executive in one of the major drug companies which planned to import thalidomide was not happy with the results of the trials. Despite tremendous pressure from her colleagues who wanted to market this drug which was so much in demand for the alleviation of pregnancy discomforts, she managed to persuade her Board to delay its release. How right she was and this saved millions of American babies from the disaster.

Not all dangerous drugs have been detected so quickly because the defects resulting from their use are not always seen immediately after the birth. In the 1940s a synthetic compound called diethylstilboestrol (DES) was developed to prevent miscarriages in the early months of pregnancy. Since it seemed to be effective in some cases for high-risk women, many doctors prescribed it routinely for every minor problem. It took till the mid-1960s to link DES with a genital cancer which was affecting adolescent girls, a disease which is very rare in young women. It was then found that the daughters of the women who had received DES in those pregnancies had a far greater risk of this type of cancer. It also affected boys, although to a lesser extent. But it took till 1971 and the Herbst Report[6] to ban DES, and to this day, these DES daughters receive regular screening in order to detect any early changes in the genital tract.

As the DES daughters reached childbearing age, further complications were linked with the drug, as it was found that in some of them, the uterus was T-shaped, causing miscarriages and premature births.

Charles Dodds, who had himself pioneered the first synthetic pill in 1938,[7] became alarmed as the hormone contraceptive became more popular in the 1960s, and he rang the warning bell about hormone therapies. 'Women who have continuous treatment with hormone contraceptives have an entirely different hormonal background due to inhibition of the pituitary gland.'[8]

It is unknown what effects these hormones will have on the baby during breastfeeding, and a 'mini-pill' or progesterone-only pill was developed which reduces the risk but is less reliable as a contraceptive.

A recent development is the progesterone vaginal ring (PVR) which is placed in the cervix via the vagina. Results of studies done by Drs S. Diaz and H. Croxatto of Chile show that this is as effective as the IUD without its risks.

Reports of this research in the *International Planned Parenthood Bulletin*[9] state:

> Rings delivering 5–15 mg daily of progesterone were tested and it was found that the effectiveness was similar to that of copper IUDs. In addition the PVR significantly prolonged the length of lactational amenorrhoea.
>
> Comparing the PVR with the copper IUD, there was no significant difference in the duration of lactation, nor was there any difference in the weight of infants or the average monthly weight increase.
>
> Since the circulating progesterone levels that cause these effects are around 15 mmol/l, within the lower half of normal luteal phase values, a baby taking 600 ml of breast milk would ingest between 1.8 and 3 micrograms of progesterone per day, which represents less than 1% of the child's endogenous production.

Table 9. Contraceptive efficacy of progesterone vaginal ring in nursing women

	Progesterone ring	Copper-T IUD	Untreated
Women	484	531	236
Woman-months*	3166	3829	1552
Pregnancies	2	3	50

* Treatments were given at day 65 postpartum. The end of the study was at months fourteen and twelve after the birth in treated and untreated women respectively.

Many couples favour the IUD and pill because they do not spoil the spontaneity of sexual relations. However, the diaphragm too can be used successfully without last-minute scrambling to the bathroom. Its use can be as routine as brushing one's teeth and its reliability was found to be 98% in a two year study by the Margaret Sanger Research Bureau.[10]

The reliability depended on its correct fitting, waiting the specified time period before its removal, and the use of the correct spermicide jelly. This last item is also under fire because there is a suggestion that if the spermicide does not actually destroy the sperm and a pregnancy occurs, it may cause damage and resultant birth defects.

No wonder that so many women are going back to nature. However, it is certainly worth obtaining the most up-to-date information from the local Family Planning clinic or the family doctor.

SPACING PREGNANCIES

In some religions, active birth control is forbidden and it can be a problem for some women if they are at the peak of fertility and produce a baby each year or two. Their bodies do not have a chance to return to their normal nutritional and hormonal state and much as these babies are traditionally welcomed, this continual state of pregnancy does take a toll on the mother.

For most families there are, however, many choices available and it is sometimes difficult for a couple to decide on child spacing.

There are distinct advantages to having one's family close together and one often sees large happy families where it is difficult to tell which is the oldest and which the youngest. In some large families, the older children are often very helpful and supportive, but in others there is resentment from the siblings that the little ones need so much time and attention.

Cynthia was training to be a childbirth educator and she called me up to book a tutorial. She said that she and her family were visiting in the area and would I mind if they all came too.

When I opened the door to greet Cynthia, she and her husband Brian both held babies in arms. And then my eyes seemed to work in steps as I faced the eldest aged fourteen who was my height and then counted seven down to the three year old toddler. Each child was equipped with a little bag containing an apple and a drink and while the bigger ones kept an eye on the toddlers and babies, Cynthia, Brian and I chatted over a cup of coffee.

When last seen, Cynthia was pregnant again and also helping her eldest daughter with the first grandchild.

Many couples feel that they can only cope if they space out the births so that they can give individual time and attention to each child for a number of years.

From the viewpoint of the woman's physical health, a two year gap is sufficient to replace any nutritional deficiencies following birth and breastfeeding.

REACTIONS OF SIBLINGS

From the child's point of view, any time that the next child is born is a difficult period for him as he ascends a rung on the family dynasty.

Preparing the siblings during pregnancy can be done through pictures, books or films. Even very young children become aware of their mother's body changes and feel very insecure. Graham became very constipated just before the birth of his baby brother. 'I have a baby in my tummy and he is trying to come out,' he vocalized his fantasies. He was obviously holding back because he was not sure if he really wanted that new baby in the family.

There are obvious steps to take to make things easier for the older child, such as making sure that the first time he sees the baby, the infant is in a pram or cot and not in the mother's arms.

Also, if the father can take time off work for a few days to concentrate on the older child, it will give the mother time to settle down with the baby.

The benefit of breastfeeding is that there is always a free hand to cuddle the older child, turn over the pages of a book, hand him a drink. The sibling will usually want to suck at the breast and he should be allowed to do so. He will probably discover that the milk is not now to his taste, but if he does enjoy it, there is no harm in him joining the baby at feed times.

A reserve of presents is a good idea because some guests will come with a present for the baby or mother, forgetting that the older child is much more appreciative of gifts.

We bought a train set for the two older boys when our third baby was born and this kept them happy for hours. When our fourth child was born, I had been kept on bedrest for some time and my husband hastily rushed out and bought some bath toys for the three boys. 'We only got rubber ducks to compensate for her,' my sons, now in their twenties, still chide me, usually in front of their sister who fortunately knows her worth.

The help that siblings can give depends very much on their age. The problem is that the older and more useful they are, the less likely it is that they will want to help! But the smaller children will take great delight in emptying the bathwater, usually while the baby is still in it, pouring out quantities of baby oil and feeding the baby with their own favourite snacks.

Where there are pets in the house, children will already have learned gentleness and responsibility, but if this is their first exposure to creatures tinier than themselves, they have to be taught that babies are rather fragile at the beginning.

Appealing to the older child's maturity is one way of helping him adjust to his new role in the family. While the father or grandparent is looking after the baby between feeds, the mother can take the older child to a film or the library, or to the shops to choose his own new coat. If he sees some of his old equipment and clothes being sorted out for the baby, he will be perhaps partly compensated if he is taken out to buy new things of his choice.

As the older child's interests develop, the father too can take him out, perhaps with another father and child to some activity that only the big guys do.

Changes such as moving him to a bigger bed or enrolling at a new playgroup should be done well before the birth or long after, so that he does not associate the change with being ousted by the baby.

Very often, siblings will be very responsible and positive, but show strange signs that they are not quite as accepting as they appear. The terrible two, Jonathan and Daniel, were aged three and two when their little brother was born. A few weeks before the birth, one cold rainy day, I asked them to help me sort out the baby clothes. They very helpfully piled up the nappies in one place and the little suits and overalls in another, while enthusing over the tiny boots and mittens. They could not believe that they had once been small enough to fit into these tiny garments. I smiled at their cooperation and left them to continue their job while I went downstairs to make the soup for lunch.

I happened to glance out of the kitchen window onto the rain-swept muddy garden, and was rather puzzled to see small white objects floating down from the sky. I ran upstairs and there were the two little boys, standing on a chair, throwing all the baby's garments out between the bars of the window, one by one, chanting: 'Baby's boots. Baby's pants. Baby's vests'.

A child sometimes makes no pretence of liking his new sibling, but at the end of the day, will protect her against all dangers.

When I came home with our fourth child from hospital, Anthony our third son was very puzzled and angry. I had gone into hospital unexpectedly, having planned to give birth at home, and there was no time to arrange reliable home help who was familiar to the children. Anthony at that time was fifteen months old and could not understand the upheaval in his life.

When I returned from hospital, he was asleep in his cot. He awoke and clung to me, whimpering. He refused to give the baby a name and insisted on calling her 'girl' for nearly a year.

When Sara was almost a year old, somebody unlocked our front gate and left it opened. Sara crawled out of the garden into the road and it was only when Anthony rushed in, pulling at my skirt, crying, 'Girl – road, girl – road,' that I realized what was happening.

He wasn't prepared to call her by name but he was prepared to save her life.

It often happens that children fight amongst themselves, but when faced by outside danger or animosity, they stand united.

Mary at two and a half had a vocabulary of a five year old, but her intellectual capacity could not handle the arrival of a baby brother, especially as he was premature and needed extra care and attention. She regressed to infantile behaviour, bedwetting, thumbsucking, bottles and nappies.

One night her little brother was rushed to hospital with a respiratory infection. After an anxious period, he recovered and returned home. From that day on, Mary accepted him happily and all the regressive symptoms ceased.

Many children fantasize that the baby will disappear. But when this happened in reality, Mary was not so happy as she thought she would be and empathized with her parents' alarm and sadness caused by her brother's illness.

Some children, on the other hand, really would like more brothers and sisters.

The birth of babies, kittens, guinea pigs, rabbits and dogs was a matter of routine in Margaret's family. There were five children but it was difficult to keep count of the other species. When Margaret told her second son, Jon, that the next door neighbour was having a new baby, he looked up from his game and said, 'Oh good, will she give us the old one then?'

Life becomes somewhat complicated when there are already other children in the family. On the one hand, the parents have much more self-confidence and their home is already equipped and organized for children. Perhaps for this reason, the younger sibling is often more relaxed and easier to cope with. The more children in the family, the more social is the environment and the adjustment of each child becomes easier. These younger babies enjoy the noise and activity going on around them and take everything in their stride.

But it does take a lot of ingenuity to organize a working day so that the mother gets enough time and space to store enough energy to provide the family with all their needs and at the same time retain her identity.

10 ❧ Mourning for the Special Baby

IF conflicts of identity and self-image are experienced by a healthy mother after a normal birth, how much more intense is the emotional upheaval after the birth of a premature baby or sick child – or even worse, after the death of a baby during pregnancy, birth or in the neonatal period.

Sometimes there are signs during pregnancy that something is wrong but although there is time to prepare, the ultimate shock is one for which nobody can be ready. Sometimes the woman is hospitalized during pregnancy, experiencing the anxieties and isolation of an antenatal ward. There is a sort of sorority in these situations so that the woman is not only stressed by her own pregnancy problems but takes to heart the complications of all her ward companions.

In some cases, there is absolutely no warning. The premature rupture of the amniotic fluid or onset of contractions may be totally unexpected, and suddenly the pregnancy is ended; the baby may be kept alive by intravenous infusions and tubes and such highly sophisticated technology that one realizes what a miracle incubator the woman's body is.

When a baby is in neonatal intensive care, there is understandably a conflict of emotions: the need to be with the baby, to express milk, to give him the best nourishment, to touch and to pray. But there can be a withdrawal, a rejection, because of fear that the baby may die or that his development may not be normal.

This is even more traumatic if the baby is deformed. There are decisions to be made. Do the parents' ideas about methods of care and quality of survival conflict with the medical caregivers? If the baby survives, what is the seriousness of the defect? Can one care

187

for the child at home or must one endure the agony of separation in an institution?

In these circumstances there is an extended time of grieving and the parents need all the resources available to help each other and themselves.

MISCARRIAGE

The ultimate grief is that of a stillbirth or miscarriage. It is a mistake to imagine that a pregnancy which ends in the first months is not mourned. There may have been fertility problems or a history of recurring miscarriage which made this a very precious pregnancy. A miscarriage at any time is an intense grieving experience which involves both parents in sadness, guilt and loss.

Most women in this situation eventually arrive at a hospital, either because the miscarriage is threatening and an ultrasound is needed to ascertain whether the foetus is alive, or because the foetus has already died and the woman is advised to have a dilation and curettage (D and C) under anaesthetic. There is some controversy over whether women should routinely have a D and C after a spontaneous abortion. On the one hand, the uterus must be free of placental or other matter in order to avoid infection, but there is some evidence that the D and C itself can cause lesions in the uterus which can cause problems in the next pregnancy. Exactly the same reasoning applies against elective abortions because however professionally done, it can endanger future pregnancies.

Whatever the reason why the woman is hospitalized, she is usually treated in the gynaecological ward and not in the maternity unit, and she is therefore related to as a 'surgical case' rather than a woman who is experiencing profound and devastating loss. Even the terminology used to describe the medical treatment after miscarriage depersonifies the baby as 'contents of the uterus' or 'foetal or placental matter'.

The woman in mourning may even share a room with women who elected to abort and there may be bitterness and guilt shared between them.

In some hospitals, women who have suffered miscarriages or stillbirth spend their recovery time in the maternity ward and this can cause raw agony. The sound of crying babies reminds one constantly of the loss, and the atmosphere in general is one of joy and celebration. Indeed, a staff member may even be unaware of what has happened and offer congratulations.

Betty was in hospital after a third miscarriage and seven years of childless marriage. 'When I started feeling cramps and bleeding at ten weeks, my doctor referred me to the hospital to see whether the baby had died or whether there was a chance that the pregnancy could be saved. I was left lying around in corridors feeling cold and isolated. My husband couldn't get any information from anyone. Eventually, the ultrasound was done and they told me that the baby had stopped developing two weeks ago and that there was no sign of life. They prepared me for the abortion saying, "You know that 10% of pregnancies end in abortion in the first twelve weeks; you'll have another baby."

'Nobody related to the fact that we had had three miscarriages and fertility problems. It was as if we should just forget that this was a baby.'

Eileen was newly married and had been starry-eyed about her pregnancy. It conformed with her image of femininity together with her neat new house and jars of pickles neatly stacked in the larder.

'We both felt that a baby would complete the home, we felt so happy. Then I fell while putting up the curtains, felt these awful cramps and went to rest. When the bleeding started, I went to hospital and everything just went wrong. After the miscarriage I was in a room with two women who had had elective abortions. It was so uncomfortable. I was feeling guilty about causing the miscarriage – I should have waited for Tom to come home and do the curtains – and I so resented these two women. They probably had very good reasons for their abortions but I couldn't look them in the eye. Looking back they must have hated me for being so self-righteous.'

The questions asked after a miscarriage are: why did it happen? was it my fault? will it happen again? how long should I wait before starting another pregnancy? It is important to ask these questions while still in hospital or make an appointment with a sympathetic GP who has access to the hospital records.

Even the health system personnel can be insensitive about the extent of grieving. Marion is a social worker and had spent much of her professional life working in a neonatal unit, and was therefore attuned to the needs of parents under stress. When her first pregnancy ended with a miscarriage, she was very depressed because her husband had a diagnosed low sperm count and their hopes of parenthood were already at risk.

After discharge from hospital, she went to her health centre for a note to stay away from work for a few days and the nurse said briskly, 'Better to get back to work, dear, and forget all about it, pull yourself together'.

'I don't want to forget all about it,' said Marion. 'I need time to grieve and adjust.'

STILLBIRTH

Stillbirth is the most shattering of experiences because very often the pregnancy has progressed quite normally; the woman has felt well, and possibly problems only arose during labour or a short while before, when foetal movements were not felt.

It is a violent cut-off and contradiction of expectations. And parents are not always given the opportunity to express their grief or work through the bereavement.

In some religions, there are rituals which give expression to mourning such as a formal funeral, a grave, a focal point. The Irish wake is vividly described in fiction and films. The custom of gathering all the relatives and friends together, singing songs and telling stories about the dear departed is therapeutic for the mourners.

Western culture eschews expressions of emotion and the hospital ward is not always the place to cry and grieve. 'Cheer up, dear, you're still young, you'll have other babies,' may be well meant but is no comfort to parents who are mourning this baby.

It is interesting to observe other cultures and how they handle their grief. One morning after I finished taking an antenatal group on a tour of the maternity ward, I heard the sound of heart-breaking wailing. An Arab woman, admitted with pregnancy problems, had just been given an ultrasound examination and told that her baby was dead. She was joined by her husband and the entire family, including her married children. Together they wept and there was no suggestion that because this was baby number eight, the grief was diminished. No doubt when she returned home to her village, the entire community would join them in their mourning.

The British personality which suffers only inwardly can have particular problems with grieving.

Some cultures are very vocal in their grief and others have

extensive mourning rituals to carry them through the stages of bereavement.

In the Jewish religion, ritual mourning follows the normal phases of shock, denial, anger, depression and acceptance. The funeral takes place as soon as possible, followed by seven days of *shiva* when the bereaved sit at home receiving visitors and reciting the Kaddish, the mourners' special prayer.

At one month, the men usually resume shaving and the mourners take up their social life, still reciting the Kaddish every morning and afternoon. Many refrain from attending celebrations or musical events until the year of mourning is at an end. Each year, on the anniversary of the death, a memorial candle is lit and burns for twenty-four hours. Synagogue services on even the most joyous of festivals include the memorial prayer. This sequence of rituals is logical in the context of the stages of mourning.

Maybe because stillbirth and neonatal death were much more common in Talmudic times, the rabbis exempted the relatives of a baby who died within twenty-eight days of birth from these rituals. Until not so long ago, the prognosis for premature babies was poor. Therefore the twenty-eighth day was considered the point at which the newborn, if he survived until then, had gained a more permanent place in life.

In these days, when such tragedies are much rarer, the parents often do feel the lack of a focal point if they do not have mourning rituals to stabilize and limit the period of grief. People do not know whether to visit; the family do not know where the baby is buried.

Also, because the expectations of a normal birth are so much higher today, parents can indulge in the fantasies and anticipation of life with the new baby. And indeed they do weave a tapestry of their unborn child, are aware of movements and uterine habits and relate them to his personality. They dream of massaging his little limbs after a quiet warm bath, singing lullabies, and later, walking with him in the forest and of swimming with him in the sea on a summer day.

Death shatters these dreams and the parents need a mourning period to adjust.

Parents can request a formal burial and there are prayers which are recited in these circumstances, but there is a lack of obligation to ritual and timing.

Miriam and Jacob now have a beautiful healthy family, but they will never forget their first pregnancy which ended in foetal death. Miriam's pregnancy had progressed normally, contrary to expectations; Miriam is a DES daughter, and one of the possible complications for these women is that the shape of the uterus is deformed, leading to difficulties in conceiving and premature birth.

Miriam's pregnancy had already reached the end of the eighth month and she and Jacob were beginning to hope that she was not one of the DES statistics. But one day she noted quite suddenly that the foetal movements had ceased, and she went to the hospital where their fears were confirmed. There was no sign of life and it was suggested that labour be induced.

Miriam's first reaction was that she wanted a full anaesthetic or a caesarean so that she would not need to endure needless pain. Eventually she understood the logic that it would be a pity to go through the risks and post-operative discomfort of a caesarean when in this case it was not being performed to save the baby.

It seems cruel to expect a woman to go through hours of labour, knowing that at the end of it there will not be a baby to make it worthwhile. But studies have shown that where women have been anaesthetized during a stillbirth, they could not believe afterwards that it had happened. They fantasized that the baby was not yet born, or that it was a mistake and that the baby was around somewhere.

Eventually, Miriam went into labour and although she received enough medication to reduce the pain, she and Jacob coped together and were ready to face reality.

Because of their belief, they did find some comfort in the rituals as they exist. 'There are special laws for parents to observe,' said Miriam.

'We requested a proper burial and that did ease our grief,' said Jacob. 'I think a full *shiva* would have been too much of a strain during Miriam's recovery period. I went to the synagogue to pray and we felt that the burial, the *niddah*, the period of ritual purity, and the *mikvah*, the ritual bath, were part of the *tumah* and *tahara* – death and resurrection process.'

'We accepted the death of our baby – it was God's will, and we felt positive about trying again but we did need an outlet for our grief,' concluded Miriam.

In 'A letter to bereaved parents'[1] couples are offered guidelines in handling their mourning experience:

> The grief experienced at this time is no less intense than that at the death of a beloved relative or friend whom you have known for many years.

People who have not lost a baby mistakenly say that as you haven't yet had time to know your baby, you will soon get over it.

Give yourselves time. Of course you knew this baby . . . Apart from the loss of the baby, there is another form of loss – of expectations, changes in life style. Your home already reflects those expectations and one of the hardest things to face is the empty house, maybe a room painted and prepared.

Where possible, the couple should be together for a few days after leaving hospital. If the bereaved mother is alone all day in the house during her own recovery period while her husband goes back to work, they may both feel depressed and lonely.

Whether or not there are other children in the family, whether or not the mother is young and healthy and able to have more children, the grief is for this lost baby.

Of course there is added pain for the couple who are older or have a history of fertility problems. I will never forget the tears of one of my clients, a woman of forty-one who after a history of miscarriages carried this last pregnancy optimistically through to the last month, when the placenta suddenly ceased to function and the baby died in the very first stage of labour. 'I did want to be a Mom,' she wept.

The mother who loses a baby at birth or during the neonatal period experiences all the physical discomforts of perhaps episiotomy, or even caesarean scar, contracting uterus and heavy, leaking breasts. It is no wonder that this is a very intense period, and the stages of mourning cannot be hurried along.

Without rituals, some couples feel very isolated in their grief. Susan and Robert have never felt the need to be affiliated to any church or centre of religion and indeed their parents too had grown away from any religious framework. They were young and healthy and optimistic and the birth of the baby seemed very remote to them until they went on a tour of the hospital and saw the babies in the nursery. Their eyes lit up and they looked at each other with new realization that there was actually a baby on the way.

The stillbirth was totally unexpected, one of those inexplicable cases of foetal death during labour. There was no time or opportunity to prepare for it and the ensuing stages of mourning were painful in the extreme.

The labour itself had been fast and comparatively easy. Susan was attended by a very sensitive midwife. 'She cried with me,' she said.

'The first two hours after the birth were the worst,' said Robert. 'Susan was waiting to be taken out of the labour room and it was so painful to hear other births and babies crying.'

In those two hours, Susan couldn't stop talking. 'She talked nonsense,' said Robert, '. . . no more babies . . . no more studying . . . what's the point of it all?' Anger is indeed a very active stage of mourning. Two days later, she was in the denial stage. 'I'll have more babies, it's not so terrible,' she said.

Homecoming was hell. The empty house, the absence of ritual, the subsequent stages of guilt, agony and loss. The family and close friends visited but the situation was unreal.

'Nobody knew what to say to us,' said Susan. 'People stopped us in the street to congratulate us and could not handle it when we told them what had happened. Others who knew crossed the street rather than cope with it.'

The most poignant experience which started them on the road to recovery was when one of the couples in the antenatal group came to visit with their baby.

They had telephoned condolences and asked if they could visit. The mother asked Susan if she would like to hold the baby. 'I was so angry at first,' said Susan. 'Then I realized that they were saying to me, accept it, there are babies in the world and you will have yours one day.

'I was so grateful that they came and it acknowledged that we were still part of their group and not ostracized because we had "failed".'

Robert felt very insecure after this experience, however, and the couple moved closer to his parents so that in a future pregnancy, 'they can look after her'.

Mothering cannot be turned off like a tap and for most there is real pain felt in the empty arms. At a midwives' seminar on grief in childbirth,[2] bereavement counsellor Rev Stewart explained, 'The hormones of lactation and mothering are flooding the body, in preparation for the demands of a newborn baby.

'When there is no baby, the process cannot be halted suddenly and those hormones go awry.'

Sherokee Ilse, who wrote *Empty Arms*,[3] discusses the value of keeping mementos such as photographs, crib cards, a lock of hair and of giving the baby a name.

Julia's anger in the first impact after stillbirth was directed at her antenatal nurse and her course teacher. 'Why didn't you tell me that this could happen?'

In fact, every nurse and childbirth educator who does her job properly raises the body awareness of the pregnant woman and teaches her to relate to foetal movement. The woman should go for a check-up if she feels any significant change, whether the movements are much stronger or weaker, as well as if they stop for any significant period of time.

However, everyone who looks after pregnant women tries not to instil fear and panic and although all the danger signs of pregnancy are outlined, they are not over-emphasized.

'If I had thought about it more,' said Julia, 'I think I would have noticed that the movements were getting weaker and gone to the hospital sooner.'

Her husband Joe did not agree. 'If every lesson of the course had been taken up with warnings of doom, I would not have gone back. I think it was clear that we should relate to danger signs without over-emphasis on this.'

'In my next pregnancy, I shall run to the hospital every time I hiccup,' Julia sighed.

Julia and Joe decided to start the next pregnancy as soon as possible, and within two months, a twin pregnancy was diagnosed. 'This was the best thing for us,' said Julia who, contrary to her expectations, is feeling calm and optimistic. She attends the high-risk clinic at the hospital, is receiving good care, and calls the same antenatal teacher to ask questions and receive encouragement.

The interval between the loss of a baby and the next pregnancy is not always a matter of choice, but parents and health professionals differ greatly in their opinions. While psychologists advise that there is a need to complete grieving for the child who cannot be replaced, others feel that the next pregnancy is a step forward and takes away the emptiness and futility of what had happened.

Whether parents decide to wait or to start a pregnancy as soon as possible, there is obviously a high state of tension and anxiety. If there has been a previous premature birth or early pregnancy complication, that stage of pregnancy is the milestone and after that the couple may relax. But where the birth was at full term, there is no release until a healthy baby is born.

Avril and Rupert had experienced a traumatic pregnancy because at thirty weeks the ultrasound detected a heart defect. It was not clear how serious it was and although there was some discussion about terminating the pregnancy, it was concluded that this was too drastic a procedure. There was no way of knowing if the baby was viable, in which case prematurity would be added to the list of problems.

Avril and Rupert had to wait another ten weeks until labour started spontaneously. The baby's heart was indeed seriously deformed and he died within a few days. During those days, when it was obvious that nothing could be done, Avril kept the baby with her in the hospital room. It gave the couple an opportunity to know him and to say goodbye.

The next pregnancy was fraught with anxiety, although tests had shown that the previous tragedy was not caused by a genetic or recurring defect. Avril reported to the hospital with every slightest change, and only began to relax when all the tests of late pregnancy were normal. 'I shan't rejoice until that baby is in my arms,' she said, and for them the pregnancy was certainly not one of optimism and anticipation.

However, when I saw her in the shopping mall several months later, happily wheeling a pram with a healthy smiling baby, it was obvious that at last she had allowed herself to rejoice.

Stages of grief are very individual, although they generally follow recognized patterns. Sometimes circumstances change reactions, but at some point the truth dawns and the parents realize that they have lost a child.

Our own fifth baby was born prematurely, and died one day later. The entire pregnancy had been problematic and I had spent many weeks in hospital. However, my fears for the baby were outweighed by anxiety for my four small children and for my husband who was having to handle the situation at home.

When the labour started prematurely and the baby was born, I denied the fact that this baby was unlikely to survive. Instead I even felt relieved that it was all over and I could go home to the business of being a mother and make up to the children for that long separation. This was in those dismal days when British hospitals did not allow children to visit and I only saw them for one hour twice a week over a period of seven weeks!

Within a few hours of the birth, I felt my physical strength returning and I went to sit by the incubator and get to know my baby. I was at that point cheerful and optimistic, still denying that this baby had almost no chance of survival.

The sympathy and support from the hospital staff was touching. The nurses and doctors who had looked after me during those anxious weeks were also mourning. A nurse whom I had disliked because she had left me sitting on a bedpan for half an hour came and spoke to me caringly and quietly. The strict visiting hours were waived so that the children could come into the nursery and see the baby.

When she died, we accepted it and felt that everything possible had been done. We will never forget the loving and devoted care given to the baby and I saw for myself that everything was done to try and save her.

I only realized the finality after I came home and my milk started to flow. Lactation starts at the twenty-fourth week of pregnancy, so mothers who lose even severely premature babies have to handle this discomfort and distress. So, four days after the birth, I sat in the bath watching the milk dripping from engorged and painful breasts, and with the milk finally flowed the tears.

THE SICK OR DEFORMED BABY

If stillbirth or neonatal death is intense in its finality how totally contrary to expectations is the birth of a sick or deformed child.

Most parents do worry about this during even the most normal pregnancy, but in Naomi's case, she really gave it little thought. She felt healthy throughout her pregnancy and she and her husband Wolf were very positive and happy. They were secure in their relationship and lifestyle even though their backgrounds were very different. Naomi was born in Australia, and Wolf and his family had left Russia through the first chink in the Iron Curtain.

The labour was very easy and together they anticipated the ecstatic moment of birth. But the midwife's face, the silence in the room, and the hasty summoning of the paediatrician stunned their elation. The baby was severely deformed with multiple external and internal defects.

'We realized immediately the seriousness of the deformities,' said Wolf. 'We were shown the baby and the situation was explained very clearly.'

The midwife told Naomi that since the baby would probably not survive, it would be better to see him and come to terms with it.

'There was a finality – we had to grieve it out,' said Naomi. 'I was so totally unprepared. I was ready for the elation and suddenly it was cut off, such a let-down.'

The doctor who stitched the episiotomy took a long time,

gently talking to them about the accidents of nature. The staff were very supportive and this helped them face the inevitable loss of their baby.

But instead of the finality and the process of grieving, Naomi and Wolf then underwent a three month ordeal. A decision was made to operate on the baby, which would technically enable it to survive for a limited period.

'But with all the problems, there was no hope for this baby, and we really did not feel that we could handle months, maybe years of hospitalization, surgery and finally the death of our child,' said Wolf. The couple refused permission for surgery but a court order was obtained. 'We were made to feel guilty for withholding consent, but we were after all the parents who had to live with the consequences,' said Naomi.

When Naomi left hospital, she faced the problem of whether or not to visit the baby and make contact. 'I was very depressed. I didn't know whether I wanted to establish a relationship, but when I eventually held him, a weight lifted from me,' she said. The apprehension was worse than the reality.

Wolf remarked that the pressure of society subconsciously influenced him. 'My family advised us to relinquish responsibility, and even our friends were divided in their support and understanding.'

'I wasn't ready to cop out,' said Naomi, 'but to hope one's baby will die is so against one's natural instincts.'

As time passed, the baby failed to develop, there was no weight gain and no crying reflex. 'I was getting attached to the baby and felt intensely sad,' said Naomi. Her father visited from overseas, and this lightened their mood. 'He held the baby and kissed him,' she said.

Finally, after three months, the baby died of kidney failure. 'It was simple after that, just a numb feeling, it was so inevitable,' said Wolf.

The couple received genetic counselling, although the autopsy shed no light on the cause of the tragedy. Wolf summed up, 'Gradually we accepted it as an accident, but sometimes I think, why me? The hardest thing was that the decisions were not left to God but to Dr X. This was my problem.'

During Naomi's next pregnancy, she was understandably afraid to get involved. It was different from the carefree optimism of that first pregnancy.

One of the strangest grieving experiences is when one of the babies of a multiple birth dies. On one hand there is rejoicing for the baby or babies who survive, while at the same time one has to handle the mourning for the baby who didn't make it. This can be even harder if one baby is born with a severe handicap and the normal bonding and care for the healthy child or children is complicated by visits to the neonatal intensive care for the sick baby.

Some parents find this paradox unbearable and have been known to leave the sick baby in the hospital and cease contact in order to concentrate on the other children in the family.

Jessie and Bob had twins, one of whom was a Down's Syndrome baby, when their other four children were in their teens. However, their handicapped child enriched all their lives in a most unexpected way.

Since Jessie was thirty-nine at the time she would have been entitled to a test of the amniotic fluid but she claimed that even if the test was positive, they would not consent to an abortion. In the case of twins this is a double dilemma because although it is theoretically possible to selectively abort one of multiple foetuses, the procedure could result in losing the other baby.

Jessie and her family were overwhelmed by support from the family, from their church community and from Bob's workplace. The child grew up in a loving warm environment and far exceeded all the predictions of her potential.

Stimulated by her big siblings, she learned to walk and talk, to the amazement of the paediatricians and family doctor. She went to a day centre during school hours and at home was part of a big busy family.

This outcome is commensurate with the findings of the Down's Children Association, founded by Rex Brinkworth in 1970, as many studies have found that physical and mental potential are improved by stimulation.

Unfortunately, some doctors and hospital nurses encourage the institutionalization of handicapped children, whereas in fact Jessie and Bob found that their daughter thrived on affection and love. However, not all families receive the support and practical help which helped Jessie and Bob live with this decision.

Part of mourning is the grief for lost expectations, which explains the phenomenon of mourning for the 'vanishing twin'. It is known in the obstetric profession that sometimes a pregnancy starts with twin embryos and for some reason, one of them does not develop and becomes absorbed in the placenta and amniotic sac. In most cases, the parents never know anything about it. But today, with the early ultrasound screening, they may know as early as eight weeks and suffer great disappointment when another check-up at twelve weeks shows only one baby.

Therefore imagine the anguish of Rose and Ted when, after being told they were expecting twins, the doctor who continued the pregnancy care never detected that one of them had ceased to develop.

Up to thirty-seven weeks of pregnancy, Rose and Ted were expecting twins, athough Rose was rather suspicious that the size of her abdomen and the strength of the foetal movements did not seem commensurate with this. Only when she went to the hospital antenatal clinic three weeks before the expected due date was it discovered that there was only one baby.

Rose and Ted were in mourning for the second twin, and it was only after the birth, when their one baby was born large and healthy, that they came to terms with their disappointment and anger.

Many years ago, parents were kept out of the neonatal intensive care unit and perhaps for days or weeks or even months, only viewed their babies through a window. It was therefore understandable that they felt very remote from the baby and that when the baby finally came home it was very difficult to form an attachment. Research into child abuse even points to this as one of the causes.

Today, parents are encouraged to spend the maximum amount of time with their premature or sick babies. Where possible, they can participate in caring for the baby, touching, stroking, and cuddling during the periods that he can be removed from the incubator.

If breast milk is expressed for the baby, it also provides the mother with the satisfaction of knowing that she is doing the utmost. The milk of a mother who has given birth prematurely is precisely suited to the needs of the premature baby and will provide the infant with extra antibodies to fight infection. If the baby is not strong enough to breastfeed, the milk can be expressed to be given from a bottle or even through a feeding tube. This process will also keep the milk flowing so that when the baby is eventually able to suck from the breast, the mother will have an adequate supply.

It is understandable that parents may fear this involvement because they feel that if the baby does not survive, the pain will be more intense. In fact, most case studies show that the opposite is true and that parents feel more reconciled to the experience if they have involved themselves with the care of the baby and got to know him.

As in other grieving situations, there are the stages of anger, guilt and denial. Added to this is dependency on the caregivers and a resentment of the equipment, monitors, tubes and incubators which are separating the parents from the baby. Research on this subject was done by A. Jackson and W. Gorman of the Department of Psychology in Dublin's National Maternity Hospital.[4]

Since the age of viability is now lowered to twenty-seven gestational weeks, many more premature babies are surviving. There is concern that the prolonged separation between parents and baby causes permanent developmental problems. Marshall Klaus and John Kennell,[5] who have written extensively on attachment, recommend immediate contact with babies in intensive care, citing studies of children who were deprived of this which resulted in failure to thrive and poor communication later on.

The Dublin study therefore concentrated on early contact, and out of thirty-one mothers of premature babies, twelve spent time with the baby briefly at the birth before treatment started, twenty-four were introduced to the staff of the intensive care unit and shown the baby in the incubator by the end of the first day, and the rest, most of whom had had caesareans and were not strong enough to make that initial visit, were taken to the unit by the fourth day.

The mothers were interviewed on discharge from hospital and showed normal reactions of stress, fatigue with some anger and criticism, but home visits some months later showed no long-term negative effects, no significant change in body image and attitudes to sex. Although mothers were very overprotective of their babies immediately after they were discharged from the intensive care unit, this did not continue long-term and did not affect behaviour, such as how many times the baby was checked at night, whether the baby was kept in the parents' room and whether babysitters were used.

SUDDEN INFANT DEATH SYNDROME

When discussing grieving after these unexpected birth outcomes, it is perhaps relevant to refer briefly to a phenomenon which is also totally unexpected: SIDS or Sudden Infant Death Syndrome.

The Medical Care Research Unit of Sheffield University recently investigated SIDS with special funding from the DHSS.[6]

Allthough SIDS or 'cot death' is usually unexpected and unexplained, the study tried to find high-risk factors or isolate a potential which would enable parents and health care professionals to pay particular attention to warning signs.

The peak age for SIDS appeared to be from four to nineteen weeks, and these deaths occurred mostly at night and in winter. It was thought that overheating of rooms or overwrapping of the baby causes excessive rise in temperature which was one of the risks involved. It was therefore recommended that although the baby's room should not be cold, for babies are at risk of hypo-thermia, the ideal temperature was 65–70°F. To check the baby, feel the back of the neck; he should be warm but not sticky and sweaty.

The Foundation for the Study of Infant Deaths reported findings by Dr Stewart Peterson of Leicester University Medical School linking SIDS with early neonatal development problems and babies' difficulties in adjusting to temperature.[7] In this research, the body temperature of 500 babies was monitored during the first few weeks of life. 'It was found that in the first three or four weeks, there was little change in temperature when babies sleep at night. They then pass through a stage in which their temperatures drop significantly when they sleep, whether it be day or night, and after that they follow the pattern of adults whose temperature drops only when asleep at night.'

Some babies adjust to the adult norm as early as eight weeks while those who mature later, with this adjustment ability emerging as late as twenty weeks, appear to share some of the other characteristics which have been associated with cot deaths.

Dr Peterson found that breastfed babies were more likely to change early to the adult temperature pattern although he found no association between bottlefeeding and cot death.

The discussion on the influence of weight gain was contro-versial because the 'purple line' adopted by paediatric doctors and nurses, set to determine that the baby was not underweight, was causing some confusion. Breastfed babies should gain weight regularly but with less dramatic increases than formula-fed babies. The study emphasized that breast is best, and that breastfed babies received extra protection from respiratory diseases and infections which are also factors in cot deaths.

New Generation,[6] the report of the Sheffield study, confirmed other sources in suggesting lying the baby on the side or the back, not on the stomach, which is usually the popular position.

Other factors found in the Sheffield study of 565 cot deaths were mothers who smoked during and after pregnancy, very short interval after the previous birth, premature birth and low birthweight, and, for reasons not clear, there seemed to be a higher risk linked with extremely young age of the mother and, even more inexplicably, a precipitate second stage of labour.

New Generation noted that Sheffield, which had a higher than average cot death rate, had set as a role model the Swedish town of Gothenburg where there was a relatively low incidence of 0.5 per 1000 babies. This compares to the British Health Minister's report of 1.8 per 1000 live births in England and Wales in 1990.

It was thought that the more intensive screening of babies at risk through well baby clinics and frequent home visits by health visitors in Sweden contributed to this improvement.

Since then, news has come from New Zealand that a concentrated effort to advise parents to put babies to sleep on their side or back has actually, in the space of six months, reduced the incidence of cot deaths.

As a result of all these reports, the Department of Health and Social Security has sent directives to all family health personnel to pass on this information to parents of young babies.[8] Because babies are more at risk during the first four to five months, the letter from the DHSS points out that once a baby is rolling over on his own, he does not need to be pressured to lie on his side. Also, parents who find that their very young babies just refuse to lie in that position should not endure sleepless nights.

THE GRIEVING FAMILY

It is not the parents alone who suffer pregnancy loss or neonatal death. There is an entire family network waiting for this baby and one should not underestimate the grieving of grandparents and other children in the family.

Fathers are as deeply involved in the loss of a baby as is the mother and yet the framework for support in this type of bereavement concentrates far more on the needs of the mother.

It is true that the mother has to be helped through a physical as well as emotional recovery, but fathers are often left in the background, do not get time off from work to mourn, and are expected to show strength and courage. The loss, the fears of future infertility, the anger or criticism aimed at hospital staff for real or imaginary negligence, the despair, are all part of mourning which is felt as much by fathers as by mothers.

For siblings, the loss is very complicated and they may suffer feelings of guilt because perhaps they had not really wanted this new baby or perhaps they didn't help mummy wash the dishes and then she got those pains and went to hospital.

They may fantasize about the reasons why it happened and relate it to what they had done and said. For little children, this is sometimes their first contact with death and they realize that it is not only old people who die. They may have coped well with the loss of a beloved pet, but this is still far from coming to terms with human death and the grief of their parents.

Dr Irwing G. Leon of Birmingham, USA, reports a case history of a child of eight whose sister was stillborn when he was eighteen months old.[9] All these years later, the child was showing symptoms of disturbance such as poor achievement at school, inattention, nightmares and he was stubborn and quarrelsome, sad and withdrawn.

The parents had never discussed the loss of the baby with him because they felt he was too young to understand. Many child guidance counsellors report fantasies of children in this situation. They wanted to know how the baby died and associated fear of strangulation with the umbilical cord. For others there is a loss of trust in their parents who promised a new baby. Another cause of distress is that there is no tangible evidence of the baby's existence. Usually in cases of bereavement, there is evidence in the form of clothes, belongings, a favourite chair or picture. Also the siblings do not see the body of the dead baby, so they may fantasize that the baby may still be around or that he was grossly deformed.

Judy Gray, in her article 'One plus'[10] suggests some guidelines for helping siblings cope with these feelings:

1. Don't avoid the subject by saying that the baby has gone away and will be back one day.
2. Don't liken death to sleep because they may fear that death will come to them when they are sleeping, and it also encourages their perception of death as temporary.
3. Be prepared for regression such as bedwetting, nightmares, dependency.

4. Encourage the child to talk about the baby and look at photographs if they are available.
5. Look for any signs of guilt and encourage the child to vent
feelings of sadness and anger.
6. Work through fantasies that babies die in hospitals.

It is therefore seen over and over again in cases of perinatal or
neonatal death that it is important for all the family to experience
the birth, see the baby and then take the stages of grieving slowly,
before getting back to normal.

Crisis is paralysing and sometimes it is hard to reach out for
help. But there are a number of support organizations which
can provide help over the telephone or by personal visits, and
resources which dispense leaflets, books and research literature on
the subject of loss in childbirth.

It is sometimes helpful to offload on someone familiar, and the
childbirth educator, health visitor or GP should be available for
this.

One never forgets. There is always a place in one's heart for
the child who did not live, but the anger and the pain diminish.
If there are no other children and the years pass, one cannot
help cherishing that very brief time of parenthood. If there are
other children, one concentrates one's energy on them and just
occasionally wonders what this lost baby would have done with
his life.

Useful Addresses

Whatever the situation for a new mother and wherever she may live, there is a network of agencies and support organizations which can answer her specific needs. Throughout the text of the book, we have referred to the work of some of these agencies. Most of them have representatives or branches throughout the country, and these addresses can be obtained from the head offices listed below:

GREAT BRITAIN

Association for Improvements in Maternity Services (AIMS)
21 Iver Lane, Iver, Bucks SL0 9LH
Tel: 0753 652781

Association for Postnatal Illness
7 Gowan Avenue, London, SW6

Bliss-Link (For bereaved parents or those with babies in special care)
17/21 Emerald Street, London WC1N 3QL
Tel: 071 831 9393

Caesarean Support Network
1 Hurst Park Drive, Huyton, Liverpool L36 ITF
Tel: 051 480 1184

Cry-sis (Support for parents of crying babies)
BM Cry-sis, London WC1N 3XX
Tel: 071 404 5011

Gingerbread (Self-help for single parents)
25 Wellington Street, London WC2 7BN

International Planned Parenthood Federation
P.O. Box 759, Inner Circle, Regent's Park, London NW1 4LQ

Joint Breastfeeding Initiative (Resource centre for National Childbirth Trust Breastfeeding Promotion Group, La Leche and Association of Breastfeeding Mothers)
Alexandra House, Oldham Terrace, London W3 6NH
Tel: 081 992 8637

MAMA (Meet a Mother Association)
5 Westbury Gardens, Luton, Beds

Marce Society (Prevention and treatment of mental illness associated with child-bearing)
Queen Margaret College, Clerwood Terrace, Edinburgh EH12 8TS
Tel: 031 317 3000

Maternity Alliance
15 Britannia Street, London WC1X 9JP
Tel: 071 837 1265

Mind – National Association for Mental Health
22 Harley Street, London WIN 2ED
Tel: 081 637 0741

Miscarriage Association
P.O. Box 24, Ossett, West Yorkshire WF5 9XG

Multiple Births Foundation
Queen Charlotte's and Chelsea Hospital, Goldhawk Road, London W6 OXG
Tel: 081 748 4666 ext. 5201

National Childbirth Trust
Alexandra House, Oldham Terrace, London W3 6NH
Tel: 081 992 8637

National Stillbirth Study Group
66 Harley Street, London WIN IAE

Nippers (Resource information and support on prematurity and special care infants)
c/o Perinatal Unit, St Mary's Hospital, Praed Street, London W2 INY
Tel: 071 725 1487

PRAMS (Postnatal Resource Association for Mothers in Stockport)
Lyndhurst, 188 Buxton Road, Stockport SK2 7AE
Tel: 061 483 8853

SANDS (Stillbirth and Neonatal Death Society)
28 Portland Place, London WIN 4DE
Tel: 071 436 5881

SATFA (Support After Termination for Foetal Abnormality)
29–30 Soho Square, London WIV 6JB
Tel: 071 439 6124

Stillbirth and Perinatal Death Association
37 Christchurch Hill, London NW3 IJY

TAMBA (Twins and Multiple Births Association)
59 Sunny Side, Worksop, Nottingham S81 7LN

Twins and Multiple Births Association Bereavement Support
32 Denton Court Road, Gravesend, Kent DA12 2HS
Tel: 0474 567320

AMERICA

American Cleft Palate Foundation
Grandview Avenue, Pittsburgh, PA 15211

Association for Psychoprophylaxis in Obstetrics
1840 Wilson Boulevard, Suite 204, Arlington, VA 22201

Caesarian Birth Association
125 North 12th Street, New Hyde Park, NY 11040

International Childbirth Education Association
PO Box 20048, Minneapolis, Minnesota 55420

International Lactation Consultants Association (research and counselling service)
PO Box 4031, University of Virginia Station, Charlottesville, VA 22903

La Leche International (worldwide network offering counselling and publications)
9616 Minneapolis Avenue, Franklin Park, IL 60131

NAPSAC (National Association of Parents and Professionals for Safe Alternatives in Childbirth)
PO Box 428, Marble Hill, MO 63764

National Downs Syndrome Congress
1800 Dempster Street, Park Ridge, IL 60068

Nursing Mothers Council of America
PO Box 50063, Palo Alto, CA 94303

Zero to Three, National Centre for Clinical Infant Programmes
2000 14th Street North, Suite 380, Arlington, VA 22201–2500

Glossary

amniotic fluid: liquid contained in a membranous sac in which the baby floats from the beginning of pregnancy until labour.

analgesic: category of drugs used for pain relief.

apgar score: assessment of baby's heart rate, respiration, muscle tone, crying, colour; done at one minute and again at five minutes after the birth. Named after Dr Virginia Apgar.

areola: pigmented area around the nipple.

colostrum: creamy fluid secreted by the breasts during pregnancy and in first days after the birth – high in protein and antibodies.

endorphins: hormones inducing euphoria and 'fight or flight' response.

engorgement: (of breasts) – painful and swollen breasts most usually found on the third to seventh day after the birth when milk supply increases.

Entonox: inhalation analgesic, sometimes called 'laughing gas' or 'gas and air'.

epidural: local analgesic injected between third and fourth lumbar vertebrae into the epidural cavity around the spinal cord.

episiotomy: incision made in the perineum to enlarge the vaginal outlet.

forceps: stainless-steel tongs placed round baby's head to conclude second stage of labour in cases of foetal distress or extreme fatigue of mother.

human chorionic gonadotrophin (HCG): pregnancy hormone which assists the construction of the placenta and relaxes the uterus in early pregnancy.

imprinting: the first experience of relating to one's own species.

induction: a method of starting or speeding up labour.

lactation: breastfeeding.

lactose intolerance: baby's stomach discomfort caused by intolerance to the sugar in breast milk.

meconium: baby's first stools, usually greenish-black in colour and sticky like tar.

Montgomery's tubercles: enlarged glands in areola from which milk is also secreted.

209

oestrogen: hormone which is increased during pregnancy.

oxytocin: hormone which stimulates contractions of the uterus and which is also instrumental in lactation.

parturient (women): period after childbirth.

perineum: the area including the urethra, vagina and labia (lips).

pethidine: analgesic drug for pain relief in labour.

pitocin (syntocinon): synthetic oxytocin used for inducing labour.

placenta (afterbirth): gland connected to the wall of the uterus during pregnancy which transfers blood supply including oxygen and nutrients from mother's blood stream via the umbilical cord to the foetus.

placenta praevia: a condition in which the placenta becomes attached to uterine wall at the outlet of the cervix.

pre-eclampsia (toxaemia): a condition which can affect the functioning of the placenta or develop into the more serious eclampsia, usually diagnosed by the presence of high blood pressure and/or protein in the urine and/or severe swelling of the limbs, body and face.

progesterone: female hormone essential for maintaining pregnancy.

prolactin: lactation hormone.

prostaglandins: hormones found in both male semen and female menstrual and amniotic fluids – used to induce labour.

psychoprophylaxis: method of pain control using breathing and relaxation techniques, based on theories of Dr Fernand Lamaze.

psychosis: severe mental illness.

transition stage: at conclusion of cervical dilation and awaiting descent of foetal head into vagina.

vacuum extraction: method of speeding up second stage of labour by applying suction to baby's head.

 *References*

Chapter 1.   The Fantasy and The Reality
1. Lamaze, F. *Painless Childbirth*, Pan, 1965.
2. Dick-Read, Grantley, *Childbirth Without Fear*, Pan, 1944.
3. Leboyer, F. *Birth Without Violence*, Knopf, 1976.
4. Odent, Michel, *Birth Reborn*, Pantheon, 1984.
5. Stewart, D. 'Possible relationship of postpartum psychiatric symptoms to childbirth education programmes', *Journal of Psychosomatic Obstetrics/ Gynaecology*, December, 1985, pp. 295–301.
6. *Journal of Health and Social Behaviour*, 1982.
7. Huyton, F. 'Metabolic adaptation of pregnancy in prevention of handicap through antenatal care', *Journal of Psychosomatic Obstetrics/Gynaecology*.
8. MacFarlane, A. *Psychology of Childbirth*, Fontana, 1977.
9. Verny, T., Kelly, J. *Secret Life of the Unborn Child*, Sphere, 1982.
10. Oakley, A. *From Here to Maternity*, Penguin, 1981.
11. Women's Co-operative Guild, *Maternity – Letters From Working Women*, ed. Llewellyn Jones, M., 1915. Reissued, Virago, 1978.

Chapter 2.   The Impact of Birth
1. Genesis 1:28.
2. Genesis 3:16.
3. Stolte, K. 'Nurses responses to changes in maternity care', *Journal of Birth*, June, 1987.
4. Marais, E. Soul of the Ape, in A. MacFarlane, *Psychology of Childbirth*, Fontana, 1977.
5. Silman, M., Siegel-Kellner, M., Naaman, T. *History of Midwifery*, Gefen, 1991.
6. Kloosterman, G. The Delivery, When and Where, in A. MacFarlane, *Psychology of Childbirth*, Fontana, 1977.
7. Jordan, B. 'The hut and the hospital: information, power and symbolism in the artifacts of birth', *Journal of Birth*, March, 1987, pp. 36–40.
8. Micah 4:9–10: Jeremiah 4:31.
9. Bloomsbury Health Authority, 1988.
10. Eidelman, A. 'Maternal Infant Recognition – Implications for Perinatal Care', *Ninth International Congress: Encounter with the Unborn*, Jerusalem, 1989.
11. Madders, J. *Stress and Relaxation*, Martin Dunitz, 1979.
12. Leboyer, F. *Birth Without Violence*, Knopf, 1976.

211

13. Klaus, M. and Kennell, J. *Bonding – Importance of Early Separation or Loss on Family Development*, Mosby, 1976.
14. Field, M. 'An Unusual Solution', *New Generation*, March, 1986, p. 44.

Chapter 3.   Three-Day Blues – or Postnatal Depression?
1. Waldenstrom, U. 'Early or late discharge after hospital birth: fatigue and emotional reactions in the postpartum period', *Journal of Psychosomatic Obstetrics/Gynaecology*, April 1988, pp. 127–35.
2. Dodshon, D. 'Loss of libido after childbirth', Seminar of Nursing Mothers Association of Australia, September, 1984.
3. Pitt, B. 'Atypical depression following childbirth', *British Psychiatry*, 1968, pp. 1325–35.
4. Chalmers, B. Chalmers, B. 'Postpartum depression – a revised perspective', *Journal of Psychosomatic Obstetrics/Gynaecology*, June, 1986, pp. 93–105.
5. Harris, B. 'This could be depressing', research at Caerphilly Miners' Hospital, report by Ann Pegum, *New Generation*, December, 1988, p. 44.
6. Dalton, K. *Depression After Childbirth*, Oxford University Press, 1989.
7. Alder, E. and Cox, J. *Journal of Psychosomatic Research*, 1983, pp. 139–44.
8. Cheney, L. 'And Sam made four', *New Generation*, September, 1989, p. 42.
9. Oakley, A. *Women Confined*, Shocken, 1980.
10. Brown, G. and Harris, T. *Social Origins of Depression*, Tavistock, 1978.
11. Frommer, A. and Pratt, G. Psychological Medicine in Obstetrics and Gynaecology, 3rd International Congress, London, 1971. Frommer, A. and O'Shea, R. 'Antenatal identification of women liable to have problems in managing their infants', *British Journal of Psychiatry*, 1973, pp. 149–56.
12. Melges, F. 'Postpartum psychiatric syndrome', *Psychosomatic Medicine*, 1968, pp. 95–108.
13. Kumar, R. and Robson, K. 'Prospective study of emotional disorders in childbearing women', *British Journal of Psychiatry*, 1984, pp. 35–47.
14 Affonso, D. and Arizmendi, T. 'Disturbances in postpartum adaptation: depressive symptomatology', *Journal of Psychosomatic Obstetrics/Gynaecology*, March, 1986, pp. 15–32.
15. Gavron, H. *The Captive Wife*, Pelican, 1966.
16. Wellburn, V. *Postnatal Depression*, Fontana, 1980.
17. Marce, L. Seminar on Mental Illness in Pregnancy and Puerperium, Report by J. Allan, *New Generation*, December, 1985, p. 42.
18. Eysenck, J. *Fact and Fiction in Psychology*, Penguin, 1970.
19. Kendell, R., McKenzie, W., West, C., McGuire, R., Case, J. 'Day to day mood changes after childbirth: further data', *Obstetrical/Gynaecological Survey* and *British Journal of Psychiatry*, 1982, pp. 111–17.
20. Sakes, B. *American Journal of Psychiatry*, 1985.
21. Petrick, J. *Journal of Obstetric/Gynaecology Nursing*, 1977.
22. Donaldson, N. 'Fourth trimester follow-up', *American Journal of Nursing*, July, 1977, pp. 1171–5.
23. Raphael-Leff, J. *Psychological Processes of Childbearing*, Chapman-Hall, 1991, and 'Facilitators and Regulators, Participators and Renouncers: Mothers and Fathers Orientations towards Pregnancy and Parenthood', *Journal of Psychosomatic Obstetrics/Gynaecology*, September, 1985, pp. 181–4.
24. Holland, P. *Postnatal Depression*, National Childbirth Trust Symposium, summarised by J. Allen, L. Waumsley and I. Willis, *New Generation*, September, 1985.

Chapter 4.   Getting Acquainted
1. Harlow, H., and Harlow, R., Dodsworth, R. and Arling, G., in *Child Behaviour and Development*, ed. N. Rebelsky, Knopf, 1970.
2. Bowlby, J. *Attachment and Loss*, Penguin, 1969.
3. Brazleton, T. *Neonatal Behaviour Assessment Scale*, Heinemann, 1973.
4. Spitz, R. and Wolf, K. How we can study the harm done, in J. Bowlby, *Child Care and the Growth of Love*, Pelican, 1965. pp. 23–9.
5. MacFarlane, A. *Psychology of Childbirth*, Fontana, 1977.
6. Klaus, M. and Kennell, J. 'Human Maternal Behavior at First Contact with her Young', *Paediatrics*, 1970.
7. Eidelman, A. 'Parturiant Women can Recognise Their Children by Touch', *Ninth International Congress on Pre- and Peri-natal Psychology and Medicine: Encounter with the Unborn*, Jerusalem, 1989.
8. Leboyer, F. *Birth Without Violence*, Knopf, 1976.
9. Richards, M. How should we approach the study of fathers? in L. McKee and M. O'Brien, (eds), *The Father Figure*, Tavistock, 1982.
10. As above.
11. Bowlby, J. *Child Care and the Growth of Love*, Pelican, 1965.
12. Freud, A., Burlingham, D. and Hellman, I. Monthly staff report (unpublished) of Hampstead Nurseries, 1944.
13. Raphael-Leff, *Psychological Processes of Childbearing*, Chapman-Hall, 1991.
14. Ludington-Hoe, S. 'Postpartum: Development of Maternicity', *American Journal of Nursing*, July, 1977, pp. 1171–5.
15. Clark, J. 'Postnatal Expectations – Frustration or Fulfilment', Seminar of Childbirth and Parenting Association, Victoria, Australia, July, 1980.
16. Ainsworth, M. *Infancy in Uganda*, John Hopkins University Press, 1967.

Chapter 5.   A New Life for Fathers
1. Mead, M. *Male and Female*, William Morrow, 1953.
2. Malinowsky, B. *Sexual Life of Savages*, Harcourt-Brace, 1927.
3. Clarke, E. Finding Father, in M. Green, *Fathering*, McGraw-Hill, 1977.
4. Heggenhougen, H. 'Father and childbirth: an anthropological perspective', *Journal of Nurse-Midwife*, 1980.
5. Richards, M. in L. McKee and M. O'Brien (eds), *The Father Figure*, Tavistock, 1982.
6. Freeman, T. 'Pregnancy as a precipitant of mental illness in men', *British Journal of Psychiatry*, 1951, No. 24, pp. 49–54.
7. Carter, J. *Journal of American Forces*, 1966.
8. Hartman, A. and Nicolay, R. 'Sexually deviant behaviour in expectant fathers', *Journal of Abnormal Psychology*, 71(3), pp. 232–4.
9. Wainwright, W. 'Fatherhood as a precipitant of mental illness', *American Journal of Psychiatry*, 1966, pp. 232–4.
10. May, K. A. and Perrin, S. P. Prelude: Pregnancy and birth, in S. Hansen and F. Bozett (eds), *Dimensions of Fatherhood*, Sage, 1985.
11. May, K. A. *Family Relations*, 1982.
12. Owen, D. The desire to father: reproductive ideologies in involuntarily childless men, in L. McKee and M. O'Brien (eds), *The Father Figure*, Tavistock, 1982.
13. D'Arcy, E. 'Congenital defects: mothers reactions to first information', *British Medical Journal*, 1968:3, pp. 796–8.
14. Gumz, E. and Gubrium, J. 'Comparative parental perceptions of a mentally retarded child', *American Journal of Mental Deficiency*, 1972:72, pp. 175–80.

15. Weaver, R. and Cranley, M. 'An exploration of paternal-fetal attachment behaviour', *Nursing Research*, 1983, 32(2), pp. 68–72.
16. Richman, J. Mens experiences of pregnancy and childbirth, in L. McKee and M. O'Brien (eds), *The Father Figure*, Tavistock, 1982.
17. Biller, H. and Meredith, D. *Father Power*, McKay, 1975.
18. Richman, J. and Goldthorpe, W. Fatherhood, the social construction of pregnancy and birth, in S. Kitzinger and J. Davis (eds), *Place of Birth*, Oxford University Press, 1978.
19. May, K. A. *Nursing Research*, 1982.
20. Liebenberg, B. *Psychological Aspects of First Pregnancy and Early Postnatal Adaptation*, Raven Press, 1973.
21. Munroe, R. Psychological interpretations of male initiation rites: the case of male pregnancy symptoms, in S. Hansen and F. Bozett (eds), *Dimensions of Fatherhood*, Sage, 1985.
22. Greenberg, M. and Morris, N. 'Engrossment: the newborn's impact upon the father', *American Journal of Orthopsychiatry*, 1974, 44, pp. 520–31.
23. Cronenwett, L. and Newmark, L. 'Fathers' responses to childbirth', *Nursing Research*, 1974, 23, pp. 210–17.
24. Grossman, F., Eichler, L. and Winickoff, S. *Pregnancy, Birth and Parenthood*, Jossey-Bass, 1980.
25. Lawrence, D. H. *The Rainbow*, Penguin, 1934.
26. Women's Co-operative Guild, *Maternity – Letters From Working Women*, ed. M. Llewellyn Jones, 1915. Reissued, Virago, 1978.
27. Greenberg, M. and Morris, N. 'Engrossment: the newborn's impact upon the father', *American Journal of Orthopsychiatry*, 1974, 44, pp. 520–31.
28. LeMasters, E. 'Parenthood as crisis', *Marriage and Family Living*, 1957, 19, pp. 252–5.
29. Hobbs, D. 'Parenthood as crisis: a third study', *Journal of Marriage and Family*, 1965, Vol. 3, pp. 720–27.
30. Raphael-Leff, J. *Psychological Processes of Childbearing*, Chapman-Hall, 1991.
31. Osofsky, H. 'Transition to parenthood: risk factors for parents and infants', *Journal of Psychosomatic Obstetrics/Gynaecology*, December, 1985, pp. 303–13.
32. McCafferty, A. Discussion on postnatal depression at National Childbirth Trust Seminar.

Chapter 6.   Mothers and Fathers

1. Clancy Shales, K. *Journal of the International Childbirth Education Association*.
2. Procacinni and Kiefaber, 'Parent burnout', *Journal of Reproductive and Infant Psychology*, 1986.
3. Moss, P., Bollard, G., Foxman, R. and Owen, C. 'Transition to Parenthood', *Journal of Reproductive and Infant Psychology*, September, 1986, 4, pp. 58–62.
4. LeMasters, E. and Dyer, E. 'Marital relations during transition', *Marriage and Family Living*, 1957, pp. 352–5.
5. Grossman, F. *Journal of Psychosomatic Obstetrics/Gynaecology*, 1985.
6. Entwhistle, D. R. and Doering, S. G. *First Birth*, Johns Hopkins University Press, 1981.
7. Seel, R. *Uncertain Father*, 1990, and 'Tailpiece', *New Generation*, March, 1984, pp. 36–7.
8. Russell, G. Problems in role-reversed families, in C. Lewis and M. O'Brien (eds), *Reassessing Fatherhood*, Sage, 1987.
9. Greif, G. *Single Fathers*, Lexington, 1987.

10. Ehrenreich, B. *Hearts of Men*, 1983.
11. Scheppler, J., University of Florida.
12. Forbes, R. *New Generation*.
13. Lewis, C. and O'Brien, M. *Reassessing Fatherhood*, Sage, 1987.
14. McKee, L. and O'Brien, M. *The Father Figure*, Tavistock, 1982.
15. Richards, M., Dunn, J. and Antonis, B. 'Caretaking in the first year of life', *Child Care Health and Development*, 1977:3, pp. 26–36.
16. Richards, M. in McKee, L. and O'Brien, M. *The Father Figure*, Tavistock, 1982.
17. Biller, N. *Father, child and sex role*, Lexington, 1971.
18. Newson, J. and Newson, E. in M. Richards, *Integration of a Child into a Social World*, Cambridge University Press, 1974.
19. Richards, M. in Lewis, C. and O'Brien, M. *Reassessing Fatherhood*, Sage, 1987.
20. Girouard, M. *The Victorian Country House*, Yale University Press, 1979.
21. King, T. *Feeding and Care of Baby*, Macmillan, 1913, reissued 1925.
22. Women's Co-operative Guild, *Maternity – Letters From Working Women*, ed. M. Llewellyn Jones, 1915. Reissued, Virago, 1978.
23. Stanway, P. and Stanway, A. *Breast is Best*, Pan, 1978.
24. *Shulchan Aruch: Code of Jewish Law*, compiled by Rabbi Solomon Ganzfried, Hebrew Publishing Co., 1961.
25. Kitzinger, S. *Women's Experiences of Sex*, Penguin, 1983.
26. Dodshon, D. 'Loss of libido after childbirth', Seminar of Nursing Mothers Association of Australia, September, 1984.
27. Osofsky, H. 'Transition to parenthood: risk factors for parents and infants', *Journal of Psychosomatic Obstetrics/Gynaecology*, December, 1985.
28. Adams, M. *Baillières Midwives' Dictionary*, 1983, p. 202.
29. Mason, D. and Ingersoll, D. *Breastfeeding and the Working Mother*, St Martins Press, 1986, p. 140–41.
30. Salk, L. *Preparing for Parenthood*, Fontana/Collins, 1974, pp. 184, 189–90.
31. Boston Womens Health Book Collective, *The New Our Bodies Ourselves*, Simon and Schuster, 1984, pp. 396, 405, 408, 411, 413, 441.

Chapter 7.   A Baby in the House – Time and Motion

1. Leboyer, F. *Birth Without Violence*, Knopf, 1976.
2. Stanway, P. *Green Babies*, Century, 1990.
3. Siegel, J. 'Kibbutznik's machine will recycle dirty diapers', *Jerusalem Post*, 18 February, 1992.
4. Calman, K. and Poole, A. 'How to reduce the risk of cot deaths', DHSS recommendations. Available from: Department of Health Store, Health Publications Unit, No. 2 Site, Manchester Road, Heywood, Lancashire, OL10 2PZ, Ref. H91/514.
5. Winnicott, D. *The Child, The Family and The Outside World*, Pelican, 1965.
6. Fisher, C., Renfrew, M. and Arms, S. *Bestfeeding*, Celestial Arts, 1991.
7. Stanway, P. and Stanway, A. *Breast is Best*, Pan, 1978.
8. Bowlby, J. *Child Care and the Growth of Love*, Pelican, 1965.
9. Newson, J. and Newson, E. *Patterns of Infant Care in the Urban Community*, Pelican, 1966.
10. Soo, I., Llewellyn-Jones, D. and Abram, S. 'Psychosomatic factors in the choice of infant feeding', *Journal of Psychosomatic Obstetrics/Gynaecology*, April, 1988, pp. 137–45.
11. Lucas, A., Morley, R., Cole, T., Lister, G. and Leison-Payne, C. *Lancet*, 1992, pp. 261–4.

12. World Health Organisation. *Code for Marketing of Infant Foods*, WHO, 1979.
13. Worthington-Roberts, B. *Nutrition in Pregnancy and Lactation*, Mosby, 1981.

Chapter 8.　Ways of Recovery: Sources of Support
1. Neugarten, B. and Weinstein, K. 'The changing American grand-parent', *Journal of Marriage and Family*, 1964, 26, pp. 199–204.
2. Kahana, R. A. and Kahana, E. 'Grandparenthood from the perspective of the developing grandchild', *Developmental Psychology*, 1970, 3(1), pp. 98–105.
3. Cunningham, Berkley, S. The experience of grandfatherhood, in Lewis, C. and O'Brien, M. *Reassessing Fatherhood*, Sage, 1987.
4. Bardon, D. 'Back to basics', *New Generation*, March, 1983, pp. 27–8.
5. Polden, M. and Whiteford, B. *Postnatal Exercises*, Century, 1992 (2nd ed.).
6. Mitchell, L. *Simple Relaxation*, John Murray, 1977.
7. Worthington-Roberts, B. *Nutrition in Pregnancy and Lactation*, Mosby, 1981.

Chapter 9.　Looking Ahead
1. Richards, M. Child Development Centre, Cambridge University, December, 1991, Personal Communication.
2. Brazleton, T. *Journal of Lamaze Parents*, 1986.
3. Bowlby, J. *Child Care and the Growth of Love*, Pelican, 1965.
4. Schonbrun, M. 'Natural methods of contraception', Seminar on Family Health, Technion Medical School, Haifa, June, 1990.
5. Seaman, Barbara and Gideon, *Women and Crisis in Sex Hormones*, Bantam, 1979.
6. Herbst, A. L., Ulfelder, J. and Poskanzer, D. C. 'Association of maternal stilboestrol therapy with tumour appearance in young women', *New England Journal of Medicine*, 1971, pp. 878–81.
7. Dodds, E. C. 'Interruption of early pregnancy by means of orally active oestrogens', *British Medical Journal*, 1938, pp. 557.
8. Dodds, E. C. 'Oral contraceptives – past and future', *Clinical Pharmacology and Therapeutics*, 1969.
9. Diaz, S. and Croxatto, H. *Bulletin of the International Planned Parenthood Association*, August, 1991, pp. 2–4.
10. Sanger, M. in Seaman, G. and B. *Women and the Crisis in Sex Hormones*, Bantam 1979.

Chapter 10.　Mourning for The Special Baby
1. Blumfield, W. 'A Letter to bereaved parents', *Journal of the International Childbirth Education Association*, September, 1984.
2. Stewart, Rev. Royal College Midwives Seminar, 1987, reported by L. Perks in *New Generation*, June, 1987.
3. Ilse, Sherokee, *Empty Arms*, 1985.
4. Jackson, A. and Gorman, W. 'Maternal attitudes to preterm birth', *Journal of Psychosomatic Obstetrics/Gynaecology*, April, 1988, Vol. 8, No. 2.
5. Klaus, M. and Kennell, K. *Bonding: Impact of Early Separation and Loss on Family Development*, Mosby, 1976.
6. Hancock, K. 'Can we prevent cot deaths?', *New Generation*, June, 1986, p. 46. Gaunt, S. *New Generation*, December, 1986, pp. 46–7.
7. Peterson, S. *Report of Foundation for the Study of Infant Deaths*, DHSS, 1992.
8. *Directives on Prevention of Sudden Infant Deaths*, DHSS, December, 1991.
9. Leon, I. 'The invisible loss: the impact of perinatal death on siblings', *Journal of Psychosomatic Obstetrics/Gynaecology*, March, 1986, pp. 1–14.
10. Gray, J. Australian Childbirth Educator, 1985.

Index